HAND BOOK
OF GASOLINE
AUTOMOBILES

1904-1906

HAND BOOK

OF GASOLINE

AUTOMOBILES

1904-1906

BY THE ASSOCIATION OF LICENSED

AUTOMOBILE MANUFACTURERS

With an Introduction by

Clarence P. Hornung

Dover Publications, Inc., New York

Published in Canada by General Publishing Company, Ltd.,
30 Lesmill Road, Don Mills, Toronto, Ontario.
Published in the United Kingdom by Constable and Company, Ltd.,
10 Orange Street, London WC 2.

This Dover edition, first published in 1969, is an unabridged and
unaltered republication of the *Hand Book of Gasoline Automobiles* as published in 1904, 1905 and 1906 by the Association of
Licensed Automobile Manufacturers. A new introduction has
been written specially for this Dover edition by Clarence P.
Hornung.

Standard Book Number: 486-22440-6
Library of Congress Catalog Card Number: 71-83311

Manufactured in the United States of America
Dover Publications, Inc.
180 Varick Street
New York, N.Y. 10014

INTRODUCTION TO THE DOVER EDITION

THE *Hand Book of Gasoline Automobiles* as issued by the Association of Licensed Automobile Manufacturers and its successors between 1904 and 1929 was the official catalog and directory of a significant portion of the early automobile industry in America.

Originally issued to provide the information needed by the prospective purchaser of an automobile, the *Hand Book* contains, in a uniform book format, illustrations and specifications of the products of the principal manufacturers throughout the United States, as well as imported gasoline-powered machines. Each volume was the official directory for the year when issued and as such provides the only dependable current guide to data and specifications. This information made it easy for a buyer to compare models and to select the one best suited to the service required, his personal taste, and the means at his command.

The 1904 edition of the *Hand Book* shows the wide variety of vehicles available. On page 70 stands the regal Mercedes manufactured by Smith & Mabley, Inc., boasting a seating capacity of five persons, steered by a wheel, possessing four cylinders, obtainable in any color desired, weighing 2,300 pounds, and costing the princely sum of $12,750 (with top). Page 78, however, contains the humbler Orient

Buckboard produced by the Waltham Manufacturing Co.; seating two, steered by a tiller, available only in the color of the wood from which it had been fashioned, and weighing 500 pounds, it cost $425 without a top, but could also be had with a top for an extra $22.

Some of the model designations encountered in these pages will be confusing to today's readers. Certain terms are holdovers from the days of the horse and carriage; phaeton and brougham, for example, were names of carriage bodies. The name of the touring car proclaims its purpose. It was longer than the phaeton to allow for a tonneau (the rear compartment behind the driver's seat). The limousine had a closed compartment seating three or more passengers, but the driver was seated in front of them at the mercy of the elements. The coupé had two doors and an enclosed compartment. The runabout was a light car seating two. Various combinations of these names were used, and the entire question of terminology became so complicated that in May 1921 the magazine *Motor* ran an article that attempted to standardize the usage of these terms.

These early cars described in the *Hand Book* are depicted in beautifully rendered and detailed photographic illustrations. We see the car lamps of brass which were brought to a high polish, seats upholstered in fine leather, and, next to the driver's seat or occasionally on the steering wheel itself, the shining horn whose blast warned the unwary pedestrian that a machine tearing down the road at 20 or 30 miles an hour was about to overtake him. Some models, such as the Packard "L" on page 53 of the 1904 volume, sport long wicker hampers alongside for the convenient transport of the boiled hams, salads, pickles, relishes, and liquid refreshments to be taken during the picnic that was part of an outing in an automobile.

At the time of the publication of the first edition of the *Hand Book* America was on the verge of realizing the true worth of the automobile. The attempts at creating a self-propelled road vehicle had been many, some dating back to the eighteenth century. In 1864 Siegfried Marcus of Austria produced an engine that operated on the principle of internal combustion using a liquid fuel.

At the Philadelphia Centennial Exposition of 1876, George B. Brayton exhibited a two-cycle engine. A patent attorney from Rochester, George B. Selden (1846-1922), saw the Brayton engine and realized the advantage of incorporating it in a self-propelled vehicle. On May 8, 1879, he filed papers with the U.S. Patent Office claiming that the automobile was, in effect, his own invention. At this point Selden was far ahead of his time. Interest in self-propelled vehicles was academic, shared only by a handful of visionaries and barnyard tinkerers. Certainly, Selden's enthusiasm could not reach out and touch the public, which only stared and ogled out of curiosity at these strange machines. But by 1893, when the Duryea Brothers of Springfield, Massachusetts, drove their buggy in countless demonstrations about town, Selden had decided that the time was ripe to assert control over the automobile. Patent No. 549,160 was granted to him on November 5, 1895, and covered all gasoline automobiles that were commercially practicable. Twenty-three days later the nation's fancy was caught by an automobile race sponsored by the *Times-Herald* in Chicago. The course running through the snow-covered streets was 54 miles long, a rugged trial for the six entries, and it was nine hours before the Duryea Brothers crossed the finish line victorious.

It took Selden several years to sell his patent. The difficulty in finding anyone who was willing to invest any capital in the automobile was considerable. Manufacture of the automobile was still on a very limited basis, the car being regarded as a toy for the monied classes. In 1900 only 4,192 automobiles were made and sold in the United States, most of them by some 42 companies. Finally, on November 4, 1899, Selden enlisted the aid of William C. Whitney and his Columbia Motor Company and Electric Vehicle Company, and assigned his patent for licensing purposes. Arrangements were made under which in the future all automobile manufacturers would be obliged to pay royalties.

To his great chagrin, Selden found that manufacturers ignored his patent. Successful litigation to enforce the patent was begun in 1900 against the Winton Motor Carriage Company, then the nation's largest maker of gasoline cars. In March 1903, after an appeal, the Winton Company, together with nine other firms, formed the Association of Licensed Automobile Manufacturers (A.L.A.M.) with all member's purchasing the right to the Selden patent at royalties ranging from 8/10 to 1 1/4 per cent of the retail price of all cars sold. Of these royalties, 2/5 went to the Electric Vehicle Company, 1/5 went to Selden, and 2/5 went to the A.L.A.M. to be used to benefit the industry. It was the A.L.A.M. that published the *Hand Book,* and the names of the 35 member companies of 1904 appear in the index to that year. Of these companies only Cadillac has survived the countless adversities of the past sixty-five years.

In 1903 Selden, in conjunction with the Electric Vehicle Company, embarked upon one of the bitterest and longest legal contests in American entrepreneurial history, the battle with the Ford Motor Company which had refused to pay royalties. Henry J. Ford (1863-1947), who had left a position with the Edison Illuminating Company of Detroit in 1899 to devote his full energies to the automobile, had ideas about the nature of the industry that were quite different from those held by other manufacturers. The automobile, intended for sale to those who were willing to pay large sums for it, was generally beyond the means of the average American. Vehicles selling for under $2,000 were inferior and unreliable. Although by 1904 the average cost of an automobile was down to $1,382, the price was still high. It was Ford's firm belief that the automobile would soon cease to be merely a novelty and become the basis of transportation. As such, he reasoned, the car should be priced as low as possible, and maintenance costs cut, in order to make it available to a wide segment of the population. Thus in 1903, the first year of its existence, the Ford Motor Company brought out the Model A to be sold for $850. In 1904 it sold 1,708 cars, but the number declined in 1905 and 1906. Then, in 1907, Ford acquired control of the company's stock and was able to put his ideas into practice without the restraining influence of his partners. That year the cheapest Ford sold for $600 (the average price for the entire industry was $2,123) and sales jumped to 8,423, a fifth of the total number of American cars produced.

In the course of the suit against Ford hundreds of witnesses were called, mountains of evidence produced. Year after year the legal maneuvering and wrangling continued. In 1906, to strenghten his claims, Selden had an automobile built in accordance with the specifications of his patent. It constituted a carriage body, an engine of the Brayton type, running gear, propeller-shaft, and driving wheels. On the side of it Selden placed the date 1877, the year of its conception, in large numbers. That the car had a good deal of trouble starting and moving did not bother Selden. This, he claimed, was the fault of the garage that had built it.

In 1909 Judge Charles Hough handed down his momentous decision in the U.S. District Court in New York City that Ford had infringed the Selden patent and was subject to payment of royalties in addition to back payments totalling an enormous amount. The Ford Company announced that it would appeal the decision, and both sides girded for battle to the finish. At a time when large monopolies were being broken, the American public was sympathetic to Ford, a man of initiative set upon by a monopoly controlling market prices and representing capital holdings of some $70,000,000. (The claim made by the A.L.A.M. in the Announcement in the 1904 edition of the *Hand Book*, that all members operated in open competition, should be taken with a grain of salt.) This second trial, ending in January 1911, brought vindication for Ford and the decision that he had not infringed the Selden patent. Ford had used a four-cycle engine, developed by Otto and Langen in Germany in 1866. On the basis of a disparaging note Selden had written about it in his diary— "another damned Dutch engine"—the Selden patent was held valid only for the Brayton two-cycle engine. Thus Ford did not have to pay Selden, and since virtually all manufacturers were using the Otto and Langen type engine, the A.L.A.M. lost its *raison d'être* and was dissolved. It has been estimated that in the seventeen years

during which the patent was in effect (1895-1912), Selden himself
made only $200,000.

If the A.L.A.M. had no great success as a monopoly, it did leave
several major accomplishments behind it. It had published the *Hand
Book* (which was to continue until 1929) and it had instituted a
program in Hartford (1910) to standardize automobile parts. Up to
that time the amount of money one could expect to spend on the
maintenance of an automobile was extremely high, and the difficulty
in securing replacement parts for individual models was a cause
of additional expense and vexation. By standardizing replacements,
maintenance could be significantly reduced, as Ford had already
shown in 1908, when he had introduced the Model T, the "universal
car" designed for simplicity. The A.L.A.M. attempted to standardize
the entire industry.

After the court decision, there was a general recognition by the
industry of the need to retain some central organization, and the
Automobile Board of Trade, consisting of former A.L.A.M. members
in addition to many other companies not formerly Selden licensees,
was formed in 1912. This new group then became the National
Automobile Chamber of Commerce in 1914. It developed a system
of cross-licensing patents (members did not have to pay royalties),
continued the *Hand Book,* sponsored research in matters affecting
the trade (including the promotion of highway safety), managed the
New York and Chicago Automobile Shows, and took active interest
in legislation pertaining to the automobile. For the quarter-century
between 1904 and 1929, a period of many vicissitudes experienced
by the growing industry especially plagued by patent suits, bank-
ruptcies, the panic of 1907, reorganizations and mergers, the annual
appearance of the *Hand Book* was an event of prime importance. In
shape, format and substance, the *Hand Book* withstood the changing
times. Numerous manufacturers zoomed across the horizon only to
disappear quickly and be replaced by others. The industry grew and
prospered, and the *Hand Book* reflected this growth. The total number of passenger cars sold in 1904 was 22,130; it was 181,000 in 1910,

1,905,560 in 1920, and 4,455,178 in 1929. In the year 1895 only 4 cars were registered in the United States; 458,500 were registered in 1910, 8,225,859 in 1920, and 23,060,421 in 1929. From the slim volume at birth in 1904, the *Hand Book* expanded until it approached 300 pages. The 1922 edition contained a Foreign Supplement printed in English, French, German, and Spanish. Translations included reference to the N.A.C.C. organization, its purposes and committees, as well as technical terms used throughout the *Hand Book*. A few years later the *Hand Book* was divided into four sections. The 1925 issue stated in its introduction: "In this Twenty-second Annual Handbook of Automobiles are illustrated 193 motor vehicles, comprising 116 private passenger automobiles, 62 commercial cars and motor trucks, 6 taxicabs and 9 motor buses; 188 are gasoline and 5 electric vehicles. A new feature of the book is the provision of special sections for taxicabs and motor buses."

The *Hand Book* is now valued as a rich and authoritative record of the formative years of the American automobile industry. The entire fraternity of antique car enthusiasts, collectors, and restorers will welcome and benefit from its general availability.

CLARENCE P. HORNUNG

New York, N.Y.
March 1969

Hand Book of
Gasoline
Automobiles

[1904]

Hand Book of

Gasoline
Automobiles

For the information of the
public who are interested
in their manufacture
and use

1904

Association ot Licensed Automobile
Manufacturers

7 East 42d Street, New York City, U. S. A.

Announcement

THIS "Hand Book" is issued primarily for convenience and information to the prospective purchaser of an automobile. The products of the principal manufacturers throughout the United States of America and the importers of gasoline machines are shown by illustrations and specifications. These specifications form a series of the leading questions that arise in the mind of the purchaser, with the answers thereto in red ink. The questions being uniform, the ease of comparison is obvious and the purchaser is enabled to select the machines which are best suited to the service required, to his personal taste, or the means at his command.

It is believed by the several manufacturers who have united in producing this publication that this disinterested method of placing before the purchaser this means of comparison will be found of great advantage.

Each manufacturer or importer conducts his business entirely independent of the other, and, of course, in open competition, but the recognition by the companies represented herein of the basic patent No. 549,160, granted to George B. Selden, November 5th, 1895, on gasoline automobiles (which controls broadly all gasoline automobiles which are accepted as commercially practicable), is a guarantee that a purchase through the several companies herein represented, or through their agents, secures to the purchaser freedom from the annoyance and expense of litigation because of infringement of this patent.

The following manufacturers and importers are licensed under the basic patent No. 549,160, granted to George B. Selden, dated November 5th, 1895, and are the owners of about 400 other patents on

Gasoline   Automobiles

Alphabetical Index

Index of Trade Names

APPERSON BROTHERS AUTOMOBILE COMPANY, KOKOMO, IND

Price

without top
$3500

with top and
standing glass
$3625

Model : " B " 1905 TOURING CAR.

Body : **Side door tonneau.**

Color : **Maroon or fancy green.**

Seating capacity : **Five** passengers.

Total weight : **2400** pounds.

Wheel base : **102** inches.

Wheel gauge : **54** inches.

Wheel diameter : **34** inches rear, **32** inches front.

Tire diameter : **4** inches.

Steering : **Wheel.**

Brakes : **Foot and hand emergency.**

Gasoline capacity : **20** gallons.

Frame : **Pressed steel.**

Horse-power : **24.**

Number of cylinders : **Four.**

Cylinders arranged : **Separately, vertical in front.**

Cooling : **Water.**

Ignition : **Jump spark.**

Drive : **Double chain.**

Transmission : **Sliding gear.**

Speeds : **Three forward and one reverse.**

Style of top : **Cape hood.**

APPERSON BROTHERS AUTOMOBILE COMPANY, KOKOMO, IND.

Price
with top
$5000

Model : "**A**" **TOURING CAR.**

Body : **Side door or rear door tonneau.**

Color : **Optional.**

Seating capacity : **Six** or **seven** passengers.

Total weight : **2800** pounds.

Wheel base : **114** inches.

Wheel gauge : **56** inches.

Wheel diameter : **34** inches.

Tire diameter : **4½** inches.

Steering : **Wheel.**

Brakes : **Foot and hand emergency.**

Gasoline capacity : **20** gallons.

Frame : **Pressed steel.**

Horse-power : **40.**

Number of cylinders : **Four.**

Cylinders arranged **Separately, vertical in front.**

Cooling : **Water.**

Ignition : **Jump spark.**

Drive : **Double chain.**

Transmission : **Sliding gear.**

Speeds : **Four forward and one reverse.**

Style of top : **Canopy.**

THE AUTOCAR COMPANY, ARDMORE, PA.

Price

$900
tops not
furnished

Model : **AUTOCAR, TYPE X.**

Body : **Two-passenger Runabout.**

Color : **Blue.**

Seating capacity : **Two** persons.

Total weight . **1200** pounds.

Wheel base : **70** inches.

Wheel gauge : **52** inches.

Wheel diameter : **28** inches.

Tire diameter : **3** inches.

Steering : **Lever.**

Brakes : **Foot lever on rear wheels ; foot lever on drive shaft.**

Gasoline capacity : **8** gallons.

Frame : **Wood, steel lined.**

Horse-power : **10-12.**

Number of cylinders : **Two.**

Cylinders arranged : **Separate and horizontal in front.**

Cooling : **Water, flange coil radiator.**

Ignition : **Jump spark and dry battery.**

Drive : **Bevel gear.**

Transmission : **Sliding gears.**

Speeds : **Three forward and one reverse.**

Style of top : **No tops furnished.**

THE AUTOCAR COMPANY, ARDMORE, PA.

Price

$1700
tops not
furnished

Model : **AUTOCAR, TYPE VIII.**

Body : **High back tonneau.**

Color : **Red or green.**

Seating capacity : **Four** persons.

Total weight : **1700** pounds.

Wheel base : **76** inches.

Wheel gauge : **54** inches.

Wheel diameter : **30** inches.

Tire diameter : **3½** inches.

Steering : **Wheel.**

Brakes : **Foot lever on rear wheels ;
foot lever on drive shaft.**

Gasoline capacity : **10** gallons.

Frame : **Wood, steel lined.**

Horse-power : **12-14.**

Number of cylinders : **Two.**

Cylinders arranged : **Separate and horizontal in front.**

Cooling : **Water, cellular radiator.**

Ignition : **Jump spark and dry battery.**

Drive : **Spur and bevel gears.**

Transmission : **Sliding gears.**

Speeds : **Three forward and one reverse.**

Style of top : **No tops furnished.**

AUTO IMPORT COMPANY, 1786 BROADWAY, NEW YORK, N. Y.

Price

with top
$8000

Model: **ROCHET-SCHNEIDER, 1905.**

Body: **Side door double phaeton.**

Color: **To suit.**

Seating capacity: **Five to seven** persons.

Total weight: **2300** pounds.

Wheel base: **112** inches.

Wheel gauge: **56** inches.

Wheel diameter: **36** inches.

Tire diameter: **5** inches.

Steering: **Wheel, worm gear.**

Brakes: **4 band brakes.**

Gasoline capacity: **30** gallons.

Frame: **Pressed steel.**

Horse-power: **24-35** (also **35-50**).

Number of cylinders: **Four.**

Cylinders arranged: **Vertical, tandem.**

Cooling: **Water, honeycomb radiator with fan and pump.**

Ignition: **Magneto, make and break.**

Drive: **Double chain.**

Transmission: **Spur gear, ball bearing.**

Speeds: **Four forward and one reverse; fourth direct.**

Style of top: **Rounded glass back and glass front.**

SIDNEY B. BOWMAN AUTOMOBILE CO., 52 W. 43D ST., NEW YORK

Price

$7000

Model: **CLEMENT-BAYARD.**

Body: **Coupé-Limousine, with detachable coupé top.**

Color: **Dark blue.**

Seating capacity: **Five** persons.

Total weight: **2500** pounds.

Wheel base: **108** inches.

Wheel gauge: **54** inches.

Wheel diameter: **34** inches.

Tire diameter: **4¼** inches.

Steering: **Wheel, irreversible worm
gear.**

Brake: **Internal expansion, double-
acting.**

Gasoline capacity: **18** gallons.

Frame: **Pressed steel.**

Horse-power: **20.**

Number of cylinders: **Four.**

Cylinders arranged: **Vertical, individual.**

Cooling: **Water, honeycomb radiator
with fan and pump.**

Ignition: **Make and break, with
magneto.**

Drive: **Bevel gear to live axle.**

Transmission: **Sliding gear, direct
drive on high gear.**

Speeds: **Four forward, one reverse.**

Style of top: **Coupé, detachable.**

CADILLAC AUTOMOBILE CO., DETROIT, MICHIGAN

Price

with top
$850
without top
$800

Model : **" B " RUNABOUT.**

Body : **Convertible to tonneau.**

Color : **Maroon.**

Seating capacity : **Two** persons.

Total weight : **1300** pounds.

Wheel base : **76** inches.

Wheel gauge : **54½** inches.

Wheel diameter : **30** inches.

Tire diameter : **3** inches.

Steering : **Wheel, rack and pinion.**

Brakes : **Rear axle double bands.**

Gasoline capacity : **6** gallons.

Frame : **Pressed steel, hot riveted.**

Horse-power : **8¼.**

Number of cylinders : **One.**

Cylinder arranged : **Horizontal.**

Cooling : **Water.**

Ignition : **Jump spark.**

Drive : **Single chain.**

Transmission : **Planetary.**

Speeds : **Two forward and reverse.**

Style of top : **Leather with apron and side curtains.**

CADILLAC AUTOMOBILE CO., DETROIT, MICHIGAN

Price
$900

Model: **"B" TOURING CAR.**

Body: **Detachable tonneau.**

Color: **Maroon.**

Seating capacity: **Four** persons.

Total weight: **1420** pounds.

Wheel base: **76** inches.

Wheel gauge: **54½** inches.

Wheel diameter: **30** inches.

Tire diameter: **3** inches.

Steering: **Wheel, with rack and pinion.**

Brakes: **Rear axle double bands.**

Gasoline capacity: **6** gallons.

Frame: **Pressed steel, hot riveted.**

Horse-power: **8¼**.

Number of cylinders: **One.**

Cylinder arranged: **Horizontal.**

Cooling: **Water.**

Ignition: **Jump spark.**

Drive: **Single chain.**

Transmission: **Planetary.**

Speeds: **Two forward and one reverse.**

CADILLAC AUTOMOBILE CO., DETROIT, MICHIGAN

Price
$900

Model: "B" DELIVERY.

Body: Not convertible.

Color: Maroon.

Seating capacity: Two persons.

Carrying capacity: 600 to 800 pounds.

Total weight: 1460 pounds.

Wheel base: 76 inches.

Wheel gauge: 54½ inches.

Wheel diameter: 30 inches.

Tire diameter: 3½ inches.

Steering: Wheel rack and pinion.

Brakes: Rear axle double bands.

Gasoline capacity: 6 gallons.

Frame: Pressed steel.

Horse-power: 8¼.

Number of cylinders: One.

Cylinder arranged: Horizontal.

Cooling: Water.

Ignition: Jump spark.

Drive: Single chain.

Transmission: Planetary.

Speeds: Two forward and one reverse.

Size of top: Inside dimensions, height 50 inches, width 40 inches, length 42 inches.

CREST   MANUFACTURING   CO.,   CAMBRIDGE,   MASS.

Price

with glass front
canopy
$1050
with tonneau
$900
without tonneau
$800

Model: **CRESTMOBILE " D " 1904.**

Body: **Tonneau, wood.**

Color: **Carmine or Brewster green.**

Seating capacity: **Two** or **four** persons.

Total weight: **1200** pounds.

Wheel base: **76** inches.

Wheel gauge: **54** inches.

Wheel diameter: **28** inches.

Tire diameter: **3** inches.

Steering: **Wheel with locking device.**

Brakes: **On differential.**

Gasoline capacity: **6** gallons.

Frame: **Tubular steel.**

Horse-power: **8½.**

Number of cylinders: **One.**

Cylinder arranged: **Vertical, in front.**

Cooling: **Air cooled, with fan.**

Ignition: **Jump spark.**

Drive: **Shaft drive with bevel gears.**

Transmission: **Individual clutches and friction bands.**

Speeds: **Two forward, one reverse.**

Style of top: **Canopy with glass front.**

THE CENTRAL AUTOMOBILE CO., 1684 BROADWAY, NEW YORK

Price
—
with top
$8800

without top
$8500

Model: **MORS TOURING CAR.**

Body: **Aluminum ; side entrance.**

Color: **Red.**

Seating capacity: **Five** persons.

Total weight: **2400** pounds.

Wheel base: **99** inches.

Wheel gauge: **56** inches.

Wheel diameter: **30** inches.

Tire diameter: **915 x 105** m/m.

Steering: **Wheel.**

Brakes: **1 service, 2 emergency.**

Gasoline capacity: **20** gallons.

Frame: **Pressed steel.**

Horse-power: **Rated 24, actual 36.**

Number of cylinders: **Four.**

Cylinders arranged: **Vertically, in front.**

Cooling: **Water.**

Ignition: **Make and break with mag-neto.**

Drive: **Double chain.**

Transmission: **Sliding gear.**

Speeds: **Four forward, one reverse.**

Style of top: **Canopy, sliding glass front.**

THE CENTRAL AUTOMOBILE CO., 1684 BROADWAY, NEW YORK

Price
———
with top
$7200
without top
$7000

Model: **NAPIER TOURING CAR.**

Body: **Aluminum; tonneau, rear entrance.**

Color: **Napier green.**

Seating capacity: **Four** persons.

Total weight: **1800** pounds.

Wheel base: **86** inches.

Wheel gauge: **52** inches.

Wheel diameter: **28** inches.

Tire diameter: **870 x 90** m/m.

Steering: **Wheel.**

Brakes: **1** service, **2** emergency.

Gasoline capacity: **15** gallons.

Frame: **Armored.**

Horse-power: **15-18.**

Number of cylinders: **Four.**

Cylinders arranged: **Vertically, in front.**

Cooling: **Water.**

Ignition: **Jump spark with battery, single point coil.**

Drive: **Double chain.**

Transmission: **Sliding gear.**

Speeds: **Four forward and reverse.**

Style of top: **Cape cart.**

THE COMMERCIAL MOTOR CO., 49–51 WEST 66TH ST., NEW YORK

Price

$4000

Model: **THE WALTER.**

Body. **Aluminum, King of Belgians, with side entrance.**

Color: **Blue or any color desired.**

Seating capacity: **Five** persons.

Total weight: **2400** pounds.

Wheel base: **96** inches.

Wheel gauge: **56½** inches.

Wheel diameter: **34** inches.

Tire diameter: **4** inches.

Steering: **Wheel, worm and segment type.**

Brakes: (3) **internal expansion on rear hubs, foot brake on differential.**

Gasoline capacity: **20** gallons.

Frame: **Pressed cold-rolled steel.**

Horse-power: **30.**

Number of cylinders: **Four.**

Cylinders arranged: **Vertical.**

Cooling: **Water, honeycomb radiator.**

Ignition: **Jump spark, storage batteries.**

Drive: **Bevel gear.**

Transmission: **Sliding gear.**

Speeds: **Three forward and reverse.**

Style of top: **None furnished, body fitted for one.**

ELECTRIC VEHICLE COMPANY, HARTFORD, CONN.

Price

with top
$1950
without top
$1750

Model:**COLUMBIA, MARK XLIII.**

Body:**Wood** tonneau, divided front seat.

Color :**Dark green or maroon.**

Seating capacity :**Four** persons.

Total weight :**1800** pounds.

Wheel base :**81¾** inches.

Wheel gauge :**55** inches.

Wheel diameter :**30** inches.

Tire diameter :**3½** inches.

Steering:**Wheel.**

Brakes :**Foot lever on driving shaft, hand lever on both rear wheels.**

Gasoline capacity :**10** gallons.

Frame :**Pressed steel.**

Horse-power :**12-14.**

Number of cylinders :**Two.**

Cylinders arranged : **Horizontal opposed, front under bonnet.**

Cooling :**Water, cellular radiator with fan.**

Ignition :**Jump spark, battery of 24 dry cells.**

Drive :**Shaft and bevel gear.**

Transmission :**Sliding gear.**

Speeds :**Three forward, one reverse.**

Style of top :**Canopy, glass front.**

ELECTRIC VEHICLE COMPANY, HARTFORD, CONN.

Price

with standard
wood body
$4000
with top
$4300

Model: **COLUMBIA, MARK XLII.**

Body: **Wood tonneau (aluminum tonneau, side door wood or aluminum, and limousine bodies at extra prices).**

Color. **Maroon, green or blue.**

Seating capacity: **Six** persons.

Total weight: **2800** pounds.

Wheel base. **106** inches.

Wheel gauge: **56** inches.

Wheel diameter: **34** inches.

Tire diameter: **4½** inches.

Steering: **Wheel.**

Brakes: **Hand lever on both rear wheels ; foot lever on countershaft.**

Gasoline capacity: **21** gallons.

Frame: **Pressed steel.**

Horse-power: **30-35.**

Number of cylinders: **Four.**

Cylinders arranged: **Forward, vertical under folding bonnet.**

Cooling: **Water, cellular radiator with fan.**

Ignition: **Jump spark ; secondary current, storage batteries.**

Drive: **Individual chains to rear wheels.**

Transmission: **Sliding gears.**

Speeds: **Four forward, one reverse.**

Style of top: **Canopy, glass front.**

ELECTRIC VEHICLE COMPANY, HARTFORD, CONN.

Price
$5000

Model : **COLUMBIA, MARK XLII.**

Body : **Limousine, wood, side door entrances.**

Color : **Optional.**

Seating capacity : **Five to seven** persons.

Total weight : **3100** pounds.

Wheel base : **110** inches.

Wheel gauge : **56** inches.

Wheel diameter : **34** inches.

Tire diameter : **4½** inches.

Steering : **Wheel.**

Brakes : **Hand lever on both rear wheels, foot lever on countershaft.**

Gasoline capacity : **21** gallons.

Frame : **Pressed steel.**

Horse-power : **30-35.**

Number of cylinders : **Four.**

Cylinders arranged : **Forward, vertical under folding bonnet.**

Cooling : **Water, cellular radiator with fan.**

Ignition : **Jump spark, secondary current storage batteries.**

Drive : **Individual chains to rear wheels.**

Transmission : **Sliding gears.**

Speeds : **Four forward, one reverse.**

Style of top : **Limousine.**

ELMORE MANUFACTURING COMPANY, CLYDE, OHIO

Price
without top
$850

Model : **ELMORE, "9."**

Body : **Wood.**

Color : **Red or blue.**

Seating capacity : **Four** persons.

Total weight : **1200** pounds.

Wheel base : **78** inches.

Wheel gauge : **56** inches.

Wheel diameter : **28** inches.

Tire diameter : **3** inches.

Steering : **Wheel-geared.**

Brakes : **2.**

Gasoline capacity : **7** gallons.

Frame : **Steel.**

Horse-power : **10.**

Number of cylinders : **One.**

Cylinder arranged : **Horizontal.**

Cooling : **Water.**

Ignition : **Jump spark, dry cells.**

Drive : **Chain.**

Transmission : **Planetary.**

Speeds : **Two speeds forward and reverse.**

ELMORE MANUFACTURING COMPANY, CLYDE, OHIO

Price
with top
$850

Model : **DELIVERY WAGON.**

Body : **Wood.**

Color : **Optional.**

Seating capacity : **Two** persons.

Total weight : **1400** pounds.

Wheel base : **78** inches.

Wheel gauge : **56** inches.

Wheel diameter : **28** inches.

Tire diameter : **3** inches.

Steering : **Wheel-geared.**

Brakes : **2.**

Gasoline capacity : **7** gallons.

Frame : **Steel.**

Horse-power : **10.**

Number of cylinders : **One.**

Cylinder arranged : **Horizontal.**

Cooling : **Water.**

Ignition : **Jump spark, dry cells.**

Drive : **Chain.**

Transmission : **Planetary.**

Speeds : **Two forward and reverse.**

Style of top : **Paneled.**

H. H. FRANKLIN MANUFACTURING CO., SYRACUSE, N. Y.

Price

with top
$1600
without top
$1400

Model: **"A" LIGHT RUNABOUT.**

Body: **Aluminum, with steel frame.**

Color: **Red, option of blue body with red running gear.**

Seating capacity: **Two** persons.

Total weight: **1100** pounds.

Wheel base: **78** inches.

Wheel gauge: **56** inches.

Wheel diameter: **28** inches.

Tire diameter: **3¼** inches.

Steering: **Wheel, Brown-Lipe worm gear.**

Brakes: **Rear wheels, hub brakes.**

Gasoline capacity: **7½** gallons.

Frame: **Angle iron.**

Horse-power: **10.**

Number of cylinders: **Four.**

Cylinders arranged: **Vertically.**

Cooling: **Air.**

Ignition: **Jump spark with dry battery.**

Drive: **Chain.**

Transmission: **Planetary.**

Speeds: **Two forward and reverse.**

Style of top: **Glass front canopy.**

H. H. FRANKLIN MANUFACTURING CO., SYRACUSE, N. Y.

Price

without top
$1650

Model: **"B" LIGHT TONNEAU.**

Body: **Aluminum, with steel frame.**

Color: **Red, option of blue body with red running gear.**

Seating capacity: **Four** persons.

Total weight: **1200** pounds.

Wheel base: **78** inches.

Wheel gauge: **56** inches.

Wheel diameter: **28** inches.

Tire diameter: **3¼** inches.

Steering: **Wheel, Brown-Lipe worm gear.**

Brakes: **Rear wheels, hub brakes.**

Gasoline capacity: **7½** gallons.

Frame: **Angle iron.**

Horse-power: **10.**

Number of cylinders: **Four.**

Cylinders arranged: **Vertically.**

Cooling: **Air.**

Ignition: **Jump spark, with dry battery.**

Drive: **Chain.**

Transmission: **Planetary.**

Speeds: **Two forward and reverse.**

H. H. FRANKLIN MANUFACTURING CO., SYRACUSE, N. Y.

Price
with top
$3250
without top
$3000

Model : "C" TOURING CAR.

Body : Aluminum, with metal frame.

Color : Red, option of blue body with red running gear.

Seating capacity : Five persons.

Total weight : 2200 pounds.

Wheel base : 96 inches.

Wheel gauge : 56 inches.

Wheel diameter : 32 inches.

Tire diameter : 4 inches.

Steering : Wheel, Brown-Lipe worm gear.

Brakes : Rear wheels, hub brakes.

Gasoline capacity : 16 gallons.

Frame : Angle iron.

Horse-power : 24.

Number of cylinders : Four.

Cylinders arranged : Vertically.

Cooling : Air.

Ignition : Jump spark, with dry battery.

Drive : Bevel gear.

Transmission : Planetary.

Speeds : Two forward and reverse.

Style of top : Glass front canopy.

THE KIRK MANUFACTURING COMPANY, TOLEDO, OHIO

Price

with top

$1800

without top

$1600

Model: **YALE**, **"D"** with top, **"C"** without top.

Body: **Wood, tonneau detachable.**

Color: **Blue.**

Seating capacity: **Five** persons.

Total weight: **1850** pounds.

Wheel base: **84** inches.

Wheel gauge: **56** inches.

Wheel diameter: **32** inches.

Tire diameter: **Front, 3½** inches; **rear, 4** inches.

Steering: **Wheel.**

Brakes: **2 on differential gear, 1 on rear wheels.**

Gasoline capacity: **12** gallons.

Frame: **Angle steel.**

Horse-power: **16.**

Number of cylinders: **Two.**

Cylinders arranged: **Horizontal, opposed.**

Cooling: **Water.**

Ignition: **Jump spark with two sets of batteries.**

Drive: **Chain.**

Transmission: **Planetary.**

Speeds: **Two forward, one reverse.**

Style of top: **Canopy.**

THE HAYNES-APPERSON CO., KOKOMO, IND

Price

with top

$1450

without top

$1400

Model : **"HAYNES" TWO PAS-SENGER TOURING CAR.**

Body : **Wood.**

Color : **Sage green body, onyx green wheels.**

Seating capacity : **Two** persons.

Total weight : **1500** pounds.

Wheel base : **76** inches.

Wheel gauge : **56** inches.

Wheel diameter : **32** inches.

Tire diameter : **3** inches.

Steering : **Adjustable wheel.**

Brakes : **Double, direct-acting.**

Gasoline capacity : **6** gallons.

Frame : **Angle iron.**

Horse-power : **12.**

Number of cylinders : **Two.**

Cylinders arranged : **Horizontal, opposed.**

Cooling : **Water, radiator.**

Ignition : **Make and break.**

Drive : **Chain.**

Transmission : **Individual clutch.**

Speeds : **Three forward and reverse.**

Style of top : **Folding.**

THE HAYNES-APPERSON CO., KOKOMO, IND.

Price

with top
$2550
without top
$2450

Model: **"HAYNES" FOUR PAS-SENGER TOURING.**

Body : **King of Belgians, aluminum seats.**

Color : **Sage green body, onyx green wheels.**

Seating capacity : **Five** persons.

Total weight : **2600** pounds.

Wheel base : **93** inches.

Wheel gauge : **56** inches.

Wheel diameter : **32** inches.

Tire diameter : **4** inches.

Steering : **Adjustable wheel.**

Brakes : **2 hub brakes, 2 direct-acting.**

Gasoline capacity : **12** gallons.

Frame : **Angle iron.**

Number of cylinders : **Two.**

Cylinders arranged : **Horizontal, op-posed.**

Cooling : **Water, fan and cellular cooler.**

Ignition : **Jump spark.**

Drive : **Chain.**

Transmission : **Individual clutch.**

Speeds : **Three forward and one reverse.**

Style of top : **Canopy with glass front.**

HOLLANDER & TANGEMAN, 5 WEST 45TH ST., NEW YORK

Price

without top
$6700
with top
extra
$150 to
$300

Model: **F I A T , 1904 or 1905.**

Body : **Choice, King of Belgians, Leo-pold or Princess Laetizia.**

Color : **Choice.**

Seating capacity : **Tonneau body, five places ; Side entrance body, seven places.**

Total weight : **Tonneau, 2050** pounds ; **Side entrance, 2200** pounds.

Wheel base : **90, 109 or 116** inches.

Wheel gauge : **56** inches.

Wheel diameter : **36** inches.

Tire diameter : **3⅝** inches.

Steering : **Irreversible wheel.**

Brakes : **(Three) expanding and band types.**

Gasoline capacity : **25** gallons.

Frame : **Pressed steel.**

Horse-power : **16-20.**

Number of cylinders : **Four.**

Cylinders arranged : **Vertical, in pairs.**

Cooling : **Daimler patented multi-cellular water radiator.**

Ignition : **Magneto, make and break.**

Drive : **Double chain.**

Transmission : **Sliding gear.**

Speeds : **Four forward, one reverse.**

Style of top : **Canopy, cape or closed.**

HOLLANDER & TANGEMAN, 5 WEST 45th ST., NEW YORK

Price

without top
$8500
with top, extra
$150 to $300

Model : **F I A T** **1904 or 1905.**

Body : **Choice, King of Belgians, Leopold or Princess Laetizia.**

Color : **Choice.**

Seating capacity : **Tonneau, five** places ; **Side entrance, seven** places.

Total weight : **Tonneau, 2150** pounds ; **Side entrance, 2300** pounds.

Wheel base : **90, 109 or 116** inches.

Wheel gauge : **55** inches.

Wheel diameter : **36** inches.

Tire diameter : **Front, 3⅝** inches ; **rear, 4⅛** inches.

Steering : **Irreversible wheel.**

Brakes : (3) **Expanding and band types.**

Gasoline capacity : **25** gallons.

Frame : **Pressed steel.**

Horse-power : **24-30** (also **60** and **90**).

Number of cylinders : **Four.**

Cylinders arranged : **Vertical, in pairs.**

Cooling : **Daimler patented multi-cellular water radiator.**

Ignition : **Magneto, make and break.**

Drive : **Double chains.**

Transmission : **Sliding gear.**

Speeds : **Four forward, one reverse.**

Style of top : **Canopy, cape or closed.**

KNOX AUTOMOBILE CO., SPRINGFIELD, MASS.

Price

with top
$1335 and **$1350**
without top
$1250

Model : **RUNABOUT** with folding front seat.

Body : **Wood.**

Color : **Standard red** or **green.**

Seating capacity : **4** persons.

Total weight : **1700** pounds.

Wheel base : **72** inches.

Wheel gauge : **54** inches.

Wheel diameter : **30** inches.

Tire diameter : **3½** inches.

Steering : **Lever and Lemp check.**

Brakes : **2 foot levers and 1 hand lever.**

Gasoline capacity : **8** gallons.

Frame : **Angle steel.**

Horse-power : **8-10.**

Number of cylinders : **One.**

Cylinder arranged : **Horizontal under center.**

Cooling : **Knox patent air cooler.**

Ignition : **Jump spark, dry cells.**

Drive : **Single chain.**

Transmission : **Planetary.**

Speeds : **Two forward, one reverse.**

Style of top : **Buggy or victoria.**

KNOX AUTOMOBILE CO., SPRINGFIELD, MASS.

Price

with top
$1675
without top
$1500

Model: **LENOX.**

Body: **Tonneau, wood.**

Color: **Standard red or green.**

Seating capacity: **Five** persons.

Total weight: **2000** pounds.

Wheel base: **78** inches.

Wheel gauge: **56** inches.

Wheel diameter: **30** inches.

Tire diameter: **4** inches.

Steering: **Lever and Lemp check.**

Brakes: **2 foot levers and 1 hand lever.**

Gasoline capacity: **16** gallons.

Frame: **Angle steel.**

Horse-power: **8-10.**

Number of cylinders: **One.**

Cylinder arranged: **Horizontal under center.**

Cooling: **Knox patent air cooler.**

Ignition: **Jump spark, dry cells.**

Drive: **Single chain.**

Transmission: **Planetary.**

Speeds: **Two forward, one reverse.**

Style of top: **Canopy, with glass front and curtains.**

KNOX AUTOMOBILE CO., SPRINGFIELD, MASS.

Price

with top
$2500

without top
$2300

Model : **TUDOR.**

Body : **King of Belgians, side or rear
entrance.**

Color : **Standard red or green.**

Seating capacity : **Five** persons.

Total weight : **2400** pounds.

Wheel base : **84** inches.

Wheel gauge : **56** inches.

Wheel diameter : **32** inches.

Tire diameter : **4** inches.

Steering : **Lever and Lemp check.**

Brakes : **2 foot levers and 1 hand
lever.**

Gasoline capacity : **14** gallons.

Frame : **Angle steel.**

Horse-power : **16-18.**

Number of cylinders : **Two.**

Cylinders arranged : **Horizontal opposed, under center.**

Cooling : **Knox patent air cooler.**

Ignition : **Jump spark, dry cells.**

Drive : **Single chain.**

Transmission : **Planetary.**

Speeds : **Two forward, one reverse.**

Style of top : **Canopy, with glass front
and curtains.**

KNOX AUTOMOBILE CO., SPRINGFIELD, MASS.

Price

with paneled top
$2500
with canvas top
$2450
without top
$2400

Model : **CRANE DELIVERY (also four other sizes of delivery cars).**

Body : **Wood.**

Color : **Standard red or green.**

Carrying capacity : **2500** pounds.

Total weight : **2800** pounds.

Wheel base : **98** inches.

Wheel gauge : **56** inches.

Wheel diameter : **32** inches.

Tire diameter : **Solid, 32 x 4** inches.

Steering : **Lever and Lemp check.**

Brakes : **2 foot levers and 1 hand lever.**

Gasoline capacity : **13** gallons.

Frame : **Angle steel.**

Horse-power : **16-18.**

Number of cylinders : **Two.**

Cylinders arranged : **Horizontal opposed, under center.**

Cooling : **Knox patent air cooler.**

Ignition : **Jump spark, dry cells.**

Drive : **Single chain.**

Transmission : **Planetary.**

Speeds : **Two forward, one reverse.**

Style of top : **Canvas or paneled.**

F. A. LA ROCHE CO., 147 W. 38TH ST., 652–664 HUDSON ST., NEW YORK

Price
—
with top
$5500

without top
$5000

Model ·   **DARRACQ,   DOUBLE PHAETON TULIP** .

Body : **Entrance on two sides.**

Color : **Royal blue, robin-egg blue and red bodies ; running gear, red.**

Seating capacity : **Five** persons.

Total weight : **Without canopy top, 1900** pounds.

Wheel base : **97** inches.

Wheel gauge : **51½** inches.

Wheel diameter : **810 x 90 m/m, front and rear.**

Tire diameter : **810 x 90 m/m, front and rear.**

Steering : **Wheel.**

Brakes : **Double acting on transmission and rear wheels.**

Gasoline capacity : **14** gallons.

Frame : **Pressed steel from one piece.**

Horse-power : **15-20.**

Number of cylinders : **Four.**

Cylinders arranged : **Vertical in pairs.**

Cooling : **Water, " Mercedes " honeycomb radiator.**

Ignition : **Jump spark.**

Drive : **Bevel gear.**

Transmission : **Sliding gears.**

Speeds : **Three forward and one reverse.**

Style of top : **Canopy ; sliding glass front and rear, side curtains.**

F. A. La ROCHE CO., 147 W. 38TH ST., 652–664 HUDSON ST., NEW YORK

Price
with top
$8500
without top
$8000

Model : **DARRACQ, DOUBLE PHAETON TULIP.**

Body : **Entrance on two sides.**

Color : **Royal blue, robin-egg blue and red bodies ; red running gear.**

Seating capacity : **Five** persons.

Total weight : **Without canopy top, 2750** pounds.

Wheel base : **100** inches.

Wheel gauge : **54** inches.

Wheel diameter : **870 x 90** m/m, **front ; 880 x 120** m/m, **rear.**

Tire diameter : **870 x 90** m/m, **front ; 880 x 120** m/m, **rear.**

Steering : **Wheel.**

Brakes : **Double acting on transmission and rear wheels.**

Gasoline capacity : **16** gallons.

Frame : **Pressed steel from one piece.**

Horse-power : **30-35.**

Number of cylinders : **Four.**

Cylinders arranged : **Vertical in pairs.**

Cooling : **Water, " Mercedes " honeycomb radiator.**

Ignition : **Jump spark, and make and break with magneto.**

Drive : **Bevel gear.**

Transmission : **Sliding gears.**

Speeds : **Three forward and one reverse.**

Style of top : **Canopy ; sliding glass front and rear, side curtains.**

THE LOCOMOBILE COMPANY OF AMERICA, BRIDGEPORT, CONN.

Price

with top
$2325

without top
$2100

Model : **TYPE " C."**

Body : **Detachable tonneau, built of wood.**

Color : **As desired by the purchaser.**

Seating capacity : **Five** persons.

Total weight : **1600** pounds.

Wheel base : **76** inches.

Wheel gauge : **50** inches.

Wheel diameter : **30** inches.

Tire diameter : **3½** inches.

Steering : **Hand wheel with irreversible worm gear.**

Brakes : (3) **Foot brake on differential ; emergency brakes on rear wheels ; sprag.**

Gasoline capacity : **10** gallons.

Frame : **One-piece rectangular channel steel frame. (Patented.)**

Horse-power : **9-12.**

Number of cylinders : **Two.**

Cylinders arranged : **Vertically and longitudinally in front.**

Cooling : **Water, by centrifugal pump. Cellular radiator.**

Ignition : **Storage batteries.**

Drive : **Double side chains.**

Transmission . **Sliding gears. Direct drive on top speed.**

Speed : **Three speeds forward, one reverse.**

Style of top : **Folding glass front, side and rear curtains, luggage carrier.**

THE LOCOMOBILE COMPANY OF AMERICA, BRIDGEPORT, CONN.

Price

with top
$4250 to $5100

depending on body.

Without top
$4000 to $4800

Model: **TYPE "D."**

Body: **Any style desired by customer.**

Color: **As desired by purchaser.**

Seating capacity: **Five** persons.

Total weight: **2500** pounds.

Wheel base: **86** inches.

Wheel gauge: **52** inches.

Wheel diameter: **34** inches.

Tire diameter: **4** inches.

Steering: **Hand wheel with irreversible worm gear.**

Brakes: (3) **Foot brake on differential; emergency brakes on rear wheels; sprag.**

Gasoline capacity: **17** gallons.

Frame: **One-piece rectangular channel steel frame. (Patented.)**

Horse-power: **16-22.**

Number of cylinders: **Four.**

Cylinders arranged: **Vertically and longitudinally in front.**

Cooling: **Water, by centrifugal pump. Cellular radiator.**

Ignition: **Storage batteries in connection with dynamo and automatic switch.**

Drive: **Double side chains.**

Transmission: **Sliding gears. Direct drive on top speed.**

Speeds: **Three forward speeds, one reverse.**

Style of top: **Canopy with folding glass front, curtains and luggage carrier.**

THE LOCOMOBILE COMPANY OF AMERICA, BRIDGEPORT, CONN.

Price

$5000
and up

Model : **TYPE "D" LIMOUSINE.**

Body : **Aluminum construction.**

Color : **As desired by the purchaser.**

Seating capacity : **Six** to **eight.**

Total weight : **2700** pounds.

Wheel base : **86** inches.

Wheel gauge : **52** inches.

Wheel diameter : **34** inches.

Tire diameter : **4** inches.

Steering : **Hand wheel with irreversible worm gear.**

Brakes : **(3) Foot brake on differential; emergency brakes on rear wheels; sprag.**

Gasoline capacity : **17** gallons.

Frame : **One-piece rectangular channel steel frame. (Patented.)**

Horse-power : **16-22.**

Number of cylinders : **Four.**

Cylinders arranged : **Vertically and longitudinally in front.**

Cooling : **Water, by centrifugal pump, cellular radiator.**

Ignition : **Storage batteries in connection with dynamo.**

Drive : **Double side chains.**

Transmission : **Sliding gears, direct drive on top speed.**

Speeds : **Three speeds forward, one reverse.**

Style of top : **Limousine.**

THE PEERLESS MOTOR CAR COMPANY, CLEVELAND, OHIO

Price

with top
$4250
without top
$4000

Model: **PEERLESS.**

Body: **Wood, side door.**

Color: **To order.**

Seating capacity: **Five** persons.

Total weight: **2550** pounds.

Wheel base: **104** inches.

Wheel gauge: **56** inches.

Wheel diameter: **34** inches.

Tire diameter: **4½** inches rear, **4** inches front.

Steering: **Wheel.**

Brakes: **Foot lever on transmission, hand lever on both rear wheels.**

Gasoline capacity: **15** gallons.

Frame: **Pressed steel.**

Horse-power: **24.**

Number of cylinders: **Four.**

Cylinders arranged: **Vertical in front.**

Cooling: **Water, cellular radiator.**

Ignition: **Commutator, storage batteries and dry cells.**

Drive: **Bevel gear.**

Transmission: **Sliding gears.**

Speeds: **Four forward and one reverse.**

Style of top: **Canopy, glass front.**

THE PEERLESS MOTOR CAR COMPANY, CLEVELAND, OHIO

Price

with top
$6250

without top
$6000

Model : **PEERLESS, TYPE 7.**

Body : **Aluminum, side door.**

Color : **To order.**

Seating capacity : **Five** persons.

Total weight : **2900** pounds.

Wheel base : **102** inches.

Wheel gauge : **56** inches.

Wheel diameter : **34** inches.

Tire diameter : Rear, **4½** inches ; front,
4 inches.

Steering : **Wheel.**

Brakes : **Hand lever on rear wheels,
foot brake on drive shaft.**

Gasoline capacity : **17** gallons.

Frame : **Pressed steel.**

Horse-power : **35·**

Number of cylinders : **Four.**

Cylinders arranged : **Vertical, in pairs.**

Cooling : **Water, cellular radiator.**

Ignition : **Make and break ; jump
spark.**

Drive : **Bevel gear.**

Transmission : **Sliding gear.**

Speeds : **Four forward and one reverse.**

Style of top : **Canopy, glass front.**

THE PEERLESS MOTOR CAR COMPANY, CLEVELAND, OHIO

Price

$5000

Model : **PEERLESS, LIMOUSINE.**

Body : **Aluminum, side door.**

Color : **To order.**

Seating capacity : **Five** persons.

Total weight : **2750** pounds.

Wheel base : **104** inches.

Wheel gauge : **56** inches.

Wheel diameter : **34** inches.

Tire diameter : **4** inches front, **4½** inches rear.

Steering : **Wheel.**

Brakes : **Foot lever on transmission, hand lever on both rear wheels.**

Gasoline capacity : **15** gallons.

Frame : **Pressed steel.**

Horse-power : **24.**

Number of cylinders : **Four.**

Cylinders arranged : **Vertical in front.**

Cooling : **Water.**

Ignition : **Commutator, storage batteries and dry cells.**

Drive : **Bevel gear.**

Transmission : **Sliding gears.**

Speeds : **Four forward and one reverse.**

Style of top : **Limousine.**

NORTHERN MANUFACTURING CO., DETROIT, MICH.

Price

with top
$800
without top
$750

Model : **NORTHERN RUNABOUT.**

Body : **Wood.**

Color : **Carmine.**

Seating capacity : **Two** persons.

Total weight : **1100** pounds.

Wheel base : **67** inches.

Wheel gauge : **56** and **60** inches.

Wheel diameter : **28** inches.

Tire diameter : **3** inches.

Steering : **Lever.**

Brakes : **On differential gear.**

Gasoline capacity : **7½** gallons.

Frame : **Angle steel.**

Horse-power : **6½.**

Number of cylinders : **One.**

Cylinder arranged : **Horizontal; under body.**

Cooling : **Water.**

Ignition : **Battery and jump spark.**

Drive : **Chain.**

Transmission : **Planetary.**

Speeds : **Two forward and reverse.**

Style of top : **Runabout pattern.**

NORTHERN MANUFACTURING CO., DETROIT, MICH

Price

with top
$1700
without top
$1500

Model: **NORTHERN TOURING CAR.**

Body: **Wood.**

Color: **Northern green.**

Seating capacity: **Five** persons.

Total weight: **2000** pounds.

Wheel base: **88** inches.

Wheel gauge: **56** inches.

Wheel diameter: **30** inches.

Tire diameter: **4** inches.

Steering: **Wheel.**

Brakes: **On rear wheel drums.**

Gasoline capacity: **10** gallons.

Frame: **Angle steel.**

Horse-power: **15 brake.**

Number of cylinders: **Two.**

Cylinders arranged: **Horizontal; opposed, under front hood.**

Cooling: **Water and fan.**

Ignition: **Jump spark and batteries.**

Drive: **Shaft.**

Transmission: **Planetary.**

Speeds: **Two forward and reverse.**

Style of top: **Canopy with glass front.**

OLDS MOTOR WORKS, DETROIT, MICHIGAN

Price
with top
$675
without top
$650

Model: **OLDSMOBILE REGULAR RUNABOUT.**

Body: **Oldsmobile curve dash.**

Color: **Black with red trimmings.**

Seating capacity: **Two** persons.

Total weight: **1100** pounds.

Wheel base: **66** inches.

Wheel gauge: **55** inches.

Wheel diameter: **28** inches.

Tire diameter: **3** inches.

Steering: **Tiller.**

Brakes: **On differential and rear wheels, operated by foot.**

Gasoline capacity: **5** gallons.

Frame: **Angle steel.**

Horse-power: **7.**

Number of cylinders: **One.**

Cylinder arranged: **Horizontal.**

Cooling: **Water, copper disc radiator.**

Ignition: **Jump spark.**

Drive: **Chain.**

Transmission: **Planetary.**

Speeds: **Two speeds forward and reverse.**

Style of top: **Buggy.**

OLDS   MOTOR   WORKS,   DETROIT,   MICHIGAN

Price
without top
$750

Model : **OLDSMOBILE TOURING RUNABOUT.**

Body : **French front.**

Color : **Brewster green.**

Seating capacity : **Two** persons.

Total weight : **1400** pounds.

Wheel base : **76** inches.

Wheel gauge : **55** inches.

Wheel diameter : **28** inches.

Tire diameter : **3** inches.

Steering : **Wheel-tilting post.**

Brakes : **On rear hubs and transmission, operated by foot.**

Gasoline capacity : **5** gallons.

Frame : **Angle steel.**

Horse-power : **7.**

Number of cylinders : **One.**

Cylinder arranged : **Horizontal, cylinder head under footboard.**

Cooling : **Water, honeycomb radiator.**

Ignition : **Jump spark.**

Drive : **Chain.**

Transmission : **Planetary.**

Speeds : **Two speeds forward and reverse.**

OLDS MOTOR WORKS, DETROIT, MICHIGAN

Price

with top
$1050
without top
$950

Model : **OLDSMOBILE LIGHT TONNEAU.**

Body : **Detachable tonneau.**

Color : **Brewster green.**

Seating capacity : **Four** persons.

Total weight : **1750** pounds.

Wheel base : **82** inches.

Wheel gauge : **55** inches.

Wheel diameter : **30** inches.

Tire diameter : **3½** inches.

Steering : **Wheel-tilting post.**

Brakes : **On rear hubs and transmission, operated by foot.**

Gasoline capacity : **7** gallons.

Frame : **Angle steel.**

Horse-power : **10.**

Number of cylinders : **One.**

Cylinder arranged : **Horizontal, cylinder head under footboard.**

Cooling : **Water, honeycomb radiator.**

Ignition : **Jump spark.**

Drive : **Chain.**

Transmission : **Planetary.**

Speeds : **Two speeds forward and reverse.**

Style of top : **Canopy.**

OLDS   MOTOR   WORKS,   DETROIT,   MICHIGAN

Price
$850

Model :   **OLDSMOBILE   LIGHT
DELIVERY WAGON.**

Body : **Paneled wood.**

Color : **Black.**

Seating capacity : **Two** persons.

Total weight : **1100** pounds.

Wheel base : **72** inches.

Wheel gauge : **55** inches.

Wheel diameter : **28** inches.

Tire diameter : **3** inches.

Steering : **Tiller.**

Brakes : **On transmission and differential.**

Gasoline capacity : **5** gallons.

Frame : **Angle steel.**

Horse-power : **5.**

Number of cylinders : **One.**

Cylinder arranged : **Horizontal.**

Cooling : **Water, copper disc radiator.**

Ignition : **Jump spark, dry batteries.**

Drive : **Chain.**

Transmission : **Planetary.**

Speeds : **Two forward and reverse.**

Style of top : **Paneled delivery.**

PACKARD MOTOR CAR COMPANY, DETROIT, MICHIGAN

Price

with top
$2300
without top
$2000

Model: **PACKARD "F."**

Body: **Wood, tonneau.**

Color: **Iroquois red.**

Seating capacity: **Five** persons.

Total weight: About **2200** pounds.

Wheel base: **88** inches.

Wheel gauge: **56½** inches.

Wheel diameter: **34** inches.

Tire diameter: **4** inches.

Steering: **Wheel with worm and seg-ment.**

Brakes: (3) **2 clamping on rear wheels, 1 on shaft drive.**

Gasoline capacity: **11** gallons.

Frame: **Channel steel.**

Horse-power: **12.**

Number of cylinders: **One.**

Cylinder arranged: **Horizontal.**

Cooling: **Water.**

Ignition: **Jump spark with dry bat-teries.**

Drive: **Chain.**

Transmission: **Sliding gear.**

Speeds: **Three forward, one reverse.**

Style of top: **Glass front canopy** (other tops special).

PACKARD MOTOR CAR COMPANY, DETROIT, MICHIGAN

Price

$3000

Top and special
equipment extra

Model: **PACKARD " L."**

Body: **Aluminum, tonneau.**

Color: **Richelieu blue and yellow.**

Seating capacity: **Five** persons.

Total weight: About **1900** pounds.

Wheel base: **94** inches.

Wheel gauge: **56½** inches.

Wheel diameter: **34** inches.

Tire diameter: **4** inches.

Steering: **Wheel with worm and segment.**

Brakes: (4) **2 internal expanding, 2 external clamping, all on rear wheels.**

Gasoline capacity: **19** gallons.

Frame: **Pressed steel.**

Horse-power: **22.**

Number of cylinders: **Four.**

Cylinders arranged: **Vertical (fore and
aft).**

Cooling: **Water.**

Ignition: **Jump spark with storage
batteries.**

Drive: **Bevel gear.**

Transmission: **Sliding gear.**

Speeds: **Three forward and reverse.**

Style of top: **Glass front canopy, cape
cart or Victoria.**

PACKARD MOTOR CAR COMPANY, DETROIT, MICHIGAN

Price
with top
$7300
without top
$7000

Model: **PACKARD " K."**

Body: **Aluminum, tonneau.**

Color: **To order.**

Seating capacity: **Five** persons.

Total weight: About **2200** pounds.

Wheel base: **92** inches.

Wheel gauge: **56½** inches.

Wheel diameter: **36** inches.

Tire diameter: **4** inches.

Steering: **Wheel with worm and segment.**

Brakes: (3) **2 clamping or rear wheels,
1 on drive shaft.**

Gasoline capacity: **19** gallons.

Frame: **Armored wood.**

Horse-power: **24.**

Number of cylinders: **Four.**

Cylinders arranged: **Vertical (fore and
aft).**

Cooling: **Water.**

Ignition: **Jump spark with storage
batteries.**

Drive: **Bevel gear.**

Transmission: **Sliding gear.**

Speeds: **Four forward and one reverse.**

Style of top: **Glass front canopy.**

PACKARD MOTOR CAR COMPANY, DETROIT, MICHIGAN

Price

$10,000

Model: **PACKARD "GREY WOLF."**

Body: **Aluminum, racing.**

Color: **Grey.**

Seating capacity: **Two** persons.

Total weight: **1310** pounds.

Wheel base: **92** inches.

Wheel gauge: **56½** inches.

Wheel diameter: **34** inches.

Tire diameter: **4** inches.

Steering: **Wheel with worm and segment.**

Brakes: **2 on rear wheels.**

Gasoline capacity: **6** gallons.

Frame: **Pressed steel.**

Horse-power: **24.**

Number of cylinders: **Four.**

Cylinders arranged: **Vertical (fore and aft.)**

Cooling: **Water.**

Ignition: **Jump spark with storage batteries.**

Drive: **Bevel gear.**

Transmission: **Sliding gear.**

Speeds: **Two forward and one reverse.**

THE GEORGE N. PIERCE CO., BUFFALO, N. Y.

Price

with top
$1300

without top
$1200

Model: **PIERCE STANHOPE.**

Body: **Stanhope, with folding front seat.**

Color: **Quaker green.**

Seating capacity : **Four** persons.

Total weight : **1200** pounds.

Wheel base : **70** inches.

Wheel gauge : **54** inches.

Wheel diameter : **30** inches.

Tire diameter : **3** inches.

Steering : **Wheel.**

Brakes : **Hub.**

Gasoline capacity : **5½** gallons.

Frame : **Tubular.**

Horse-power : **8 Brake.**

Number of cylinders : **One.**

Cylinder arranged : **Vertically.**

Cooling : **Water, natural circulation.**

Ignition : **High-tension electric.**

Drive : **Spur gear.**

Transmission : **Planetary.**

Speeds : **Two forward and reverse.**

Style of top : **Victoria.**

THE   GEORGE   N.   PIERCE   CO.,   BUFFALO,   N. Y.

Price

with top
$4250

without top
$4000

Model: **GREAT ARROW TOUR-ING CAR.**

Body: **Tonneau, aluminum.**

Color: **Quaker green.**

Seating capacity: **Five** persons.

Total weight: **2400** pounds.

Wheel base: **93** inches.

Wheel gauge: **56** inches.

Wheel diameter: **34** inches.

Tire diameter: **4** inches.

Steering: **Wheel.**

Brakes: **Internal and external on hubs.**

Gasoline capacity: **15** gallons.

Frame: **Pressed steel.**

Horse-power: **24** to **28 Brake.**

Number of cylinders: **Four.**

Cylinders arranged: **Verticallv.**

Cooling: **Water with pump, Whitlock radiator and fan.**

Ignition: **High-tension electric.**

Drive: **Bevel gear.**

Transmission: **Sliding gear.**

Speeds: **Three forward and reverse.**

Style of top: **Canopy.**

POPE MANUFACTURING COMPANY, HARTFORD, CONN.

Price
$650

Model : **POPE-TRIBUNE.**

Body : **Wood, runabout type.**

Color : **Olive green.**

Seating capacity : **Two** persons.

Total weight : **750** pounds.

Wheel base : **65** inches.

Wheel gauge : **54** inches.

Wheel diameter : **28** inches.

Tire diameter : **2½** inches.

Steering : **Wheel.**

Brakes : **1 on engine, 1 on differential.**

Gasoline capacity : **3½** gallons.

Frame : **Angle steel.**

Horse-power : **6.**

Number of cylinders : **One.**

Cylinder arranged : **Vertical.**

Cooling : **Cylinder head by water, cylinder body by air.**

Ignition : **Jump spark, dry batteries.**

Drive : **Shaft with bevel gears.**

Transmission : **Sliding gear.**

Speeds : **Two forward, one reverse.**

Style of top : **None furnished.**

POPE MANUFACTURING COMPANY, HARTFORD, CONN.

Price

$1050

Model: **POPE - HARTFORD "A"
RUNABOUT**.

Body: **Wood (detachable tonneau)**.

Color: **Red, blue, olive green or sage
green ; yellow gear if desired**.

Seating capacity: **Two** persons.

Total weight: **1400** pounds.

Wheel base: **78** inches.

Wheel gauge: **54** inches.

Wheel diameter: **30** inches.

Tire diameter: **3½** inches.

Steering: **Wheel, with tilting post**.

Brakes: **Direct, double-acting on differential**.

Gasoline capacity: **10** gallons.

Frame: **Angle steel**.

Horse-power: **10**.

Number of cylinders : **One**.

Cylinder arranged: **Horizontal**.

Cooling: **Water**.

Ignition : **Jump spark, dry batteries**.

Drive : **Single chain**.

Transmission: **Spur gear**.

Speeds: **Two forward, one reverse**.

Style of top : **None furnished**.

POPE MANUFACTURING COMPANY, HARTFORD, CONN.

Price

$1200

Model: **POPE-HARTFORD "B."**

Body: **Wood, tonneau.**

Color: **Red, blue, olive green or sage green; yellow gear if desired.**

Seating capacity: **Four** persons.

Total weight: **1600** pounds.

Wheel base: **78** inches.

Wheel gauge: **54** inches.

Wheel diameter: **30** inches.

Tire diameter: **3½** inches.

Steering: **Wheel, with tilting post.**

Brakes: **Direct, double-acting on differential.**

Gasoline capacity: **10** gallons.

Frame: **Angle steel.**

Horse-power: **10.**

Number of cylinders: **One.**

Cylinder arranged: **Horizontal.**

Cooling: **Water.**

Ignition: **Jump spark, dry batteries.**

Drive: **Single chain.**

Transmission: **Spur gear.**

Speeds: **Two forward, one reverse.**

Style of top: **None furnished.**

POPE MOTOR CAR COMPANY, TOLEDO, OHIO

Price

$3500

Model: **POPE-TOLEDO VI.**

Body: **Wood.**

Color: **Red, olive green or blue, with red or yellow running gear.**

Seating capacity: **Five persons.**

Total weight: **2400** pounds.

Wheel base: **94** inches.

Wheel gauge: **54** inches.

Wheel diameter: **34** inches.

Tire diameter: **4** inches.

Steering: **Tilting wheel, irreversible; worm and segment type.**

Brakes: **Main brake on differential, internal expanding on rear wheels.**

Gasoline capacity: **14** gallons.

Frame: **Pressed steel.**

Horse-power: **24.**

Number of cylinders: **Four.**

Cylinders arranged: **Vertical.**

Cooling: **Water.**

Ignition: **Jump spark with batteries.**

Drive: **Double chain, countershaft.**

Transmission: **Sliding gear, ball bearing.**

Speeds: **Three forward, one reverse.**

POPE MOTOR CAR COMPANY, TOLEDO, OHIO

Price

with top
$3750
without top
$3500

Model: **POPE-TOLEDO VI.**

Body: **Wood.**

Color: **Red, olive green or blue, with red or yellow running gear.**

Seating capacity: **Five** persons.

Total weight: 2400 pounds.

Wheel base: **94** inches.

Wheel gauge: **54** inches.

Wheel diameter: **34** inches.

Tire diameter: **4** inches.

Steering: **Tilting wheel, irreversible; worm and segment type.**

Brakes: **Main brake on differential, internal expanding on rear wheels.**

Gasoline capacity: **14** gallons.

Frame: **Pressed steel.**

Horse-power: **24.**

Number of cylinders: **Four.**

Cylinder arranged: **Vertical.**

Cooling: **Water.**

Ignition: **Jump spark with batteries.**

Drive: **Double chain, countershaft.**

Transmission: **Sliding gear, ball bearing**

Speeds: **Three forward and reverse.**

Style of top: **Glass front canopy, mahogany lined, Mackintosh curtains.**

POPE MOTOR CAR COMPANY, TOLEDO, OHIO

Price

$7500

Model : **POPE-TOLEDO RACER.**

Body : **Aluminum and wood.**

Color : **Silver grey.**

Seating capacity : **Two** persons.

Total weight : **2200** pounds.

Wheel base : **102** inches.

Wheel gauge : **54** inches.

Wheel diameter : **32** inches.

Tire diameter : **4** inches.

Steering : **Wheel, irreversible ; worm and segment type.**

Brakes : **Double-acting on both rear wheels, and on differential.**

Gasoline capacity : **10** gallons.

Frame : **Pressed steel.**

Horse-power : **60.**

Number of cylinders : **Four.**

Cylinders arranged : **Vertically, fore and aft.**

Cooling : **Water.**

Ignition : **Jump spark, high tension.**

Drive : **Outside chains.**

Transmission : **Sliding gear, ball bearing.**

Speeds : **Three forward, one reverse.**

Style of top : **None.**

POPE – ROBINSON CO., HYDE PARK, MASS.

Price

with top
$4600

without top
$4500

Model : **POPE-ROBINSON.**

Body : **Aluminum.**

Color : **To order.**

Seating capacity : **Five** persons.

Total weight : **4750** pounds.

Wheel base : **96** inches.

Wheel gauge : **56** inches.

Wheel diameter : **34** inches.

Tire diameter : **4½** inches.

Steering : **Wheel.**

Brakes : **Double-acting; on differential
and rear wheels.**

Gasoline capacity : **21** gallons.

Frame : **Channel steel, riveted.**

Horse-power : **24.**

Number of cylinders : **Four.**

Cylinders arranged : **Vertical.**

Cooling : **Water, tubular radiator.**

Ignition : **Make and break, two storage
batteries.**

Drive : **Double chain.**

Transmission : **Sliding gear.**

Speeds : **Three forward, one reverse.**

Style of top : **Cape.**

STANDARD AUTOMOBILE CO. OF N. Y., 136 W. 38TH ST., N. Y.

Price

$4500 to
$5000
top extra

Model : " DECAUVILLE " 1905.

Body : **Double phaeton, with revolving front seat ; or to order.**

Color : **To order.**

Seating capacity : **Five** persons.

Total weight : **2100** pounds.

Wheel base : **84** to **102** inches.

Wheel gauge : **54** inches.

Wheel diameter : **32** or **34** inches.

Tire diameter : **3½** or **4** inches.

Steering : **Wheel.**

Brakes : **Three.**

Gasoline capacity : **15** gallons.

Frame : **Pressed steel, with steel pan supporting engine and transmission.**

Horse-power : **12-16.**

Number of cylinders : **Four.**

Cylinders arranged : **Vertically in front.**

Cooling : **Water.**

Ignition : **Jump spark.**

Drive : **Bevel gear.**

Transmission : **Sliding gear.**

Speeds : **Three forward and reverse.**

Style of top : **Any style desired.**

STANDARD AUTOMOBILE CO. OF N. Y., 136 W. 38TH ST., N. Y.

Price

$6000 to
$7500
top extra

Model: **"DECAUVILLE" 1905.**

Body: **Double phaeton or to order.**

Color: **To order.**

Seating capacity: **Five** or **six** persons

Total weight: **2200** pounds.

Wheel base: **96** to **108** inches.

Wheel gauge: **56** inches.

Wheel diameter: **34** inches.

Tire diameter: **4¼** inches.

Steering: **Wheel.**

Brakes: **Three.**

Gasoline capacity: **15** gallons.

Frame: **Pressed steel, with steel pan supporting engine and transmission.**

Horse-power: **18-24.**

Number of cylinders: **Four.**

Cylinders arranged: **Vertically in front.**

Cooling: **Water.**

Ignition: **Jump spark.**

Drive: **Bevel gear.**

Transmission: **Sliding gear.**

Speeds: **Three forward and reverse.**

Style of top: **Any style desired.**

STANDARD AUTOMOBILE CO. OF N. Y., 136 W. 38TH ST., N. Y.

Price
$6500
to $7500

Model : " DECAUVILLE " 1905.

Body : Single brougham.

Color : Any color desired.

Seating capacity : Four persons.

Total weight : 2100 pounds.

Wheel base : 102 and 108 inches.

Wheel gauge : 54 inches.

Wheel diameter : 34 inches.

Tire diameter : 4⅛ inches.

Steering : Wheel.

Brakes : Three.

Gasoline capacity : 12 gallons.

Frame : Pressed steel, with steel pan supporting engine and transmission.

Horse-power : 12-16 (also 18-24).

Number of cylinders : Four.

Cylinders arranged : Vertically in front.

Cooling : Water.

Ignition : Jump spark.

Drive : Bevel gear.

Transmission : Sliding gear.

Speeds : Three forward, one reverse.

Style of top : Brougham.

THE STANDARD MOTOR CONSTRUCTION CO., JERSEY CITY, N. J.

Price

with top

$3250

without top

$3000

Model: **U. S. LONG DISTANCE STANDARD TOURIST.**

Body: **Wood.**

Color: **To order.**

Seating capacity: **Five** persons.

Total weight: **2000** pounds.

Wheel base: **95** inches.

Wheel gauge: **54** inches.

Wheel diameter: **34** inches.

Tire diameter: **4** inches.

Steering: **Wheel.**

Brakes: **On each rear hub and one on shaft.**

Gasoline capacity: **15** gallons.

Frame: **Pressed steel.**

Horse-power: **25.**

Number of cylinders: **Four.**

Cylinders arranged: **Vertical.**

Cooling: **Water, honeycomb radiator with fan and pump.**

Ignition: **Make and break with magneto.**

Drive: **Bevel gear.**

Transmission: **Sliding gears.**

Speeds: **Three forward, one reverse.**

Style of top: **Canopy top with glass front and curtains.**

J. STEVENS ARMS & TOOL CO., CHICOPEE FALLS, MASS.

Price

with top
$1300
without top
$1250

Model: "L" STEVENS-DURYEA.

Body: Wood, folding front seat.

Color: Maroon.

Seating capacity: Two or four persons.

Total weight: 1350 pounds.

Wheel base: 69 inches.

Wheel gauge: 54 inches.

Wheel diameter: 28 inches.

Tire diameter: 3 inches.

Steering: One spoke of wheel steerer.

Brakes: Two.

Gasoline capacity: 6 gallons.

Frame: Tubular.

Horse-power: 7.

Number of cylinders: Two.

Cylinders arranged: Horizontal.

Cooling: Water.

Ignition: Jump spark.

Drive: Chain.

Transmission: Individual clutch system.

Speeds: Three forward and reverse.

Style of top: Victoria or buggy.

SMITH & MABLEY, INCORPORATED, 513–519 7TH AVE., NEW YORK

Price

with top
$12,750
without top
$12,450

Model : **MERCEDES.**

Body : **Vedrine K. of B.**

Color : **Any color desired.**

Seating capacity : **Five** persons.

Total weight : **2300** pounds.

Wheel base : **96** inches.

Wheel gauge : **52** inches.

Wheel diameter : **36** inches.

Tire diameter : **Front 910 x 90m/m; rear 920 x 120 m/m.**

Steering : **Wheel.**

Brakes : **On differential, countershaft and emergency on rear wheels.**

Gasoline capacity : **25** gallons.

Frame : **Pressed steel.**

Horse-power : **28/32 (also 18/28,40/45, 60, 90).**

Number of cylinders : **Four.**

Cylinders arranged : **Vertical.**

Cooling : **Water, cellular radiator and fan.**

Ignition : **Make and break, magneto.**

Drive : **Double chain.**

Transmission : **Sliding gear.**

Speeds : **Four forward, one reverse.**

Style of top : **Canopy, glass front and rear.**

SMITH & MABLEY, INCORPORATED, 513–519 7TH AVE., NEW YORK

Price
with top
$8250
without top
$7950

Model : **PANHARD - LEVASSOR, 1904, long chassis.**

Body : **Aluminum, side entrance.**

Color : **Any color desired.**

Seating capacity : **Five** persons.

Total weight : **2500** pounds.

Wheel base : **105** inches.

Wheel gauge : **53½** inches.

Wheel diameter : **Front 34¼** inches, **rear 36⅛** inches.

Tire diameter : **Front 870 x 90** m/m ; rear **920 x 120** m/m.

Steering : **Wheel, by worm and gear direct.**

Brakes : **Differential and emergency on rear wheels.**

Gasoline capacity : **17-18** gallons.

Frame : **Armored wood.**

Horse-power : **24** (other types **7, 8, 10, 15, 18, 35, 60**).

Number of cylinders : **Four.**

Cylinders arranged : **Vertical.**

Cooling : **Water, cellular radiator and fan.**

Ignition : **Magneto and jump spark.**

Drive : **Chains to both rear wheels.**

Transmission : **Sliding gear.**

Speeds : **Four forward, one reverse.**

Style of top : **Canopy with glass front and storm curtains.**

SMITH & MABLEY, INCORPORATED, 513–519 7TH AVE., NEW YORK

Price

with top
**$6000 to
$6300**

without top
$5900

Model : **RENAULT 1904, long chassis (also 6 other types).**

Body : **King of Belgians, with side
door entrance.**

Color : **Any color desired.**

Seating capacity : **Five** persons.

Total weight : **2200** pounds.

Wheel base : **102** inches.

Wheel gauge : **50** inches.

Wheel diameter : **34** inches.

Tire diameter : **870 x 90** m/m.

Steering : **Wheel.**

Brakes : **On** differential, and emergency on rear wheels.

Gasoline capacity : **15** gallons.

Frame : **Tubular steel.**

Horse-power : **14.**

Number of cylinders : **Four.**

Cylinders arranged : **Vertical.**

Cooling : **Water.**

Ignition : **Jump spark ;** coil or magneto.

Drive : **Bevel gear.**

Transmission : **Sliding gear.**

Speeds : **Three forward and one re-**
verse.

Style of top : **Leather Cape Town**
hood, or canopy.

SMITH & MABLEY, INCORPORATED, 513–519 7TH AVE., NEW YORK

Price

Chassis only
$5250

with body top
and equipment
$6750

Model: **SMITH & MABLEY " SIM- PLEX " 1904 B. A.**

Body: **King of Belgians (any style to order).**

Color: **Any color desired.**

Seating capacity: **Five** persons.

Total weight: **2400** pounds. **(chassis).**

Wheel base: **105** inches.

Wheel gauge: **54** inches.

Wheel diameter: **36** inches.

Tire diameter: **910 x 90** m/m.

Steering: **Wheel.**

Brakes: **On differential, and emergency on rear wheels.**

Gasoline capacity: **30** gallons. **pressure feed.**

Frame: **Angle steel.**

Horse-power: **30 (also special 75).**

Number of cylinders: **Four.**

Cylinders arranged: **Vertical.**

Cooling: **Water, cellular radiator and fan.**

Ignition: **Jump spark, storage battery or magneto.**

Drive: **Side chains.**

Transmission: **Sliding gear.**

Speeds: **Four forward and one reverse.**

Style of top: **Canopy glass front.**

THE F. B. STEARNS CO., CLEVELAND, OHIO

Price
$4000

Model: **STEARNS** 1905.

Body : **French type, side doors.**

Color : **Optional.**

Seating capacity : **Seven** persons.

Total weight : **2675** pounds.

Wheel base : **111** inches.

Wheel gauge : **56** inches.

Wheel diameter : **34** inches.

Tire diameter : **4½** inches.

Steering : **Wheel.**

Brakes : **Hand lever, inner expansion on both rear hubs, foot brake on differential.**

Gasoline capacity : **18** gallons.

Frame : **Pressed steel.**

Horse-power : **36.**

Number of cylinders : **Four.**

Cylinders arranged : **Vertical, in pairs in front.**

Cooling : **Water, tubular radiator, fan.**

Ignition : **High tension, storage battery.**

Drive : **Double chain.**

Transmission : **Sliding gear.**

Speeds : **Four forward, one reverse.**

Style of top : **As desired, extra equipment.**

STUDEBAKER AUTOMOBILE CO., SOUTH BEND, IND.

Price

with top

$1750

without top

$1600

Model: " C."

Body: Tonneau.

Colors: Dark maroons or dark blue.

Seating capacity: Five persons.

Total weight: 1800 pounds.

Wheel base: 82 inches.

Wheel gauge: 56 inches.

Wheel diameter: 30 inches.

Tire diameter: 3½ inches.

Steering: Wheel, irreversible.

Brakes: Two sets, one on rear hubs, other on differential.

Gasoline capacity: 10 gallons.

Frame: Armored wood.

Horse-power: 16.

Number of cylinders: Two.

Cylinders arranged: Horizontal, opposed, under center.

Cooling: Water, pump.

Ignition: Jump spark.

Drive: Chain.

Transmission: Planetary.

Speeds: Two forward, one reverse.

Style of top: Canopy.

E. R. THOMAS MOTOR CO., BUFFALO, N. Y.

Price

with top
$2650
without top
$2500

Model: **THOMAS FLYER No. 22.**

Body: **Tonneau, King of Belgians.**

Color: **Automobile red or Brewster green.**

Seating capacity: **Five** persons.

Total weight: **2200** pounds.

Wheel base: **84** inches.

Wheel gauge: **56½** inches.

Wheel diameter: **32** inches.

Tire diameter: **4** inches.

Steering: **Wheel.**

Brakes: **Foot lever on countershaft, hand lever emergency on both rear wheels.**

Gasoline capacity: **12** gallons.

Frame: **Channel steel.**

Horse-power: **24.**

Number of cylinders: **Three.**

Cylinders arranged: **Vertical in front.**

Cooling: **Water, cellular type radiator.**

Ignition: **Jump spark.**

Drive: **Double side chains.**

Transmission: **Sliding gear.**

Speeds: **Three forward and reverse.**

Style of top: **Canopy.**

E. R. THOMAS MOTOR CO., BUFFALO, N. Y.

Price
$3000

Model : **THOMAS FLYER No. 23.**

Body : **Limousine, Summer or Winter.**

Color : **Brewster green.**

Seating capacity : **Six** persons.

Total weight : **2400** pounds.

Wheel base : **92** inches.

Wheel gauge : **56½** inches.

Wheel diameter : **32** inches.

Tire diameter : **4½** inches.

Steering : **Wheel.**

Brakes : **Foot lever on countershaft, hand lever emergency on both rear wheels.**

Gasoline capacity : **12** gallons.

Frame : **Channel steel.**

Horse-power : **24.**

Number of cylinders : **Three.**

Cylinders arranged : **Vertical in front.**

Cooling : **Water, cellular type radiator.**

Ignition : **Jump spark.**

Drive : **Double side chains.**

Transmission : **Sliding gear.**

Speeds : **Three forward and reverse.**

Style of top : **Limousine, open for Summer, closed for Winter.**

WALTHAM MANUFACTURING CO., WALTHAM, MASS.

Price

with top
$447

without top
$425

Model : **ORIENT BUCKBOARD.**

Body : **Wood.**

Color : **Natural wood.**

Seating capacity : **Two** persons.

Total weight : **500** pounds.

Wheel base : **80** inches.

Wheel gauge : **42** inches.

Wheel diameter : **26** inches.

Tire diameter : **2½** inches.

Steering : **Tiller.**

Brakes : **One.**

Gasoline capacity : **3** gallons.

Frame : **Tubular.**

Horse-power : **4.**

Number of cylinders : **One.**

Cylinder arranged : **In rear.**

Cooling : **Air.**

Ignition : **Jump spark.**

Drive : **Spur gear.**

Transmission : **Planetary.**

Speeds : **Two.**

Style of top : **Canopy.**

WALTHAM MANUFACTURING CO., WALTHAM, MASS.

Price

with top
$475

without top
$450

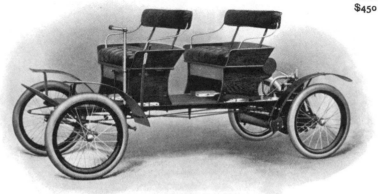

Model: **ORIENT SURREY.**

Body: **Wood.**

Color: **Natural wood.**

Seating capacity : **Four** persons.

Total weight : **550** pounds.

Wheel base: **80** inches.

Wheel gauge : **42** inches.

Wheel diameter: **26** inches.

Tire diameter : **2½** inches.

Steering : **Side lever.**

Brakes : **One.**

Gasoline capacity : **3** gallons.

Frame : **Tubular.**

Horse-power : **4.**

Number of cylinders : **One.**

Cylinder arranged : **In rear.**

Cooling : **Air.**

Ignition : **Jump spark.**

Drive : **Spur gear.**

Transmission : **Planetary.**

Speeds : **Two.**

Style of top : **Canopy.**

THE WINTON MOTOR CARRIAGE CO., CLEVELAND, O.

Price

with top
$2500
without top
$2300

Model : **TWO-CYLINDER TOUR-ING CAR.**

Body : **Tonneau, rear entrance.**

Color : **Winton red and primrose yellow.**

Seating capacity : **Five** persons.

Total weight : **2600** pounds.

Wheel base : **94½** inches.

Wheel gauge : **56½** inches.

Wheel diameter: **Front, 32 inches. Rear, 34 inches.**

Tire diameter : **Front, 4** inches. **Rear, 4½** inches.

Steering : **Wheel, worm gear.**

Brakes : (3) **Emergency brake on engine sprocket ; hub brakes on drive wheels.**

Gasoline capacity : **10** gallons.

Frame : **Sheet steel riveted.**

Horse-power : **20.**

Number of cylinders : **Two.**

Cylinders arranged : **Horizontal opposed, under body.**

Cooling : **Water, gear-driven centrifugal pump ; tubular radiator.**

Ignition : **Jump spark.**

Drive : **Center chain.**

Transmission : **Individual clutches.**

Speeds : **Two forward and reverse.**

Style of top : **Canopy, with sliding front and curtains.**

THE WINTON MOTOR CARRIAGE CO., CLEVELAND, O.

Price
with top
$3200
without top
$3000

Model: **THE WINTON QUAD.**

Body: **Side entrance tonneau.**

Color: **Winton red and Brewster green.**

Seating capacity: **Five** persons.

Total weight: **2300** pounds.

Wheel base: **104** inches.

Wheel gauge: **56½** inches.

Wheel diameter: **Front, 32** inches. **Rear, 34** inches.

Tire diameter: **Front, 4** inches. **Rear, 4½** inches.

Steering: **Wheel, worm gear.**

Brakes: (3) **Emergency brake on drive shaft; two outside hub brakes.**

Gasoline capacity: **10** gallons.

Frame: **Pressed steel.**

Horse-power: **24.**

Number of cylinders: **Four.**

Cylinders arranged: **Horizontal, under footboard, all on same side of crank shaft.**

Cooling: **Water, gear-driven centrifugal pump, double radiators.**

Ignition: **Jump spark, four-coil, rolling contact breaker.**

Drive: **Bevel gear through longitudinal shaft.**

Transmission: **Individual clutches.**

Speeds: **Two forward and reverse.**

Style of top: **Canopy, with sliding front and curtains.**

WORTHINGTON AUTOMOBILE CO., 547 FIFTH AVE., NEW YORK

Price
with top
$2950
without top
$2750

Model : **METEOR.**

Body : **Tonneau, wood or aluminum.**

Color : **Imperial blue, gold striping.**

Seating capacity : **Five** persons.

Total weight : **1800** pounds.

Wheel base : **91** inches.

Wheel gauge : **56** inches.

Wheel diameter : **32** inches.

Tire diameter : **4** inches.

Steering : **Wheel.**

Brakes : **Hand lever, internal expanding on both rear wheels, foot lever on drive shaft.**

Gasoline capacity : **14** gallons.

Frame : **Pressed steel.**

Horse-power : **18.**

Number of cylinders : **Four.**

Cylinders arranged : **Vertical in front.**

Cooling : **Water, cellular radiator.**

Ignition : **Jump spark.**

Drive : **Bevel gear.**

Transmission : **Sliding gear.**

Speeds : **Three forward and reverse.**

Style of top : **Canopy or hood.**

WORTHINGTON AUTOMOBILE CO., 547 FIFTH AVE., NEW YORK

Price

with top
$3750

without top
$3500

Model: **BERG.**

Body: **Tonneau, wood or aluminum.**

Color: **Imperial blue with gold strip-ing.**

Seating capacity: **Five** persons.

Total weight: **2200** pounds.

Wheel base: **96** inches.

Wheel gauge: **56** inches.

Wheel diameter: **34** inches

Tire diameter: **4** inches.

Steering: **Wheel.**

Brakes: **Hand lever on rear wheels, foot lever on differential.**

Gasoline capacity: **14** gallons.

Frame: **Armored wood.**

Horse-power: **24.**

Number of cylinders: **Four.**

Cylinders arranged: **Vertical in front.**

Cooling: **Water, with tubular cooler and water tank.**

Ignition: **Jump spark.**

Drive: **Double chain.**

Transmission: **Sliding gear.**

Speeds: **Four forward and reverse.**

Style of top: **Canopy or hood.**

Hand Book of

Gasoline

Automobiles

[1905]

Hand Book of

Gasoline
Automobiles

For the information of the
public who are interested
in their manufacture
and use

1905

Association ot Licensed Automobile
Manufacturers

7 East 42d Street, New York City, U. S. A.

Second Annual Announcement

THIS " Hand Book," like its predecessor, is issued primarily for the convenience and information of the prospective purchaser of an automobile. The successful results which attended the initial issue for 1904 have fully justified the " Hand Book " in its present standardized form as a permanent annual publication. The products of the principal manufacturers throughout the United States of America and the importers of gasoline machines are shown by illustrations and specifications. These specifications form a series of the leading questions that arise in the mind of the purchaser, with the answers thereto in red ink. The questions being uniform, the ease of comparison is obvious and the purchaser is enabled to select the machines which are best suited to the service required, to his personal taste, or the means at his command.

It is believed by the several manufacturers who have united in producing this publication that this disinterested method of placing before the purchaser this means of comparison will be found of great advantage.

Each manufacturer or importer conducts his business entirely independent of the other, and, of course, in open competition, but the recognition by the companies represented herein of the basic patent No. 549,160, granted to George B. Selden, November 5th, 1895, on gasoline automobiles (which controls broadly all gasoline automobiles which are accepted as commercially practicable), is a guarantee that a purchase through the several companies herein represented, or through any one of their agents, secures to the purchaser freedom from the annoyance and expense of litigation because of infringement of this patent.

The following manufacturers and importers are licensed under the basic patent No. 549,160, granted to George B. Selden, dated November 5th, 1895, and are the owners of about 400 other patents on

Gasoline Automobiles

The Commissioner of patents in his annual report for the year 1895, said: "Selden, in 1895, received a patent, November 5th, No. 549,160, which may be considered the pioneer invention in the application of the compression gas engine to road or horseless carriage use."

Alphabetical Index

Index of Trade Names

APPERSON BROTHERS AUTOMOBILE COMPANY, KOKOMO, IND.

Price
with top
$3650
without top
$3500

Model : **TOURING MODEL " B."**

Body : **Wood.**

Color : **Optional.**

Seating capacity : **Five** persons.

Total weight : **2400** pounds.

Wheel base : **102** inches.

Wheel tread : **56** inches.

Tire dimensions, front : **815 x 105** m/m.

Tire dimensions, rear : **875 x 105** m/m.

Steering : **Worm and segmit, irreversible.**

Brakes : **Foot and hand emergency.**

Gasoline capacity : **23** gallons.

Frame : **Pressed steel.**

Horse-power : **24.**

Number of cylinders : **Four.**

Cylinders arranged : **Vertical separately.**

Cooling : **Water, radiator and fan.**

Ignition : **Jump spark.**

Drive : **Shaft or double chain.**

Transmission : **Sliding gear.**

Speeds : **Either three or four forward and one reverse.**

Style of top : **Full cape top.**

Descriptive catalogue sent upon application to the above-named company.

APPERSON BROTHERS AUTOMOBILE COMPANY, KOKOMO, IND.

Price

with top
$4150
without top
$4000

Model: **TOURING CAR MODEL "A."**

Body: **Wood.**

Color: **Optional.**

Seating capacity: **Seven** persons.

Total weight: **2600** pounds.

Wheel base: **108** inches.

Wheel tread: **56** inches.

Tire dimensions, front: **815 x 105** m/m.

Tire dimensions, rear: **875 x 120** m/m.

Steering: **Worm and segmit, irreversible.**

Brakes: **Foot and hand emergency.**

Gasoline capacity: **23** gallons.

Frame: **Pressed steel.**

Horse-power: **40.**

Number of cylinders: **Four.**

Cylinders arranged: **Separately.**

Cooling: **Water, radiator and fan.**

Ignition: **Jump spark.**

Drive: **Double chain.**

Transmission: **Sliding gear.**

Speeds: **Four forward and one reverse.**

Style of top: **Full cape top.**

Descriptive catalogue sent upon application to the above-named company.

APPERSON BROTHERS AUTOMOBILE COMPANY, KOKOMO, IND.

Price

with limousine
body
$6500

with standard
wood body
$5150

Model : **APPERSON SPECIAL.**

Body : Wood.

Color : Optional.

Seating capacity : Seven persons.

Total weight : 2800 pounds.

Wheel base : 114 inches.

Wheel tread : 56 inches.

Tire dimensions, front : 815 x 105 m/m.

Tire dimensions, rear : 875 x 120 m/m.

Steering : Worm and segmit, irreversible.

Brakes : Foot and hand emergency, double acting.

Gasoline capacity : 23 gallons.

Frame : Pressed steel.

Horse-power : 50.

Number of cylinders : Four.

Cylinders arranged : Vertical in front.

Cooling : Water, radiator, pump and fan.

Ignition : Jump spark.

Drive : Double chain.

Transmission : Sliding gear.

Speeds : Four forward and one reverse.

Style of top : Full collapsible or victoria on open car.

Descriptive catalogue sent upon application to the above-named company.

AUTO IMPORT COMPANY, 1786 BROADWAY, NEW YORK, N. Y.

Price

$8000
with top
inclusive

Model: ROCHET - SCHNEIDER, 1905.

Body: With double side doors, any style.

Color: To suit.

Seating capacity: Five to seven persons.

Total weight: 2200 pounds.

Wheel base: 9 feet 6½ inches.

Wheel tread: 4 feet 7 inches.

Tire dimensions, front: 920 x 120 m/m.

Tire dimensions, rear: 920 x 120 m/m.

Steering : Wheel, worm gear.

Brakes : Four double-acting, metal to metal.

Gasoline capacity : 30 gallons.

Frame : Pressed steel, one piece including under frame.

Horse-power : 24-35 (also 35-50).

Number of cylinders: Four.

Cylinders arranged : 24-35 vertical tandem (35-50 individual).

Cooling: Water, new form honeycomb radiator with fan and pump.

Ignition : Magneto, low tension.

Drive : Double-roller chains.

Transmission : Spur gear ball bearing.

Speeds : Four forward, one reverse ; fourth speed direct.

Style of top : As desired.

Descriptive catalogue sent upon application to the above-named company.

THE AUTOCAR COMPANY, ARDMORE, PA.

Price

without top
$900

Model: **TYPE X.**

Body: **Runabout.**

Color: **Blue.**

Seating capacity: **Two to three per-sons.**

Total weight: **1200** pounds.

Wheel base: **70** inches.

Wheel tread: **52** inches.

Tire dimensions, front: **28 x 3** inches.

Tire dimensions, rear: **28 x 3** inches.

Steering: **Side lever.**

Brakes: **Two external band hub brakes, one pinion shaft brake.**

Gasoline capacity: **9** gallons.

Frame: **Armored wood.**

Horse-power: **10-12.**

Number of cylinders: **Two.**

Cylinders arranged: **Horizontal op-posed, in front.**

Cooling: **Water, tubular radiator, fan and centrifugal pump.**

Ignition: **Jump spark and dry cells.**

Drive: **Gear driven.**

Transmission: **Slide gear.**

Speeds: **Three forward, one reverse.**

Style of top: **No top furnished.**

Descriptive catalogue sent upon application to the above-named company.

THE AUTOCAR COMPANY, ARDMORE, PA.

Price
without top
$1400

Model: **TYPE VIII.**

Body: **Rear-entrance tonneau, divided front seat.**

Color: **Green or red.**

Seating capacity: **Four persons.**

Total weight: **1700** pounds.

Wheel base: **76** inches.

Wheel tread: **54** inches.

Tire dimensions, front: **30 x 3½** inches.

Tire dimensions, rear: **30 x 3½** inches.

Steering: **Wheel.**

Brakes: **Two external band hub brakes, one pinion shaft brake.**

Gasoline capacity: **10** gallons.

Frame: **Armored wood.**

Horse-power: **12-14.**

Number of cylinders: **Two.**

Cylinders arranged: **Horizontal opposed, in front.**

Cooling: **Water, cellular radiator, fan and centrifugal pump.**

Ignition: **Jump spark and dry cells.**

Drive: **Gear driven.**

Transmission: **Slide gear.**

Speeds: **Three forward, one reverse.**

Style of top: **No top furnished.**

Descriptive catalogue sent upon application to the above-named company.

13

THE AUTOCAR COMPANY, ARDMORE, PA.

Price

without top
$2000

Model: **TYPE XI.**

Body: **Double side-entrance tonneau, divided front seat.**

Color: **Blue.**

Seating capacity: **Four to five persons.**

Total weight: **1900** pounds.

Wheel base: **96** inches.

Wheel tread: **54** inches.

Tire dimensions, front: **30 x 3 ½** inches.

Tire dimensions, rear: **30 x 3 ½** inches.

Steering: **Wheel.**

Brakes: **Two external band hub brakes, emergency brake on main transmission shaft.**

Gasoline capacity: **15** gallons.

Frame: **Wood armored with pressed steel.**

Horse-power: **16-20.**

Number of cylinders: **Four.**

Cylinders arranged: **Vertical tandem in front.**

Cooling: **Water, cellular radiator, fan and centrifugal pump.**

Ignition: **Jump spark and storage battery.**

Drive: **Gear driven.**

Transmission: **Slide gear.**

Speeds: **Three forward, one reverse.**

Style of top: **Special top designed, not furnished by company.**

Descriptive catalogue sent upon application to the above-named company.

BUICK MOTOR COMPANY, JACKSON, MICHIGAN

Price

$1200

Model: BUICK " C."

Body: Wood, side-door entrance.

Color: Royal blue body; running gear, ivory white.

Seating capacity: Five persons.

Total weight: 1740 pounds.

Wheel base: 85 inches.

Wheel tread: 56 inches.

Tire dimensions, front: 30 x 3½ inches.

Tire dimensions, rear: 30 x 3½ inches.

Steering: Wheel with tilting column.

Brakes: Raymond double acting on differential.

Gasoline capacity: 16 gallons.

Frame: Angle steel.

Horse-power: 22.

Number of cylinders: Two.

Cylinders arranged: Horizontal, double opposed.

Cooling: Water.

Ignition: Jump spark with dry cells.

Drive: Single chain.

Transmission: Planetary.

Speeds: Two forward, one reverse.

Style of top: Canopy or cape cart.

Descriptive catalogue sent upon application to the above-named company.

15

SIDNEY B. BOWMAN AUTOMOBILE CO., 50-52 W. 43D ST., N. Y.

Price

with top
brougham
$6500
without top
$5750

Model : **CLEMENT-BAYARD.**

Body : Double side-entrance tonneau, landaulet or brougham.

Color : Blue and yellow, green and yellow, red and red.

Seating capacity : Six persons.

Total weight : 2500 pounds ; open body, 2250 pounds.

Wheel base : 108 inches.

Wheel tread : 56 inches.

Tire dimensions, front : 34 x 4¼ inches.

Tire dimensions, rear : 34 x 4¼ inches.

Steering : Wheel, through irreversible worm gear.

Brakes : Two, internal expansion, double acting.

Gasoline capacity : 12 to 18 gallons.

Frame : Pressed steel.

Horse-power : 24 (also 20, $5250).

Number of cylinders : Four.

Cylinders arranged : Separate, vertically

Cooling : Water, honeycomb radiator with fan and pump.

Ignition : Jump spark with high-tension magneto.

Drive : Bevel gear through live axle.

Transmission : Sliding gears, direct drive on high.

Speeds : Four forward, one reverse.

Style of top : Cape or canopy.

Descriptive catalogue sent upon application to the above-named company.

SIDNEY B. BOWMAN AUTOMOBILE CO., 50–52 W. 43D ST., N. Y.

Price

with top
$7500
without top
$7250

Model : **CLEMENT-BAYARD.**

Body : Double side-entrance body, landaulet or brougham.

Color : Blue and yellow, green and yellow, red and red.

Seating capacity : Five persons.

Total weight : 2300 pounds, with top 2500 pounds.

Wheel base : 112 inches.

Wheel tread : 56 inches.

Tire dimensions, front : 34 x 4¼ inches.

Tire dimensions rear : 34 x 4¼ inches.

Steering : Wheel, through irreversible worm gear.

Brakes : Two, internal expansion, double acting.

Gasoline capacity. 12-18 gallons.

Frame : Pressed steel, frame and pan one piece, special design.

Horse-power : 30.

Number of cylinders : Four.

Cylinders arranged : Separate, vertically.

Cooling : Water, honeycomb radiator with fan and pump.

Ignition : Jump spark with high-tension magneto.

Drive : Chain.

Transmission : Sliding gears, direct drive on high.

Speeds : Four forward, one reverse.

Style of top : Cape or canopy.

Descriptive catalogue sent upon application to the above-named company.

SIDNEY B. BOWMAN AUTOMOBILE CO., 50–52 W. 43D ST., N. Y.

Price

with top
$8900
without top
$8750

Model: **CLEMENT-BAYARD.**

Body: Double side-entrance tonneau, landaulet or brougham.

Color: Blue and yellow, green and yellow, red and red.

Seating capacity: Five, possible seven persons.

Total weight: 2500 pounds.

Wheel base: 115 inches.

Wheel tread: 56 inches.

Tire dimensions, front: 36 x 4¼ inches.

Tire dimensions, rear: 36 x 4¾ inches.

Steering: Wheel through irreversible worm gear.

Brakes: Internal expansion, double acting.

Gasoline capacity: 15-20 gallons.

Frame: Pressed steel, frame and pan one piece, special design.

Horse-power: 45.

Number of cylinders: Four

Cylinders arranged: Separate, vertically.

Cooling: Water, honeycomb radiator with fan and pump.

Ignition: Jump spark with high-tension magneto.

Drive: Chain.

Transmission: Sliding gears, direct drive on high, ball bearing.

Speeds: Four forward, one reverse.

Style of top: Cape or canopy.

Descriptive catalogue sent upon application to the above-named company.

18

CADILLAC AUTOMOBILE CO., DETROIT, MICHIGAN

Price
with top
$800
without top
$750

Model: "E" LIGHT RUNABOUT.

Body : Wood.

Color : Brewster green.

Seating capacity : Two persons.

Total weight : 1100 pounds.

Wheel base : 74 inches.

Wheel tread : 56½ inches, option on 61 inches.

Tire dimensions, front : 28 x 3 inches.

Tire dimensions, rear : 28 x 3 inches.

Steering : Wheel.

Brakes : Double acting on differential

Gasoline capacity : 7 gallons.

Frame : Pressed steel.

Horse-power : 9.

Number of cylinders : One.

Cylinder arranged : Horizontal under body.

Cooling : Water.

Ignition : Jump spark.

Drive : Chain.

Transmission : Planetary.

Speeds : Two forward and reverse.

Style of top : Leather.

Descriptive catalogue sent upon application to the above-named company.

CADILLAC AUTOMOBILE CO., DETROIT, MICHIGAN

Price
without top
$900

Model: "B" DETACHABLE TON-
NEAU TOURING CAR.

Body : **Wood.**

Color : **Brewster green, primrose
running gear.**

Seating capacity : **Four** persons.

Total weight : **1460** pounds.

Wheel base : **76** inches.

Wheel tread : **56½** inches.

Tire dimensions, front : **30 x 3** inches.

Tire dimensions, rear : **30 x 3** inches.

Steering : **Wheel.**

Brakes : **Double acting on differential.**

Gasoline capacity : **7** gallons.

Frame : **Pressed steel.**

Horse-power : **9.**

Number of cylinders : **One.**

Cylinder arranged : **Horizontal under
body.**

Cooling : **Water.**

Ignition : **Jump spark.**

Drive : **Direct chain.**

Transmission : **Planetary.**

Speeds : **Two forward and reverse.**

Descriptive catalogue sent upon application to the above-named company.

CADILLAC AUTOMOBILE CO., DETROIT, MICHIGAN

Price

without top

$950

Model: "F" LIGHT TOURING CAR.

Body: Wood, double side-door entrance, individual seats.

Color: Brewster green, primrose running gear.

Seating capacity: Four persons.

Total weight: 1350 pounds.

Wheel base: 76 inches.

Wheel tread: 56½ inches, option on 61 inches.

Tire dimensions, front: 30 x 3½ inches.

Tire dimensions, rear: 30 x 3½ inches.

Steering: Wheel with rack and pinion.

Brakes: Double acting on differential.

Gasoline capacity: 7 gallons.

Frame: Pressed steel.

Horse-power: 9.

Number of cylinders: One.

Cylinder arranged: Horizontal under body.

Cooling: Water.

Ignition: Jump spark.

Drive: Chain.

Transmission: Planetary.

Speeds: Two forward and reverse.

Descriptive catalogue sent upon application to the above-named company.

CADILLAC AUTOMOBILE CO., DETROIT, MICHIGAN

Price

without top
$2800

Model : " D " CADILLAC.

Body : Wood.   Option on aluminum, extra, $250.

Color : Brewster green, primrose running gear.

Seating capacity : Five persons.

Total weight : Approximately 2600 pounds.

Wheel base : 100 inches.

Wheel tread : 56½ inches.

Tire dimensions, front : 34 x 4½ inches.

Tire dimensions, rear : 34 x 4½ inches.

Steering : Wheel, special irreversible.

Brakes : Double-acting, foot brake on drive shaft, emergency hand brake on wheels.

Gasoline capacity : 25 gallons.

Frame : Pressed steel.

Horse-power : 30.

Number of cylinders : Four.

Cylinders arranged : Vertical in front.

Cooling : Water, cellular radiator.

Ignition : Jump spark.

Drive : Direct through bevel gears.

Transmission : Planetary.

Speeds : Three forward and reverse.

Descriptive catalogue sent upon application to the above-named company.

CADILLAC AUTOMOBILE CO., DETROIT, MICHIGAN

Price

$950

Model: "F" DELIVERY.

Body: Not convertible.

Color: Maroon.

Seating capacity: Twopersons.

Carrying capacity: 600 to 800pounds.

Total weight: 1460pounds.

Wheel base: 76inches.

Wheel tread: 56½inches.

Tire dimensions, front: 30 x 3½ inches.

Tire dimensions, rear: 30 x 3½inches.

Steering: Wheel, rack and pinion.

Brakes: Rear axle, double bands.

Gasoline capacity: 7gallons.

Frame: Pressed steel.

Horse-power: 9.

Number of cylinders: One.

Cylinder arranged: Horizontal.

Cooling: Water.

Ignition: Jump spark.

Drive: Single chain.

Transmission: Planetary.

Speeds: Two forward and one reverse.

Size of top, inside dimensions: height, 50inches; width, 40 inches; length, 42inches.

Descriptive catalogue sent upon application to the above-named company.

ELECTRIC VEHICLE COMPANY, HARTFORD, CONN

Price

$1500
with top
$1700

Model : **COLUMBIA MARK XLIII.**

Body : **Rear-entrance tonneau.**

Color : **Dark green or maroon.**

Seating capacity : **Four persons.**

Total weight : **1800** pounds.

Wheel base : **81½** inches.

Wheel tread : **55** inches.

Tire dimensions, front : **30 x 3½** inches.

Tire dimensions, rear : **30 x 3½** inches.

Steering : **Wheel.**

Brakes : **Foot brake on propeller shaft ; hand brake on rear hubs.**

Gasoline capacity : **10** gallons.

Frame : **Pressed steel.**

Horse-power : **12-14.**

Number of cylinders : **Two.**

Cylinders arranged : **Opposed, horizontal forward under folding bonnet.**

Cooling : **Water, cellular radiator with fan.**

Ignition : **Jump spark, 24 dry cells.**

Drive : **Propeller shaft.**

Transmission : **Sliding gears, direct drive on high gear.**

Speeds : **Three forward, one reverse.**

Style of top : **Canopy, glass front.**

Descriptive catalogue sent upon application to the above-named company.

ELECTRIC VEHICLE COMPANY, HARTFORD, CONN.

Price

$1750

Model: **COLUMBIA MARK XLIV.**

Body: Side-entrance tonneau, divided front seat.

Color: Body, dark green; gear, yellow.

Seating capacity: **Four** persons.

Total weight: 1800 pounds.

Wheel base: 81½ inches.

Wheel tread: 55 inches.

Tire dimensions, front: 30 x 3½ inches.

Tire dimensions, rear: 30 x 3½ inches

Steering: **Wheel.**

Brakes: **Two, external and internal on rear hubs.**

Gasoline capacity: 10 gallons.

Frame: **Pressed steel.**

Horse-power: 18.

Number of cylinders: **Two.**

Cylinders arranged: **Horizontal opposed, forward under folding bonnet.**

Cooling: Water, cellular radiator with fan.

Ignition: **Jump spark, 25 dry cells.**

Drive: **Propeller shaft.**

Transmission: **Sliding gears; direct drive on high gear.**

Speeds: **Three forward, one reverse.**

Descriptive catalogue sent upon application to the above-named company.

ELECTRIC VEHICLE COMPANY, HARTFORD, CONN

Price

$4000

Model: **COLUMBIA MARK XLV. (STANDARD)**.

Body: Side-entrance tonneau.

Color: Body, dark green; gear, yellow.

Seating capacity: Five persons.

Total weight: 2900 pounds.

Wheel base: 108 inches.

Wheel tread: 55 inches.

Tire dimensions, front: 34 x 4 inches.

Tire dimensions, rear: 34 x 4½ inches.

Steering: Wheel, irreversible worm and sector.

Brakes: Foot brake on front sprockets; hand brake on rear sprockets.

Gasoline capacity: 24 gallons.

Frame: Pressed steel.

Horse-power: 35-40.

Number of cylinders: Four.

Cylinders arranged: Vertical, forward under folding bonnet.

Cooling: Water, cellular radiator with fan.

Ignition: Jump spark, storage battery.

Drive: Double side chain.

Transmission: Sliding gears; direct drive on high gear.

Speeds: Four forward, one reverse.

Descriptive catalogue sent upon application to the above-named company.

ELECTRIC VEHICLE COMPANY, HARTFORD, CONN.

Price

$5000

Model: **COLUMBIA MARK XLV. (LANDAULET)**.

Body: Landaulet.

Color: Optional.

Seating capacity: Four persons.

Total weight: 3400 pounds.

Wheel base: 112 inches.

Wheel tread: 55 inches.

Tire dimensions, front: 34 x 4 inches.

Tire dimensions, rear: 34 x 4½ inches.

Steering: Wheel, irreversible worm and sector.

Brakes: Foot brake on front sprockets; hand brake on rear sprockets.

Gasoline capacity: 24 gallons.

Frame: Pressed steel.

Horse-power: 35-40.

Number of cylinders: Four.

Cylinders arranged: Vertical, forward under folding bonnet.

Cooling: Water, cellular radiator with fan.

Ignition: Jump spark, storage battery.

Drive: Double side chain.

Transmission: Sliding gears; direct drive on high gear.

Speeds: Four forward, one reverse.

Style of top: Folding landaulet.

Descriptive catalogue sent upon application to the above-named company.

ELECTRIC VEHICLE COMPANY, HARTFORD, CONN

Price

$5000

**Model: COLUMBIA MARK XLV.
(ROYAL VICTORIA).**

Body : Victoria with hood.

Color : Optional.

Seating capacity : Five persons.

Total weight : 3100 pounds.

Wheel base : 112 inches.

Wheel tread : 55 inches.

Tire dimensions, front : 34 x 4 inches.

Tire dimensions, rear : 34 x 4½ inches.

Steering : Wheel, irreversible worm
and sector.

Brakes : Foot brake on front
sprockets ; hand brake on rear
sprockets.

Gasoline capacity : 24 gallons.

Frame : Pressed steel.

Horse-power : 35-40.

Number of cylinders : Four.

Cylinders arranged : Vertical, forward
under folding bonnet.

Cooling : Water, cellular radiator with
fan.

Ignition : Jump spark, storage battery.

Drive : Double side chain.

Transmission : Sliding gears ; direct
drive on high gear.

Speeds : Four forward, one reverse.

Style of top : Hand - buffed leather
hood.

Descriptive catalogue sent upon application to the above-named company.

ELECTRIC VEHICLE COMPANY, HARTFORD, CONN.

Price

$5500

Model: **COLUMBIA MARK XLV.
(LIMOUSINE).**

Body: **Limousine.**

Color: **Optional.**

Seating capacity: **Seven** persons.

Total weight: **3400** pounds.

Wheel base: **112** inches.

Wheel tread: **55** inches.

Tire dimensions, front: **34 x 4** inches.

Tire dimensions, rear: **34 x 4½** inches.

Steering: **Wheel, irreversible worm
and sector.**

Brakes: **Foot brake on front
sprockets; hand brake on rear
sprockets.**

Gasoline capacity: **24** gallons.

Frame: **Pressed steel.**

Horse-power: **35-40.**

Number of cylinders: **Four.**

Cylinders arranged: **Vertical, forward
under folding bonnet.**

Cooling: **Water, cellular radiator with
fan.**

Ignition: **Jump spark, storage battery.**

Drive: **Double side chain.**

Transmission: **Sliding gears; direct
drive on high gear.**

Speeds: **Four forward, one reverse.**

Style of top: **Limousine, wood.**

Descriptive catalogue sent upon application to the above-named company.

ELMORE MANUFACTURING COMPANY, CLYDE, OHIO

Price

$950

Model: 10.

Body: Rear-entrance detachable tonneau.

Color: Automobile red.

Seating capacity: Four persons.

Total weight: 1300 pounds.

Wheel base: 78 inches.

Wheel tread: 56-60 inches.

Tire dimensions, front: 28 x 3 inches.

Tire dimensions, rear: 28 x 3½ inches.

Steering: Wheel, geared.

Brakes: Two on differential; emergency on transmission.

Gasoline capacity: 10 gallons.

Frame: Trussed angle steel.

Horse-power: 10.

Number of cylinders: One.

Cylinder arranged: Horizontal.

Cooling: Water.

Ignition: Jump spark.

Drive: Single chain.

Transmission: Planetary.

Speeds: Two forward and reverse.

Descriptive catalogue sent upon application to the above-named company.

ELMORE   MANUFACTURING   COMPANY,   CLYDE,   OHIO

Price

with top
$1350
without top
$1250

Model : II.

Body: Detachable double side-entrance tonneau.

Color : Imperial blue, Yale blue panel.

Seating capacity : Five persons.

Total weight : 1500 pounds.

Wheel base : 83 inches.

Wheel tread : 56-60 inches.

Tire dimensions, front : 30 x 3 inches.

Tire dimensions, rear : 30 x 3½ inches.

Steering : Wheel geared.

Brakes : Two on differential, emergency on transmission.

Gasoline capacity : 10 gallons.

Frame : Trussed angle steel.

Horse-power : 16.

Number of cylinders : Two.

Cylinders arranged : Horizontal.

Cooling : Water.

Ignition : Jump spark.

Drive : Single chain.

Transmission : Planetary.

Speeds : Two forward and reverse.

Style of top : Canopy or cape top.

Descriptive catalogue sent upon application to the above-named company.

H. H. FRANKLIN MANUFACTURING CO., SYRACUSE, N. Y

Price

without top
$1400

Model: **FRANKLIN TYPE "E," GENTLEMAN'S RUNABOUT.**

Body: **Aluminum with divided seats.**

Color: **Franklin green or Franklin red.**

Seating capacity: **Two persons.**

Total weight: **1050 pounds.**

Wheel base: **74** inches.

Wheel tread: **Standard.**

Tire dimensions, front: **28 x 3** inches.

Tire dimensions, rear: **28 x 3** inches.

Steering: **Wheel.**

Brakes: **Two equalizing bands on rear wheels.**

Gasoline capacity: **5** gallons.

Frame: **Angle iron and wood.**

Horse-power: **12.**

Number of cylinders: **Four.**

Cylinders arranged: **Vertical under hood.**

Cooling: **Air cooled.**

Ignition: **Jump spark.**

Drive: **Chain.**

Transmission: **Planetary.**

Speeds: **Two forward and reverse.**

Descriptive catalogue sent upon application to the above-named company.

H. H. FRANKLIN MANUFACTURING CO., SYRACUSE, N. Y.

Price

without top
$1500

Model : **FRANKLIN TYPE "A,"** with or without tonneau.

Body : **Aluminum with divided seats.**

Color : **Franklin green or red.**

Seating capacity : **Two or four persons**

Total weight : **1175** pounds.

Wheel base : **82** inches.

Wheel tread : **Standard.**

Tire dimensions, front : **28 x 3** inches.

Tire dimensions, rear : **760 x 90** m/m.

Steering : **Wheel.**

Brakes : **Two ; equalizing bands on rear wheels.**

Gasoline capacity : **7** gallons.

Frame : **Angle iron.**

Horse-power : **12.**

Number of cylinders : **Four.**

Cylinders arranged : **Vertical under hood.**

Cooling : **Air cooled.**

Ignition : **Jump spark.**

Drive : **Chain.**

Transmission : **Planetary.**

Speeds : **Two forward and reverse.**

Descriptive catalogue sent upon application to the above-named company.

H. H. FRANKLIN MANUFACTURING CO., SYRACUSE, N. Y.

Price

without top

$1650

Model: FRANKLIN TYPE "B," FOUR - PASSENGER LIGHT CAR.

Body: Aluminum with rear-entrance tonneau and divided front seats.

Color: Franklin green or Franklin red.

Seating capacity: Four persons.

Total weight: 1275 pounds.

Wheel base: 82 inches.

Wheel tread: Standard.

Tire dimensions, front: 28 x 3 inches.

Tire dimensions, rear: 760 x 90 m/m.

Steering: Wheel.

Brakes: Two ; equalizing bands on rear wheels.

Gasoline capacity: 7 gallons.

Frame: Angle iron and wood.

Horse-power: 12.

Number of cylinders: Four.

Cylinders arranged: Vertical under hood.

Cooling: Air cooled.

Ignition: Jump spark.

Drive: Chain.

Transmission: Planetary.

Speeds: Two forward and reverse.

Descriptive catalogue sent upon application to the above-named company.

H. H. FRANKLIN MANUFACTURING CO., SYRACUSE, N. Y.

Price

without top
$1700

Model: **FRANKLIN TYPE "F," FOUR - PASSENGER LIGHT CAR.**

Body: **Aluminum, front entrance to tonneau through tilting seat.**

Color: **Franklin red or Franklin green.**

Seating capacity: **Four** persons.

Total weight: **1275** pounds.

Wheel base: **82** inches.

Wheel tread: **Standard.**

Tire dimensions, front: **28 x 3** inches.

Tire dimensions, rear: **760 x 90** m/m.

Steering: **Wheel.**

Brakes: **Two; equalizing bands on rear wheels.**

Gasoline capacity: **7** gallons.

Frame: **Angle iron.**

Horse-power: **12.**

Number of cylinders: **Four.**

Cylinders arranged: **Vertical under hood.**

Cooling: **Air cooled.**

Ignition: **Jump spark.**

Drive: **Chain.**

Transmission: **Planetary.**

Speeds: **Two forward and reverse.**

Descriptive catalogue sent upon application to the above-named company.

H. H. FRANKLIN MANUFACTURING CO., SYRACUSE, N. Y.

Price

without top
$2500

Model: **FRANKLIN TYPE " D,"
LIGHT TOURING CAR.**

Body: **Aluminum, with side door
entrance tonneau; divided front
seats.**

Color: **Franklin green or Franklin
red.**

Seating capacity: **Five** persons.

Total weight: **1800** pounds.

Wheel base: **100** inches.

Wheel tread: **Standard.**

Tire dimensions, front: **30 x 4** inches.

Tire dimensions, rear: **30 x 4** inches.

Steering: **Wheel.**

Brakes: **One on countershaft and two
equalizing bands on rear wheels.**

Gasoline capacity: **12** gallons.

Frame: **Wood.**

Horse-power: **20.**

Number of cylinders: **Four.**

Cylinders arranged: **Vertical under
hood.**

Cooling: **Air cooled.**

Ignition: **Jump spark.**

Drive: **Shaft.**

Transmission: **Sliding gear.**

Speeds: **Three forward and one reverse.**

Descriptive catalogue sent upon application to the above-named company.

H. H. FRANKLIN MANUFACTURING CO., SYRACUSE, N. Y.

Price

without top
$3500

Model: **FRANKLIN TYPE "C."**

Body: **Aluminum, with side door entrance tonneau and divided front seats.**

Color: **Franklin green or Franklin red.**

Seating capacity: **Five** persons.

Total weight: **2400** pounds.

Wheel base: **110** inches.

Wheel tread: **Standard.**

Tire dimensions, front: **34 x 4** inches.

Tire dimensions, rear: **34 x 4½** inches.

Steering: **Wheel.**

Brakes: **One on countershaft and two equalizing bands on rear wheels.**

Gasoline capacity: **18** gallons.

Frame: **Wood.**

Horse-power: **30.**

Number of cylinders: **Four.**

Cylinders arranged: **Vertical under hood.**

Cooling: **Air cooled.**

Ignition: **Jump spark.**

Drive: **Shaft.**

Transmission: **Sliding gear.**

Speeds: **Three forward and one reverse.**

Descriptive catalogue sent upon application to the above-named company.

37

CREST MANUFACTURING CO., DORCHESTER, MASS.

Price

with glass
front canopy
$1050
with tonneau
$900
without tonneau
$800

Model : **CRESTMOBILE "D" 1905.**

Body : **Wood tonneau.**

Color : **Carmine or Brewster green.**

Seating capacity : **Two or four persons.**

Total weight : **1200** pounds.

Wheel base : **76** inches.

Wheel tread : **54** inches.

Tire dimensions, front : **28 x 3** inches

Tire dimensions, rear : **28 x 3** inches.

Steering : **Wheel with locking device.**

Brakes : **On differential.**

Gasoline capacity : **6** gallons.

Frame : **Tubular steel.**

Horse-power : **8½.**

Number of cylinders : **One.**

Cylinder arranged : **Vertical, in front.**

Cooling : **Air cooled, with fan.**

Ignition : **Jump spark.**

Drive : **Shaft drive with bevel gears.**

Transmission : **Individual clutches and friction bands.**

Speeds : **Two forward, one reverse.**

Style of top : **Canopy with glass front.**

Descriptive catalogue sent upon application to the above-named company

THE HAYNES-APPERSON CO., KOKOMO, IND.

Price

with top
$1350

Model: **TWO - PASSENGER TOURING CAR.**

Body: **Folding front seat.**

Color: **Olive green.**

Seating capacity: **Two and four persons**

Total weight: **1500** pounds.

Wheel base: **81** inches.

Wheel tread: **56** inches.

Tire dimensions, front: **32 x 3½** inches.

Tire dimensions, rear: **32 x 3½** inches.

Steering: **Irreversible wheel.**

Brakes: **Two on differential.**

Gasoline capacity: **6** gallons.

Frame: **Angle iron.**

Horse power: **16-18.**

Number of cylinders: **Two.**

Cylinders arranged: **Horizontal, opposed.**

Cooling: **Water.**

Ignition: **Jump spark.**

Drive: **Chain.**

Transmission: **Individual clutch.**

Speeds: **Three forward, one reverse.**

Descriptive catalogue sent upon application to the above-named company.

THE HAYNES-APPERSON CO., KOKOMO, IND.

Price

without top

$1500

Model: **LIGHT TOURING CAR.**

Body: **Four-passenger, divided front seat, side entrance.**

Color: **Dark green.**

Seating capacity: **Four persons.**

Total weight: **1500 pounds.**

Wheel base: **81 inches.**

Wheel tread: **56 inches.**

Tire dimensions, front: **32 x 3½ inches.**

Tire dimensions, rear: **32 x 3½ inches.**

Steering: **Irreversible wheel.**

Brakes: **One on each rear hub.**

Gasoline capacity: **6 gallons.**

Frame: **Pressed steel.**

Horse-power: **16-18.**

Number of cylinders: **Two.**

Cylinders arranged: **Horizontal, opposed.**

Cooling: **Water and fan**

Ignition: **Jump spark.**

Drive: **Shaft, with roller gear and sprocket.**

Transmission: **Individual clutch direct on high gear.**

Speeds: **Three forward, one reverse.**

Descriptive catalogue sent upon application to the above-named company.

THE HAYNES-APPERSON CO., KOKOMO, IND.

Price

with top
$3200
without top
$3000

Model : **FOUR-CYLINDER.**

Body : **Side entrance, folding top, divided seats.**

Color : **Dark green.**

Seating capacity : **Five** persons.

Total weight : **2800** pounds.

Wheel base : **108** inches.

Wheel tread : **56** inches.

Tire dimensions, front : **34 x 4½** inches.

Tire dimensions, rear : **34 x 4½** inches.

Steering : **Irreversible wheel.**

Brakes : **Rear hubs, also emergency on driving shaft.**

Gasoline capacity : **14** gallons.

Frame : **Pressed steel.**

Horse-power : **35-40.**

Number of cylinders : **Four.**

Cylinders arranged : **Vertical, separate.**

Cooling : **Water and fan.**

Ignition : **Jump spark.**

Drive : **Shaft with roller gear and sprocket.**

Transmission : **Individual clutch direct on high gear.**

Speeds : **Three forward, one reverse.**

Descriptive catalogue sent upon application to the above-named company.

HOLLANDER & TANGEMAN, 5 WEST 45th ST., NEW YORK

Price

with limousine
body
$7200
with touring body
$6700
with top, extra
$150 to $300

Model: F I A T, 1905.

Body: Choice King of Belgians, Leopold or Princess Laetizia.

Color: Choice.

Seating capacity: Tonneau body, five persons; side-entrance, seven persons.

Total weight: Tonneau, 2050 pounds; side-entrance, 2200 pounds.

Wheel base: 111 inches and 125 inches.

Wheel tread: 56 inches.

Tire dimensions, front: 910 x 90 m/m.

Tire dimensions, rear: 915 x 105 m/m.

Steering: Irreversible wheel.

Brakes: Four; expanding and band types (water cooled).

Gasoline capacity: 30 gallons.

Frame: Pressed steel.

Horse-power: 16-20.

Number of cylinders: Four.

Cylinders arranged: Vertical, in pairs.

Cooling: Daimler patented multi-cellular water radiator.

Ignition: Magneto, make and break.

Drive: Double chain.

Transmission: Sliding gear.

Speeds: Four forward, one reverse.

Style of top: Canopy, cape or closed.

Descriptive catalogue sent upon application to the above named company.

HOLLANDER & TANGEMAN, 5 WEST 45th ST., NEW YORK

Price

with limousine
body
$9000
with touring body
$8500
with top, extra
$150 to $300

Model : **F I A T**, 1905.

Body : **Choice King of Belgians, Leopold or Princess Laetizia.**

Color : **Choice.**

Seating capacity: **Tonneau, five persons ; side-entrance, seven persons.**

Total weight : **Tonneau, 2150** pounds; **side-entrance, 2300** pounds.

Wheel base : **114** inches and **128** inches.

Wheel tread : **56** inches.

Tire dimensions, front : **910 x 90** m/m.

Tire dimensions, rear : **915 x 105** and **920 x 120** m/m.

Steering : **Irreversible wheel.**

Brakes : **Four ; expanding and band type (water cooled).**

Gasoline capacity :   **30** gallons.

Frame : **Pressed steel.**

Horse-power: **24-32, also 60, 90 and 100.**

Number of cylinders : **Four.**

Cylinders arranged : **Vertical, in pairs.**

Cooling : **Daimler patented multi-cellular water radiator.**

Ignition : **Magneto make and break.**

Drive : **Double chain.**

Transmission : **Sliding gear.**

Speeds : **Four forward, one reverse.**

Style of top : **Canopy, cape or closed.**

Descriptive catalogue sent upon application to the above-named company.

THE KIRK MANUFACTURING COMPANY, TOLEDO, OHIO

Price

side entrance
$1100
rear entrance
$1000

Model: **YALE " E,"** rear entrance; **"G,"** side entrance.

Body: **Wood, divided front seat.**

Color: **Body, blue; gear, straw color.**

Seating capacity: **Five** persons.

Total weight: **1500** pounds.

Wheel base: **" E,"** 83 inches; **"G,"** 85 inches.

Wheel tread: **56** inches.

Tire dimensions, front: 30 x 3½ inches.

Tire dimensions, rear: 30 x 3½ inches.

Steering: **Non-reversible worm gear type.**

Brakes: **Two internal brakes on rear wheels.**

Gasoline capacity: **10** gallons.

Frame: **Angle steel, wood reinforcement.**

Horse-power: **14-16.**

Number of cylinders: **Two.**

Cylinders arranged: **Horizontal, opposed.**

Cooling: **Water, tubular radiator.**

Ignition: **Jump spark.**

Drive: **Chain.**

Transmission: **Planetary.**

Speeds: **Two forward and reverse.**

Style of top: **Extra: victoria, cape, extension or canopy.**

Descriptive catalogue sent upon application to the above-named company.

THE KIRK MANUFACTURING COMPANY, TOLEDO, OHIO

Price

$2500

Model : **YALE " F."**

Body : **Wood.**

Color : **Body, blue ; gear, straw color.**

Seating capacity : **Five** persons.

Total weight : **2300** pounds.

Wheel base : **104** inches.

Wheel tread : **56** inches.

Tire dimensions, front : **32 x 4** inches.

Tire dimensions, rear : **32 x 4** inches.

Steering : **Non-reversible ; compound screw and nut** (all encased).

Brakes : **One on transmission, two internal, expanding on rear wheels.**

Gasoline capacity : **20** gallons.

Frame : **Angle steel.**

Horse-power : **24-28.**

Number of cylinders : **Four.**

Cylinders arranged : **Vertical, in front.**

Cooling : **Water, tubular radiator with radiating fins.**

Ignition : **Jump spark.**

Drive : **Bevel gear.**

Transmission : **Sliding gears.**

Speeds : **Three forward and reverse.**

Style of top : **Extra : victoria, cape, extension or canopy.**

Descriptive catalogue sent upon application to the above-named company.

KNOX AUTOMOBILE CO., SPRINGFIELD, MASS.

Price

with top
$1335 and
$1350
without top
$1250

Model: " E " RUNABOUT with folding front seat.

Body: **Wood.**

Color: **Carmine, green or blue.**

Seating capacity: **Four** persons.

Total weight: **1700** pounds.

Wheel base: **72** inches.

Wheel tread: **54** inches.

Tire dimensions, front: **30 x 3½** inches.

Tire dimensions, rear: **30 x 3½** inches.

Steering: **Lever and Lemp check.**

Brakes: **Two foot levers and one hand lever.**

Gasoline capacity: **8** gallons.

Frame: **Angle steel.**

Horse-power: **8-10.**

Number of cylinders: **One.**

Cylinder arranged: **Horizontal, under center.**

Cooling: **Air cooled, Knox Company's patent.**

Ignition: **Jump spark from dry cells.**

Drive: **Single chain.**

Transmission: **Planetary.**

Speeds: **Two forward, one reverse.**

Style of top: **Buggy or victoria.**

Descriptive catalogue sent upon application to the above-named company.

KNOX AUTOMOBILE CO. SPRINGFIELD, MASS.

Price
with close top
$1615
with open top
$1600
without top
$1500

Model: " F-I " RUNABOUT.

Body: **Folding, front seat.**

Color: **Carmine, green or blue.**

Seating capacity: **Four** persons.

Total weight: **1850** pounds.

Wheel base: **81** inches.

Wheel tread: **56** inches.

Tire dimensions, front: **30 x 4** inches.

Tire dimensions, rear: **30 x 4** inches.

Steering: **Irreversible lever or wheel.**

Brakes: **Two foot and one hand.**

Gasoline capacity: **16** gallons.

Frame: **Angle steel.**

Horse-power: **14-16.**

Number of cylinders: **Two.**

Cylinders arranged: **Horizontal opposed, under center.**

Cooling: **Air cooled, Knox Company's patent.**

Ignition: **Jump spark from dry cells.**

Drive: **Single chain.**

Transmission: **Planetary.**

Speeds: **Two forward, one reverse.**

Style of top: **Leather.**

Descriptive catalogue sent upon application to the above-named company.

KNOX AUTOMOBILE CO., SPRINGFIELD, MASS.

Price

with close top
$1865
with open top
$1850
without top
$1750

Model: **"F-3" SURREY.**

Body: **Folding rear seat.**

Color: **Carmine, green or blue.**

Seating capacity: **Four** persons.

Total weight: **1950** pounds.

Wheel base: **87** inches.

Wheel tread: **56** inches.

Tire dimensions, front: **30 x 4** inches.

Tire dimensions, rear: **30 x 4** inches.

Steering: **Irreversible lever or wheel.**

Brakes: **Two foot and one hand.**

Gasoline capacity: **16** gallons.

Frame: **Angle steel.**

Horse-power: **14-16.**

Number of cylinders: **Two.**

Cylinders arranged: **Horizontal opposed, under center.**

Cooling: **Air cooled, Knox Company's patent.**

Ignition: **Jump spark from dry cells.**

Drive: **Single chain.**

Transmission: **Planetary.**

Speeds: **Two forward, one reverse.**

Style of top: **Leather.**

Descriptive catalogue sent upon application to the above-named company.

KNOX AUTOMOBILE CO., SPRINGFIELD, MASS.

Price

with top
$2000
without top
$1900

Model : " F " TONNEAU.

Body : **Side entrance.**

Color : **Carmine, green or blue.**

Seating capacity : **Five** persons.

Total weight : **2000** pounds.

Wheel base : **90** inches.

Wheel tread : **56** inches.

Tire dimensions, front : **30 x 4** inches.

Tire dimensions, rear : **30 x 4** inches.

Steering : **Irreversible lever or wheel.**

Brakes : **Two foot and one hand.**

Gasoline capacity : **16** gallons.

Frame : **Angle steel.**

Horse-power : **14-16.**

Number of cylinders : **Two.**

Cylinders arranged : **Horizontal opposed, under center.**

Cooling : **Air cooled, Knox Company's patent.**

Ignition : **Jump spark from dry cells.**

Drive : **Single chain.**

Transmission : **Planetary.**

Speeds : **Two forward, one reverse.**

Style of top : **Khaki cloth.**

Descriptive catalogue sent upon application to the above-named company.

KNOX AUTOMOBILE COMPANY, SPRINGFIELD, MASS

Price
with top
$1800

Model: **No. 41.**

Body: **Wood.**

Color: **Standard red or green.**

Carrying capacity: **1500 pounds.**

Total weight: **2700** pounds.

Wheel base: **78** inches.

Wheel tread: **56** inches.

Tire dimensions, front: **32 x 3½** inches, solid.

Tire dimensions, rear: **32 x 3½** inches, solid.

Steering: **Irreversible lever and Lemp check.**

Brakes: **Two foot levers and one hand lever.**

Gasoline capacity: **13** gallons.

Frame: **Angle steel.**

Horse-power: **8-10.**

Number of cylinders: **One.**

Cylinder arranged: **Horizontal, under center.**

Cooling: **Air cooled, Knox Company's patent.**

Ignition: **Jump spark from dry cells.**

Drive: **Single chain.**

Transmission: **Planetary.**

Speeds: **Two forward, one reverse.**

Style of top: **Metal grill.**

Descriptive catalogue sent upon application to the above-named company.

KNOX AUTOMOBILE CO., SPRINGFIELD, MASS.

Price

with paneled top
$2500
with canvas top
$2450
without top
$2400

Model: No. 39.

Body: Wood.

Color: Standard red or green.

Carrying capacity: 2500 pounds.

Total weight: 3300 pounds.

Wheel base: 96 inches.

Wheel tread: 56 inches.

Tire dimensions, front: 32 x 3½ inches, solid.

Tire dimensions rear: 32 x 3½ inches, solid.

Steering: Lever and Lemp check.

Brakes: Two foot levers and one hand lever.

Gasoline capacity: 13 gallons.

Frame: Angle steel.

Horse-power: 16-18.

Number of cylinders: Two.

Cylinders arranged: Horizontal opposed, under center.

Cooling: Air cooled, Knox Company's patent.

Ignition: Jump spark from dry cells.

Drive: Single chain.

Transmission: Planetary.

Speeds: Two forward, one reverse.

Style of top: Canvas or paneled.

Descriptive catalogue sent upon application to the above-named company.

F. A. LA ROCHE CO., 652–664 HUDSON ST., NEW YORK CITY

Price

with top
$5500
without top
$5000

Model: **DARRACQ, Double Phaeton Tulip.**

Body: **Entrance, two sides.**

Color: **Royal blue, dark green, Mercedes red.**

Seating capacity: **Five** persons.

Total weight: **2050** pounds.

Wheel base: **110** inches (**long chassis**).

Wheel tread: **52** inches.

Tire dimensions, front: **810 x 90** m/m.

Tire dimensions, rear: **810 x 90** m/m.

Steering: **Irreversible and adjustable (worm gear).**

Brakes: **Three; internal expansion double-acting on driving shaft and rear wheels.**

Gasoline capacity: **15** gallons.

Frame: **Pressed steel of one piece throughout (special Darracq patent).**

Horse-power: **15-20.**

Number of cylinders: **Four.**

Cylinders arranged: **Vertical, in pairs.**

Cooling: **Water, Mercedes honeycomb radiator and pump.**

Ignition: **Combination jump spark and make and break with magneto.**

Drive: **Bevel gear (shaft).**

Transmission: **Sliding gears.**

Speeds: **Three forward and one reverse.**

Style of top: **Canopy, detachable glass back and sliding glass front.**

Descriptive catalogue sent upon application to the above-named company.

F. A. LA ROCHE CO., 652–664 HUDSON ST., NEW YORK CITY

Price

with top
$6000

Model: **DARRACQ**, double side entrance.

Body: **Demi-limousine with combination top.**

Color: **Royal blue, dark green, Mercedes red.**

Seating capacity: **Five** persons.

Total weight: **2200** pounds.

Wheel base: **112** inches (**extra long chassis**).

Wheel tread: **52** inches.

Tire dimensions, front: **810 x 90** m/m.

Tire dimensions, rear: **820 x 120** m/m.

Steering: **Irreversible and adjustable (worm gear).**

Brakes: **Three; internal expansion double-acting on driving shaft and rear wheels.**

Gasoline capacity: **15** gallons.

Frame: **Pressed steel of one piece throughout (special Darracq patent).**

Horse-power: **15–20.**

Number of cylinders: **Four.**

Cylinders arranged: **Vertical, in pairs.**

Cooling: **Water, Mercedes honeycomb radiator and pump.**

Ignition: **Jump spark and make and break with magneto.**

Drive: **Bevel gear (shaft).**

Transmission: **Sliding gears.**

Speeds: **Three forward and one reverse.**

Style of top: **Canopy, stationary glass back and sliding glass front.**

Descriptive catalogue sent upon application to the above-named company.

THE LOCOMOBILE COMPANY OF AMERICA, BRIDGEPORT, CONN.

Price

$2800
chassis
$2550
tops
extra

Model: **LOCOMOBILE, TYPE "E."**

Body: **Wood, side entrances.**

Color: **As desired by the purchaser.**

Seating capacity: **Five persons.**

Total weight: **1800 pounds.**

Wheel base: **92 inches.**

Wheel tread: **50 inches.**

Tire dimensions, front: **32 x 4 inches.**

Tire dimensions, rear: **32 x 4 inches.**

Steering: **Wheel with irreversible worm-gear mechanism.**

Brakes: **Foot brake on differential shaft; emergency brakes on rear wheels. (All double-acting.)**

Gasoline capacity: **17 gallons.**

Frame: **Pressed steel.**

Horse-power: **15-20.**

Number of cylinders: **Four.**

Cylinders arranged: **Vertically and longitudinally, in front.**

Cooling: **Water, by gear-driven centrifugal pump and cellular radiator.**

Ignition: **Make and break, magneto.**

Drive: **Double chain.**

Transmission: **Sliding gear system.**

Speeds: **Three forward, one reverse.**

Style of top: **Any style desired by the customer.**

Descriptive catalogue sent upon application to the above-named company.

THE LOCOMOBILE COMPANY OF AMERICA, BRIDGEPORT, CONN.

Price

$3300
chassis
$2550

Model : LOCOMOBILE, TYPE "E."

Body : Wood, side entrances.

Color : As desired by the purchaser.

Seating capacity : Five persons.

Total weight : 1800 pounds.

Wheel base : 92 inches.

Wheel tread : 50 inches.

Tire dimensions, front : 32 x 4 inches.

Tire dimensions, rear : 32 x 4 inches.

Steering : Wheel with irreversible worm-gear mechanism.

Brakes : Foot brake on differential shaft ; emergency brakes on rear wheels. (All double-acting.)

Gasoline capacity : 17 gallons.

Frame : Pressed steel.

Horse-power : 15-20.

Number of cylinders : Four.

Cylinders arranged : Vertically and longitudinally, in front.

Cooling : Water, by gear-driven centrifugal pump and cellular radiator.

Ignition : Make and break, magneto.

Drive : Double chain.

Transmission : Sliding gear system.

Speeds : Three forward, one reverse.

Style of top : Any style desired by the customer.

Descriptive catalogue sent upon application to the above-named company.

THE LOCOMOBILE COMPANY OF AMERICA, BRIDGEPORT, CONN.

Price

$3700
chassis
$3400
tops
extra

Model: **LOCOMOBILE, TYPE "D."**

Body: **Wood, side entrances.**

Color: **As desired by the purchaser.**

Seating capacity: **Seven** persons.

Total weight: **2300** pounds.

Wheel base: **96** inches.

Wheel tread: **52** inches.

Tire dimensions, front: **34 x 4½** inches.

Tire dimensions, rear: **34 x 4½** inches.

Steering: **Wheel, with irreversible worm-gear mechanism.**

Brakes: **Foot brake on differential shaft; emergency brakes on rear wheels. (All double-acting.)**

Gasoline capacity: **17** gallons.

Frame: **Channel steel.**

Horse-power: **20-25.**

Number of cylinders: **Four.**

Cylinders arranged: **Vertically and longitudinally, in front.**

Cooling: **Water, by gear-driven centrifugal pump and cellular radiator.**

Ignition: **Jump spark with storage batteries.**

Drive: **Double chain.**

Transmission: **Sliding gear system.**

Speeds: **Three forward, one reverse.**

Style of top: **Any style of top desired by the customer.**

Descriptive catalogue sent upon application to the above-named company.

THE LOCOMOBILE COMPANY OF AMERICA, BRIDGEPORT, CONN.

Price

$5000
chassis
$4600
tops
extra

Model: **LOCOMOBILE, TYPE " H."**

Body : **Wood, side entrances.**

Color : **As desired by the purchaser.**

Seating capacity : **Seven** persons.

Total weight : **2700** pounds.

Wheel base : **106** inches.

Wheel tread : **54** inches.

Tire dimensions, front : **34 x 4½** inches.

Tire dimensions, rear : **34 x 4½** inches.

Steering : **Wheel with irreversible worm-gear mechanism.**

Brakes : **Foot brake on differential shaft ; emergency brakes on rear wheels. (All double-acting.)**

Gasoline capacity : **25** gallons.

Frame : **Pressed steel.**

Horse-power : **30-35.**

Number of cylinders : **Four.**

Cylinders arranged : **Vertically and longitudinally, in front.**

Cooling : **Water, by gear-driven centrifugal pump and cellular radiator.**

Ignition : **Make and break, magneto.**

Drive : **Double chain.**

Transmission : **Sliding gear system.**

Speeds : **Three forward, one reverse.**

Style of top : **Any style of top desired by the customer.**

Descriptive catalogue sent upon application to the above-named company.

57

THE LOCOMOBILE COMPANY OF AMERICA, BRIDGEPORT, CONN.

Price

$6000
chassis
$4600

Model: **LOCOMOBILE, TYPE "H."**

Body : **Wood, side entrances.**

Color : **As desired by the purchaser.**

Seating capacity : **Seven** persons.

Total weight : **3000** pounds.

Wheel base : **106** inches.

Wheel tread : **54** inches.

Tire dimensions, front : **34 x 4½** inches.

Tire dimensions, rear : **34 x 4½** inches.

Steering : **Wheel with irreversible worm-gear mechanism.**

Brakes : **Foot brake on differential shaft ; emergency brakes on rear wheels. (All double-acting.)**

Gasoline capacity : **25** gallons.

Frame : **Pressed steel.**

Horse-power : **30-35.**

Number of cylinders : **Four.**

Cylinders arranged : **Vertically and longitudinally, in front.**

Cooling : **Water, by gear-driven centrifugal pump and cellular radiator.**

Ignition : **Make and break, magneto.**

Drive : **Double chain.**

Transmission : **Sliding gear system.**

Speeds : **Three forward, one reverse.**

Style of top : **Any style of top desired by the customer.**

Descriptive catalogue sent upon application to the above-named company.

THE LOCOMOBILE COMPANY OF AMERICA, BRIDGEPORT, CONN.

Price

$8000
chassis
$6700

Model: **LOCOMOBILE, TYPE "F."**

Body: **Wood or aluminum, side entrances.**

Color: **As desired by the purchaser.**

Seating capacity: **Seven persons.**

Total weight: **3000 pounds.**

Wheel base: **110 inches.**

Wheel tread: **54 inches.**

Tire dimensions, front: **36 x 5 inches.**

Tire dimensions, rear: **36 x 5 inches.**

Steering: **Wheel, with irreversible worm-gear mechanism.**

Brakes: **Foot brake on differential shaft; emergency brakes on rear wheels. (All double-acting.)**

Gasoline capacity: **25 gallons.**

Frame: **Pressed steel.**

Horse-power: **40-45.**

Number of cylinders: **Four.**

Cylinders arranged: **Vertically and longitudinally, in front.**

Cooling: **Water, by gear-driven centrifugal pump and cellular radiator.**

Ignition: **Make and break, magneto.**

Drive: **Double chain.**

Transmission: **Sliding gear system.**

Speeds: **Four forward, one reverse.**

Style of top: **Any style of top desired by the customer.**

Descriptive catalogue sent upon application to the above-named company.

NORTHERN MANUFACTURING CO., DETROIT, MICH.

Price

with top
$700

without top
$650

Model : 1905 **NORTHERN RUN-ABOUT.**

Body : **Wood.**

Color : **Carmine.**

Seating capacity : **Two, or four with dos-a-dos seat.**

Total weight : **1100** pounds.

Wheel base : **70** inches.

Wheel tread : **56** inches.

Tire dimensions, front : **28 x 3** inches.

Tire dimensions, rear : **28 x 3** inches.

Steering : **Center lever.**

Brakes · **On rear axle differential and transmission reverse.**

Gasoline capacity : **7½** gallons.

Frame : **Angle steel.**

Horse-power : **7.**

Number of cylinders : **One.**

Cylinder arranged : **Horizontal under body.**

Cooling : **Water, 18-tube radiator and pump.**

Ignition : **Jump spark and batteries.**

Drive : **Chain.**

Transmission : **Planetary.**

Speeds : **Two forward and reverse.**

Style of top : **Full leather carriage top.**

Descriptive catalogue sent upon application to the above-named company.

NORTHERN   MANUFACTURING   CO.,   DETROIT,   MICH.

Price

with top
$1575
without top
$1500

Model: **NORTHERN TWO-PAS-
SENGER TOURING CAR.**

Body: **Wood.**

Color: **Body dark green, gear cream
yellow.**

Seating capacity. **Two** persons.

Total weight: **1800** pounds.

Wheel base: **88** inches.

Wheel tread: **56** inches.

Tire dimensions, front: **30 x 4** inches.

Tire dimensions, rear: **30 x 4** inches.

Steering: **Wheel and gear.**

Brakes: **Hub and transmission.**

Gasoline capacity: **10** gallons.

Frame: **Angle steel.**

Horse power: **18.**

Number of cylinders: **Two.**

Cylinders arranged: **Double, opposed
under hood.**

Cooling: **Water, radiator and pump.**

Ignition: **Jump spark and battery.**

Drive: **Shaft and bevel gears.**

Transmission: **Planetary.**

Speeds: **Two forward and reverse.**

Style of top: **Leather carriage top.**

Descriptive catalogue sent upon application to the above-named company.

NORTHERN MANUFACTURING CO., DETROIT, MICH.

Price

with top
$1800
(cape
pattern)
without top
$1700

Model: 1905 **NORTHERN TOUR-ING CAR.**

Body: **Wood, side entrance.**

Color: **Dark green body and cream yellow running gear.**

Seating capacity: **Five** persons.

Total weight: 2000 pounds.

Wheel base: 100 inches.

Wheel tread: 56 inches.

Tire dimensions, front: 30 x 4 inches.

Tire dimensions, rear: 30 x 4 inches.

Steering: **Wheel and gear.**

Brakes: **Hub and transmission.**

Gasoline capacity: 10 gallons

Frame: **Angle steel.**

Horse-power: 17.

Number of cylinders: **Two.**

Cylinders arranged: **Double, opposed under hood.**

Cooling: **Water, radiator in front; circulation by pump.**

Ignition: **Jump spark, batteries.**

Drive: **Shaft and bevel gears.**

Transmission: **Planetary.**

Speeds: **Two forward and reverse.**

Style of top: **Cape or canopy.**

Descriptive catalogue sent upon application to the above-named company.

NORTHERN MANUFACTURING CO., DETROIT, MICH.

Price

$2500

Model: **NORTHERN LIMOUSINE.**

Body: **Wood.**

Color: **Coach blue and green.**

Seating capacity: **Five persons.**

Total weight: **2200** pounds.

Wheel base : **100** inches.

Wheel tread : **56** inches.

Tire dimensions, front : **30 x 4** inches.

Tire dimensions, rear : **30 x 4** inches.

Steering: **Wheel and gear.**

Brakes : **Hub and transmission.**

Gasoline capacity : **10** gallons.

Frame : **Angle steel.**

Horse-power : **17.**

Number of cylinders : **Two.**

Cylinders arranged : **Double, opposed under front hood.**

Cooling : **Water, radiator under front hood and pump.**

Ignition : **Jump spark and battery.**

Drive : **Shaft and bevel gears.**

Transmission : **Planetary.**

Speeds : **Two forward and reverse.**

Descriptive catalogue sent upon application to the above-named company.

OLDS   MOTOR   WORKS,   DETROIT,   MICHIGAN

Price

with top
$675
without top
$650

Model : **OLDSMOBILE STAND-ARD RUNABOUT.**

Body : **Oldsmobile curved dash.**

Color : **Black with red trimmings, gilt striping.**

Seating capacity : **Two** persons.

Total weight : **1100** pounds.

Wheel base : **66** inches.

Wheel tread : **55** inches.

Tire dimensions, front : **28 x 3** inches.

Tire dimensions, rear : **28 x 3** inches.

Steering : **Tiller.**

Brakes : **Transmission and rear hub, operated by foot pedal.**

Gasoline capacity : **5** gallons.

Frame : **Angle steel.**

Horse-power : **7.**

Number of cylinders : **One.**

Cylinder arranged : **Horizontal, under body.**

Cooling : **Water, copper disk radiator.**

Ignition : **Jump spark.**

Drive : **Chain.**

Transmission : **Planetary.**

Speeds : **Two forward, and one reverse.**

Style of top : **Buggy.**

Descriptive catalogue sent upon application to the above-named company.

OLDS   MOTOR   WORKS,   DETROIT,   MICHIGAN

Price

without top

$750

Model: **OLDSMOBILE TOURING RUNABOUT.**

Body: **Wood.**

Color: **Brewster green.**

Seating capacity: **Two** persons.

Wheel base: **76** inches.

Wheel tread: **55** inches.

Tire dimensions, front: **28 x 3** inches.

Tire dimensions, rear: **28 x 3** inches.

Steering: **Wheel, tilting post.**

Brakes: **On rear hubs and transmission, operated by foot pedal.**

Gasoline capacity: **5** gallons.

Frame: **Angle steel.**

Horse-power: **7.**

Number of cylinders: **One.**

Cylinder arranged: **Horizontal, under body.**

Cooling: **Water, honeycomb radiator.**

Ignition: **Jump spark.**

Drive: **Chain.**

Transmission: **Planetary.**

Speeds: **Two forward and one reverse.**

Descriptive catalogue sent upon application to the above-named company.

O L D S   M O T O R   W O R K S ,   D E T R O I T ,   M I C H I G A N

Price

without
top
$1400

Model: **OLDSMOBILE TOURING CAR.**

Body: **Side entrance.**

Seating capacity: **Five** persons.

Total weight: **2350** pounds.

Wheel base: **90** inches.

Wheel tread: **55** inches.

Tire dimensions, front: **30 x 3½** inches.

Tire dimensions, rear: **30 x 4** inches.

Steering: **Wheel, tilting post.**

Brakes: **On rear hubs and transmission, operated by foot.**

Gasoline capacity: **15** gallons.

Frame: **Angle steel.**

Horse-power: **20.**

Number of cylinders: **Two.**

Cylinders arranged: **Double opposed, under body.**

Cooling: **Water, honeycomb radiator.**

Ignition: **Jump spark.**

Drive: **Chain.**

Transmission: **Planetary.**

Speeds: **Two forward and one reverse.**

Style of top: **Canopy.**

Descriptive catalogue sent upon application to the above-named company.

OLDS MOTOR WORKS, DETROIT, MICHIGAN

Price
$2200

Model: **OLDSMOBILE COACH.**

Body: **Wood.**

Seating capacity: **Eleven** persons.

Wheel base: **83** inches.

Wheel tread: **55** inches.

Tire dimensions, front: **30 x 4½** inches, solid.

Tire dimensions, rear: **30 x 4½** inches, solid.

Steering: **Wheel.**

Brakes: **Transmission, controlled by foot; internal hub, by hand lever.**

Gasoline capacity: **11** gallons.

Frame: **Pressed steel.**

Horse-power: **16.**

Number of cylinders: **Two.**

Cylinders arranged: **Vertical, under seat.**

Cooling: **Water, disk radiator on front of dash.**

Ignition: **Jump spark.**

Drive: **Double side chain.**

Transmission: **Planetary, mounted on countershaft.**

Speeds: **Two forward and reverse.**

Descriptive catalogue sent upon application to the above-named company.

OLDS MOTOR WORKS, DETROIT, MICHIGAN

Price

$1000

Model : **OLDSMOBILE LIGHT DELIVERY CAR.**

Body : **Wood, with paneled or latticed wire sides.**

Seating capacity : **Two** persons ; carrying capacity, **1000** pounds.

Wheel base : **82** inches.

Wheel tread : **55** inches.

Tire dimensions, front : **30 x 3½** inches, solid.

Tire dimensions, rear : **30 x 3½** inches, solid.

Steering : **Wheel, tilting post.**

Brakes : **On rear hubs and transmission, operated by foot.**

Gasoline capacity : **7** gallons.

Frame : **Angle steel.**

Horse-power : **10.**

Number of cylinders : **One.**

Cylinder arranged : **Horizontal, cylinder head under footboard.**

Cooling : **Water, honeycomb radiator.**

Ignition : **Jump spark.**

Drive : **Chain.**

Transmission : **Planetary.**

Speeds : **Two forward and one reverse.**

Descriptive catalogue sent upon application to the above-named company.

OLDS MOTOR WORKS, DETROIT, MICHIGAN

Price
$2000

Model: **OLDSMOBILE HEAVY DELIVERY CAR.**

Body: **Wood, paneled or latticed wire sides.**

Seating capacity: **Two** persons; carrying capacity, **2000** pounds.

Wheel base: **83** inches.

Wheel tread: **55** inches.

Tire dimensions, front: **30 x 4½** inches, solid.

Tire dimensions, rear: **30 x 4½** inches, solid.

Steering: **Wheel.**

Brakes: **Transmission, controlled by foot; internal hub, by hand lever.**

Gasoline capacity: **11** gallons.

Frame: **Pressed steel.**

Horse-power: **16.**

Number of cylinders: **Two.**

Cylinders arranged: **Vertical, under seat.**

Cooling: **Water, disk radiator on front of dash.**

Ignition: **Jump spark.**

Drive: **Double side chain.**

Transmission: **Planetary, mounted on countershaft.**

Speeds: **Two forward and one reverse.**

Descriptive catalogue sent upon application to the above-named company.

PACKARD MOTOR CAR COMPANY, DETROIT, MICHIGAN

Price

$3000
with top
$3100 to
$3300

Model : " L."

Body : **Aluminum, rear-entrance tonneau.**

Color : **Richelieu blue and cream
yellow.**

Seating capacity : **Five** persons.

Total weight : **2200** pounds.

Wheel base : **94** inches.

Wheel tread : **56½** inches.

Tire dimensions, front : **34 x 4** inches.

Tire dimensions, rear : **34 x 4** inches.

Steering : **Wheel with worm and segment, irreversible.**

Brakes : **(Four) two expanding, two
clamping; all operating direct on
rear wheels.**

Gasoline capacity : **20** gallons.

Frame : **Pressed steel.**

Horse-power : **22 brake.**

Number of cylinders : **Four.**

Cylinders arranged : **Vertically (fore
and aft).**

Cooling : **Water (positive circulating).**

Ignition : **Jump spark.**

Drive : **Bevel gear.**

Transmission : **Sliding gear.**

Speeds : **Three forward, one reverse.**

Style of top : **Cape cart, victoria or
glass front canopy.**

Descriptive catalogue sent upon application to the above-named company.

PACKARD   MOTOR   CAR   COMPANY,   DETROIT,   MICHIGAN

Price
$3400

Model :   T W O - P A S S E N G E R
SPECIAL.

Body : Wood with aluminum seats.

Color :   Richelieu   blue   and   cream
yellow.

Seating capacity : Two persons.

Total weight : 2150 pounds.

Wheel base :   106 inches.

Wheel tread :   56½ inches.

Tire dimensions, front :   34 x 4 inches.

Tire dimensions, rear :   34 x 4 inches.

Steering : Wheel with worm and segment, irreversible.

Brakes : Four, two expanding, two
clamping ; all operating direct on
rear wheels.

Gasoline capacity : 20 gallons.

Frame : Pressed steel.

Horse-power : 28 brake.

Number of cylinders : Four.

Cylinders   arranged :   Vertically (fore
and aft).

Cooling : Water (positive circulating).

Ignition : Jump spark.

Drive : Bevel gear.

Transmission : Sliding gear.

Speeds : Three forward, one reverse.

Style of top : Top not furnished.

Descriptive catalogue sent upon application to the above-named company.

PACKARD   MOTOR   CAR   COMPANY,   DETROIT,   MICHIGAN

Price

with top
$3600 to
$3800
without top
$3500

Model: " N."

Body: **Aluminum, double side entrance.**

Color: **Richelieu blue and cream yellow.**

Seating capacity: **Five** persons.

Total weight: **2350** pounds.

Wheel base: **106** inches.

Wheel tread: **56½** inches.

Tire dimensions, front: **34 x 4** inches.

Tire dimensions, rear: **34 x 4** inches.

Steering: **Wheel with worm and segment, irreversible.**

Brakes: **Four; two expanding, two clamping; all operating direct on rear wheels.**

Gasoline capacity: **20** gallons.

Frame: **Pressed steel.**

Horse-power: **28 brake.**

Number of cylinders: **Four.**

Cylinders arranged: **Vertically (fore and aft).**

Cooling: **Water (positive circulating).**

Ignition: **Jump spark.**

Drive: **Bevel gear.**

Transmission: **Sliding gear.**

Speeds: **Three forward, one reverse.**

Style of top: **Cape cart, extension cape cart, victoria or glass front canopy.**

Descriptive catalogue sent upon application to the above-named company.

PACKARD   MOTOR   CAR   COMPANY,   DETROIT,   MICHIGAN

Price

with top
$3675

Model : "N."

Body : **Aluminum, double side entrance.**

Color : **Richelieu blue and cream yellow.**

Seating capacity : **Five** persons.

Total weight : **2400** pounds.

Wheel base : **106** inches

Wheel tread : **56½** inches.

Tire dimensions, front : **34 x 4** inches.

Tire dimensions, rear : **34 x 4** inches.

Steering : **Wheel with worm and segment, irreversible.**

Brakes : **Four ; two expanding, two clamping ; all operating direct on rear wheels.**

Gasoline capacity : **20** gallons.

Frame : **Pressed steel.**

Horse-power : **28 brake.**

Number of cylinders : **Four.**

Cylinders arranged : **Vertically (fore and aft).**

Cooling : **Water (positive circulating).**

Ignition : **Jump spark.**

Drive : **Bevel gear.**

Transmission : **Sliding gear.**

Speeds : **Three forward, one reverse.**

Style of top : **Extension cape cart.**

Descriptive catalogue sent upon application to the above-named company.

PACKARD MOTOR CAR COMPANY, DETROIT, MICHIGAN

Price

$4100

Model: **INSIDE-DRIVEN BROUG-HAM.**

Body : **Wood.**

Color: **Body, Richelieu blue and black ; running gear, cream yellow.**

Seating capacity : **Twopersons.**

Total weight : **2400** pounds.

Wheel base : **106** inches.

Wheel tread : **56½** inches.

Tire dimensions, front : **34 x 4** inches.

Tire dimensions, rear : **34 x 4** inches.

Steering : **Wheel with worm and segment, irreversible.**

Brakes : **Four, two expanding, two clamping ; all operating direct on rear wheels.**

Gasoline capacity : **20** gallons.

Frame : **Pressed steel.**

Horse-power : **28** brake.

Number of cylinders : **Four.**

Cylinders arranged : **Vertically (fore and aft).**

Cooling : **Water (positive circulating).**

Ignition : **Jump spark.**

Drive : **Bevel gear.**

Transmission : **Sliding gear.**

Speeds : **Three forward, one reverse.**

Style of top : **Brougham body only.**

Descriptive catalogue sent upon application to the above-named company.

PACKARD MOTOR CAR COMPANY, DETROIT, MICHIGAN

Price

$4600

Model: **PACKARD LIMOUSINE.**

Body: **Double side-entrance limousine.**

Color: **Body, Richelieu blue and black; running gear, cream yellow.**

Seating capacity: **Four persons.**

Total weight: **2550 pounds.**

Wheel base: **106 inches.**

Wheel tread: **56½ inches.**

Tire dimensions, front: **34 x 4 inches.**

Tire dimensions, rear: **34 x 4½ inches.**

Steering: **Wheel with worm and segment, irreversible.**

Brakes: **Four, two expanding, two clamping; all operating direct on rear wheels.**

Gasoline capacity: **20 gallons.**

Frame: **Pressed steel.**

Horse-power: **28 brake.**

Number of cylinders: **Four.**

Cylinders arranged: **Vertically (fore and aft).**

Cooling: **Water (positive circulating).**

Ignition: **Jump spark.**

Drive: **Bevel gear.**

Transmission: **Sliding gear.**

Speeds: **Three forward, one reverse.**

Descriptive catalogue sent upon application to the above-named company.

THE GEORGE N. PIERCE CO., BUFFALO, N. Y.

Price
with top
$1300
without top
$1200

Model: **PIERCE STANHOPE.**

Body: **Stanhope, with folding front seat.**

Color: **Quaker green.**

Seating capacity: **Four** persons.

Total weight: **1250** pounds.

Wheel base: **70** inches.

Wheel tread: **54** inches.

Tire dimensions, front: **30 x 3** inches.

Tire dimensions, rear: **30 x 3** inches.

Steering: **Wheel.**

Brakes: **Hub.**

Gasoline capacity: **5** gallons.

Frame: **Shelby tubular steel.**

Horse-power: **8 brake.**

Number of cylinders: **One.**

Cylinder arranged: **Vertically.**

Cooling: **Water, natural circulation.**

Ignition: **High-tension electric.**

Drive: **Spur gear.**

Transmission: **Planetary.**

Speeds: **Two forward and reverse.**

Style of top: **Buggy, victoria or canopy with glass front.**

Descriptive catalogue sent upon application to the above-named company.

THE   GEORGE   N.   PIERCE   CO.,   BUFFALO,   N. Y.

Price

with top
Canopy
$3750
Victoria
$3650
Cape
$3650
without top
$3500

Model : **PIERCE GREAT AR-
ROW.**

Body : **King of Belgians, cast aluminum, side entrance.**

Color : **Blue, with red running gear.**

Seating capacity : **Five persons.**

Total weight : **2500** pounds.

Wheel base : **100** inches.

Wheel tread : **56** inches.

Tire dimensions, front : **34 x 4** inches.

Tire dimensions, rear : **34 x 4** inches.

Steering : **Wheel.**

Brakes : **Internal and external on
drums on both rear wheels.**

Gasoline capacity : **17** gallons.

Frame : **Pressed special carbon steel,
channel section.**

Horse-power : **24 to 28 brake.**

Number of cylinders : **Four.**

Cylinders arranged : **Vertically.**

Cooling : **Water with pump, tubular
disc radiator and fan.**

Ignition : **Jump spark.**

Drive : **Bevel gear.**

Transmission : **Sliding gear.**

Speeds : **Three forward and reverse.**

Style of top : **Canopy with glass front,
victoria and cape.**

Descriptive catalogue sent upon application to the above-named company.

THE GEORGE N. PIERCE CO., BUFFALO, N. Y.

Price
—
with top
Canopy
$4250
Victoria
$4150
Cape
$4150
without
top
$4000

Model: **PIERCE GREAT AR-ROW.**

Body: **King of Belgians, cast alumi-num, side entrance.**

Color: **Quaker green with red running gear.**

Seating capacity: **Five persons.**

Total weight: **2700 pounds.**

Wheel base: **104 inches.**

Wheel tread: **56 inches.**

Tire dimensions, front: **34 x 4 inches.**

Tire dimensions, rear: **34 x 4½ inches.**

Steering: **Wheel.**

Brakes: **Internal and external on drums on both rear wheels.**

Gasoline capacity: **18 gallons.**

Frame: **Pressed special carbon steel, channel section.**

Horse-power: **28 to 32 brake.**

Number of cylinders: **Four.**

Cylinders arranged: **Vertically.**

Cooling: **Water with pump, tubular disc radiator and fan.**

Ignition: **Jump spark.**

Drive: **Bevel gear.**

Transmission: **Sliding gear.**

Speeds: **Three forward and reverse.**

Style of top: **Canopy with glass front, victoria and cape.**

Descriptive catalogue sent upon application to the above-named company.

THE GEORGE N. PIERCE CO., BUFFALO, N. Y.

Price
$5000

Model : **LANDAULET GREAT ARROW.**

Body : **Aluminum, side entrance.**

Color : **Special.**

Seating capacity : **Seven** persons.

Total weight : **2900** pounds.

Wheel base : **109** inches.

Wheel tread : **56** inches.

Tire dimensions, front : **34 x 4** inches.

Tire dimensions, rear : **34 x 4½** inches.

Steering : **Wheel.**

Brakes : **Internal and external on drums on both rear wheels.**

Gasoline capacity : **18** gallons.

Frame : **Pressed special carbon steel, channel section.**

Horse-power : **28 to 32 brake.**

Number of cylinders : **Four.**

Cylinders arranged : **Vertically.**

Cooling : **Water with pump, tubular disc radiator and fan.**

Ignition : **Jump spark.**

Drive : **Bevel gear.**

Transmission : **Sliding gear.**

Speeds : **Three forward and reverse.**

Style : **Landaulet.**

Descriptive catalogue sent upon application to the above-named company.

THE   GEORGE   N.   PIERCE   CO.,   BUFFALO,   N. Y.

Price

$5000

Model: **SUBURBAN GREAT AR-
ROW.**

Body: **Aluminum, side entrance.**

Color: **Special.**

Seating capacity: **Seven** persons.

Total weight: **2950** pounds.

Wheel base: **109** inches.

Wheel tread: **56** inches.

Tire dimensions, front: **34 x 4** inches.

Tire dimensions, rear: **34 x 4½** inches.

Steering: **Wheel.**

Brakes: **Internal and external on
drums on both rear wheels.**

Gasoline capacity: **18** gallons.

Frame: **Pressed special carbon steel,
channel section.**

Horse-power: **28 to 32 brake.**

Number of cylinders: **Four.**

Cylinders arranged: **Vertically.**

Cooling: **Water with pump, tubular
disc radiator and fan.**

Ignition: **Jump spark.**

Drive: **Bevel gear.**

Transmission: **Sliding gear.**

Speeds: **Three forward and reverse.**

Style: **Suburban.**

Descriptive catalogue sent upon application to the above-named company.

THE GEORGE N. PIERCE CO., BUFFALO, N. Y.

Price

$5000

Model: **OPERA COACH GREAT ARROW.**

Body: **Aluminum, rear entrance.**

Color: **Special.**

Seating capacity: **Eight** persons.

Total weight: **2950** pounds.

Wheel base: **109** inches.

Wheel tread: **56** inches.

Tire dimensions, front: **34 x 4** inches.

Tire dimensions, rear: **34 x 4½** inches.

Steering: **Wheel.**

Brakes: **Internal and external on drums on both rear wheels.**

Gasoline capacity: **18** gallons.

Frame: **Pressed special carbon steel, channel section.**

Horse-power: **28 to 32.**

Number of cylinders: **Four.**

Cylinders arranged: **Vertically.**

Cooling: **Water with pump, tubular disc radiator and fan.**

Ignition: **Jump spark.**

Drive: **Bevel gear.**

Transmission: **Sliding gear.**

Speeds: **Three forward and reverse.**

Style: **Opera coach.**

Descriptive catalogue sent upon application to the above-named company.

THE PEERLESS MOTOR CAR COMPANY, CLEVELAND, OHIO

Price

with top
according
to kind.
Without
top
$3200

Model : **No. 9.**

Body : **King of Belgians (side doors.)**

Color : **Optional.**

Seating capacity : **Five** persons.

Total weight : **Approximate 2400** pounds

Wheel base : **102** inches.

Wheel tread : **Standard.**

Tire dimensions, front : **34 x 4** inches.

Tire dimensions, rear : **34 x 4½** inches.

Steering : **Wheel.**

Brakes : **Foot lever operating on wheels, emergeney operating on wheels.**

Gasoline capacity : **18** gallons.

Frame : **Pressed steel.**

Horse-power : **24.**

Number of cylinders : **Four.**

Cylinders arranged : **Vertical in front.**

Cooling : **Water, vertical tubular radiator.**

Ignition : **Jump spark by magneto or storage batteries.**

Drive : **Bevel gear.**

Transmission : **Sliding gears.**

Speeds : **Four forward, one reverse.**

Style of top : **Optional.**

Descriptive catalogue sent upon application to the above-named company.

THE PEERLESS MOTOR CAR COMPANY, CLEVELAND, OHIO

Price
$4000

Body: **LIMOUSINE (side doors).**

Color: **Optional.**

Seating capacity: **Five** persons (**three inside**).

Wheel base: **102** inches.

Wheel tread: **Standard.**

Tire dimensions, front: **34 x 4** inches.

Tire dimensions, rear: **34 x 4½** inches.

Steering: **Wheel.**

Brakes: **Foot lever operating on wheels, emergency operating on wheels.**

Gasoline capacity: **18** gallons.

Frame: **Pressed steel.**

Horse-power: **24.**

Number of cylinders: **Four.**

Cylinders arranged: **Vertical in front.**

Cooling: **Water, vertical tubular radiator.**

Ignition: **Jump spark by magneto or storage batteries.**

Drive: **Bevel gear.**

Transmission: **Sliding gears.**

Speeds: **Four forward, one reverse.**

Style of top: **Limousine.**

Descriptive catalogue sent upon application to the above-named company.

THE   PEERLESS   MOTOR   CAR   COMPANY,   CLEVELAND,   OHIO

Price

$4000

Body :   **LIMOUSINE** (side doors).

Color :   Optional.

Seating capacity :   Seven persons (five inside).

Wheel base :   102 inches.

Wheel tread :   Standard.

Tire dimensions, front :   34 x 4 inches.

Tire dimensions, rear :   34 x 4½ inches.

Steering :   Wheel.

Brakes :   Foot lever operating on wheels, emergency operating on wheels.

Gasoline capacity :   18 gallons.

Frame :   Pressed steel.

Horse-power :   24.

Number of cylinders :   Four.

Cylinders arranged :   Vertical in front.

Cooling :   Water, vertical tubular radiator.

Ignition :   Jump spark by magneto or storage batteries.

Drive :   Bevel gear.

Transmission :   Sliding gears.

Speeds :   Four forward, one reverse.

Style of top :   Limousine.

Descriptive catalogue sent upon application to the above-named company.

THE PEERLESS MOTOR CAR COMPANY, CLEVELAND, OHIO

Price
$4000

Model: **No. II.**

Body: **King of Belgians (side doors),**

Color: **Optional.**

Seating capacity: **Five** persons.

Total weight: **Approximate 2800** pounds.

Wheel base: **104** inches.

Wheel tread: **Standard.**

Tire dimensions, front: **34 x 4** inches.

Tire dimensions, rear: **34 x 4½** inches.

Steering: **Wheel.**

Brakes: **Foot lever operating on wheels, emergency operating on wheels.**

Gasoline capacity: **18** gallons.

Frame: **Pressed steel.**

Horse-power: **35.**

Number of cylinders: **Four.**

Cylinders arranged: **Vertical in front.**

Cooling: **Water, vertical tubular radiator.**

Ignition: **Jump spark by magneto or storage batteries.**

Drive: **Bevel gear.**

Transmission: **Sliding gears.**

Speeds: **Four forward and one reverse.**

Style of top: **Optional.**

Descriptive catalogue sent upon application to the above-named company.

THE   PEERLESS   MOTOR   CAR   COMPANY,   CLEVELAND,   OHIO

Price
with top
$6250
without top
$6000

Model : **No. 12.**

Body : **Victoria detachable tonneau.**

Color : **Optional.**

Seating capacity : **Five** persons.

Total weight : **Approximate 2900** pounds.

Wheel base : **107** inches.

Wheel tread : **Standard.**

Tire dimensions, front : **36 x 4** inches.

Tire dimensions, rear : **36 x 4½** inches.

Steering : **Wheel.**

Brakes : **Foot lever operating on wheels, emergency operating on wheels.**

Gasoline capacity : **18** gallons.

Frame : **Pressed steel.**

Horse-power : **60.**

Number of cylinders : **Four.**

Cylinders arranged : **Vertical in front.**

Cooling : **Water, vertical tubular radiator.**

Ignition : **Jump spark by magneto or storage batteries.**

Drive : **Bevel gear.**

Transmission : **Sliding gears.**

Speeds : **Four forward and one reverse.**

Style of top : **Victoria.**

Descriptive catalogue sent upon application to the above-named company.

POPE MANUFACTURING COMPANY, HARTFORD, CONN.

Price

$900

Model: **POPE-TRIBUNE**, side-door tonneau, Model 4.

Body: **Wood, detachable tonneau, divided front seat.**

Color: **Cumberland blue, cream running gear.**

Seating capacity: **Four** persons.

Total weight: **1575** pounds.

Wheel base: **82** inches.

Wheel tread: **56** inches.

Tire dimensions, front: **30 x 3½** inches.

Tire dimensions, rear: **30 x 3½** inches.

Steering: **Wheel.**

Brakes: **Two in rear wheel drums one on propeller shaft.**

Gasoline capacity: **8** gallons.

Frame: **Angle steel.**

Horse-power: **12.**

Number of cylinders: **Two.**

Cylinders arranged: **Vertical tandem.**

Cooling: **Water, pump driven from secondary shaft.**

Ignition: **Jump spark.**

Drive: **Direct with bevel gears.**

Transmission: **Individual clutch.**

Speeds: **Three forward, one reverse.**

Style of top: **None furnished.**

Descriptive catalogue sent upon application to the above-named company.

POPE MANUFACTURING COMPANY, HARTFORD, CONN.

Price

$1600

Model: **POPE - HARTFORD, Model D.**

Body: **Laminated wood, with divided front seat and side-door tonneau.**

Color: **Royal purple, cream running gear.**

Seating capacity : **Five** persons.

Total weight: **2000** pounds.

Wheel base : **88** inches.

Wheel tread : **56** inches.

Tire dimensions, front : **30 x 3½** inches.

Tire dimensions, rear : **30 x 3½** inches.

Steering: **Wheel, worm and sector.**

Brakes : **Two in rear wheel drums ; one on propeller shaft.**

Gasoline capacity : **11** gallons.

Frame : **Armored oak.**

Horse-power : **16.**

Number of cylinders : **Two.**

Cylinders arranged : **Horizontal opposed, crosswise.**

Cooling : **Water, pump driven from secondary shaft.**

Ignition : **Jump spark from two sets of dry cell batteries.**

Drive : **Direct with bevel gears.**

Transmission : **Sliding gear.**

Speeds : **Three forward, one reverse.**

Style of top : **None furnished.**

Descriptive catalogue sent upon application to the above-named company.

POPE MOTOR CAR COMPANY, TOLEDO, OHIO

Price
with top
$3050
without top
$2800

Model : **POPE-TOLEDO, TYPE X**

Body : **Side entrance, wood ; seats and tonneau, mirror-finished steel.**

Color : **Auto red, Brewster green, royal blue, royal blue and cream.**

Seating capacity : **Five persons.**

Total weight : **1800** pounds.

Wheel base : **88** inches.

Wheel tread : **54** inches.

Tire dimensions, front : **32 x 3½** inches, detachable.

Tire dimensions, rear : **32 x 3½** inches, detachable.

Steering : **Irreversible, worm and segment type.**

Brakes : **Main brake on drive shaft, two powerful band brakes on rear wheels.**

Gasoline capacity : **8** gallons.

Frame : **Channel steel of new design.**

Horse-power : **20.**

Number of cylinders : **Four.**

Cylinders arranged : **Vertically.**

Cooling : **Water, planetic radiator.**

Ignition : **Jump spark.**

Drive : **Double chain, countershaft.**

Transmission : **Sliding gear, ball bearing.**

Speeds : **Three forward and reverse.**

Style of top : **Canopy, victoria, extension cape cart.**

Descriptive catalogue sent upon application to the above-named company.

POPE   MOTOR   CAR   COMPANY,   TOLEDO,   OHIO

Price
with top
$3750
without top
$3500

Model: **POPE-TOLEDO, TYPE VIII.**

Body : **Side entrance, wood ; seats and tonneau, mirror-finished steel.**

Color : **Auto red, Brewster green, royal blue, royal blue and cream.**

Seating capacity: **Five** persons.

Total weight : **2450** pounds.

Wheel base : **100** inches.

Wheel tread : **56** inches.

Tire dimensions, front : **34 x 4** inches, detachable.

Tire dimensions, rear : **34 x 4** inches, detachable.

Steering : **Tilting wheel, irreversible worm and segment type.**

Brakes : **Main brake on drive shaft, internal expanding on rear wheels.**

Gasoline capacity : **14** gallons.

Frame : **Channel steel of new design.**

Horse-power : **30.**

Number of cylinders : **Four.**

Cylinders arranged : **Vertically.**

Cooling : **Water, planetic radiator.**

Ignition : **Jump spark.**

Drive : **Double chain, countershaft.**

Transmission : **Sliding gear, ball bearing.**

Speeds : **Three forward and reverse.**

Style of top : **Canopy, victoria, extension cape cart.**

Descriptive catalogue sent upon application to the above-named company.

POPE MOTOR CAR COMPANY, TOLEDO, OHIO

Price

with top

$6250

without top

$6000

Model: **POPE-TOLEDO, TYPE IX.**

Body: **Side entrance, wood; seats and tonneau, mirror-finished steel.**

Color: **Auto red, Brewster green, royal blue, royal blue and cream.**

Seating capacity: **Five** persons.

Total weight: **2650** pounds.

Wheel base: **104** inches.

Wheel tread: **56** inches.

Tire dimensions, front: **34 x 4½** inches, detachable.

Tire dimensions, rear: **34 x 4½** inches, detachable.

Steering: **Tilting wheel, irreversible worm and segment type.**

Brakes: **Main brake on drive shaft, internal expanding on rear wheels.**

Gasoline capacity: **14** gallons.

Frame: **Channel steel of new design.**

Horse-power: **45.**

Number of cylinders: **Four.**

Cylinders arranged: **Vertically.**

Cooling: **Water, planetic radiator.**

Ignition: **Jump spark.**

Drive: **Double chain, countershaft.**

Transmission: **Sliding gear, ball bearing.**

Speeds: **Three forward and reverse.**

Style of top: **Canopy, victoria, extension cape cart.**

Descriptive catalogue sent upon application to the above-named company.

THE SANDUSKY AUTOMOBILE COMPANY, SANDUSKY, OHIO

Price
$650

Model : "COURIER" "F."

Body : Wood.

Color : Red.

Seating capacity : Two persons.

Total weight : 1100 pounds.

Wheel base : 70 inches.

Wheel tread : 54 inches.

Tire dimensions, front : 28 x 3 inches.

Tire dimensions, rear : 28 x 3 inches.

Steering : Wheel.

Brakes : On differential gear.

Gasoline capacity : 5 gallons.

Frame : Angle steel.

Horse-power : 7.

Number of cylinders : One.

Cylinder arranged : Horizontal, under body.

Cooling : Water.

Ignition : Jump spark and battery.

Drive : Chain.

Transmission : Sliding gear.

Speeds : Two forward and one reverse.

Style of top : Runabout.

Descriptive catalogue sent upon application to the above-named company.

THE SANDUSKY AUTOMOBILE COMPANY, SANDUSKY, OHIO

Price

with tonneau
$800
without tonneau
$700

Model: **"COURIER" "H."**

Body: **Detachable tonneau.**

Color: **Dark green.**

Seating capacity: **Four** persons.

Total weight: **1150** pounds.

Wheel base: **76** inches.

Wheel tread: **56** inches.

Tire dimensions, front: **28 x 3** inches.

Tire dimensions, rear: **28 x 3** inches.

Steering: **Wheel.**

Brakes: **Rear axle, double bands.**

Gasoline capacity: **6** gallons.

Frame: **Angle steel.**

Horse-power: **8.**

Number of cylinders: **One.**

Cylinder arranged: **H o r i z o n t a l, under body.**

Cooling: **Water.**

Ignition: **Jump spark and battery.**

Drive: **Chain.**

Transmission: **Sliding gear.**

Speeds: **Two forward and one reverse.**

Descriptive catalogue sent upon application to the above-named company.

STANDARD AUTOMOBILE CO. OF N. Y., 136 W. 38TH ST., N. Y.

Price

with top
$6500

Model : **DECAUVILLE, 16-20.**

Body : **Side-entrance landaulet.**

Color : **Any.**

Seating capacity : **Five** persons.

Total weight : **2200** pounds.

Wheel base : **106** inches.

Wheel tread : **52** inches.

Tire dimensions, front : **875 x 105** m/m.

Tire dimensions, rear : **875 x 105** m/m.

Steering : **Wheel.**

Brakes : **Three.**

Gasoline capacity : **15** gallons.

Frame : **Pressed steel.**

Horse-power : **16-20.**

Number of cylinders : **Four.**

Cylinders arranged : **Vertically.**

Cooling : **Water.**

Ignition : **Jump spark by magneto and battery.**

Drive : **Bevel gear.**

Transmission : **Sliding gear.**

Speeds : **Three forward and reverse.**

Style of top : **Any.**

Descriptive catalogue sent upon application to the above-named company

STANDARD AUTOMOBILE CO. OF N. Y., 136 W. 38TH ST., N. Y.

Price

$7400
with top
$7900

Model : **DECAUVILLE**, 24-28.

Body : **Side entrance.**

Color : **Any.**

Seating capacity : **Eight** persons.

Total weight : **2250** pounds.

Wheel base : **110** inches.

Wheel tread : **57** inches.

Tire dimensions, front : **880 x 120** m/m.

Tire dimensions, rear : **880 x 120** m/m.

Steering : **Wheel.**

Brakes : **Three.**

Gasoline capacity : **20** gallons.

Frame : **Pressed steel.**

Horse-power : **24-28.**

Number of cylinders : **Four.**

Cylinders arranged : **Vertically.**

Cooling : **Water.**

Ignition : **Jump spark by magneto and battery.**

Drive : **Bevel gear.**

Transmission : **Sliding gear.**

Speeds : **Four forward and reverse.**

Style of top : **Any.**

Descriptive catalogue sent upon application to the above-named company.

STUDEBAKER AUTOMOBILE CO., SOUTH BEND, IND.

Price
$1250

Model : **STUDEBAKER No. 9502.**

Body : **Rear entrance.**

Color : **Dark blue, maroon or dark green.**

Seating capacity : **Five** persons.

Total weight : **1950** pounds.

Wheel base : **82** inches.

Wheel tread : **56½** inches.

Tire dimensions, front : **30 x 3½** inches.

Tire dimensions, rear : **30 x 3½** inches.

Steering : **Wheel.**

Brakes : **Two sets, one on rear hubs, other on differential.**

Gasoline capacity : **10** gallons.

Frame : **Armored wood.**

Horse-power : **15.**

Number of cylinders : **Two.**

Cylinders arranged : **Horizontal opposed.**

Cooling : **Water, gear-driven pump.**

Ignition : **Jump spark.**

Drive : **Chain.**

Transmission : **Planetary.**

Speeds : **Two forward, one reverse.**

Style of top : **As desired, as extra equipment.**

Descriptive catalogue sent upon application to the above-named company.

STUDEBAKER AUTOMOBILE CO., SOUTH BEND, IND.

Price

$1350

Model: **STUDEBAKER No. 9502.**

Body: **Side entrance.**

Color: **Dark green or dark blue.**

Seating capacity: **Five persons.**

Total weight: **1950** pounds.

Wheel base : **82** inches.

Wheel tread : **56½** inches.

Tire dimensions, front: **30 x 3½** inches.

Tire dimensions, rear: **30 x 3½** inches.

Steering : **Wheel.**

Brakes: **Two sets, one on rear hubs, other on differential.**

Gasoline capacity : **10** gallons.

Frame : **Armored wood.**

Horse-power : **15.**

Number of cylinders: **Two.**

Cylinders arranged: **Horizontal opposed.**

Cooling : **Water, gear-driven pump.**

Ignition : **Jump spark.**

Drive: **Chain.**

Transmission : **Planetary.**

Speeds: **Two forward, one reverse.**

Style of top: **As desired, as extra equipment.**

Descriptive catalogue sent upon application to the above-named company.

STUDEBAKER AUTOMOBILE CO., SOUTH BEND, IND.

Price
$3000

Model : **STUDEBAKER No. 9503.**

Body : **Side entrance.**

Color : **Dark blue or dark green.**

Seating capacity : **Five persons.**

Total weight : **2100** pounds.

Wheel base : **96** inches.

Wheel tread : **54** inches.

Tire dimensions, front : **32 x 4** inches.

Tire dimensions, rear : **32 x 4** inches.

Steering : **Wheel.**

Brakes : **Hand lever, internal expand-ing on both rear wheels, foot lever on driving shaft.**

Gasoline capacity : **14** gallons.

Frame : **Pressed steel.**

Horse-power : **20.**

Number of cylinders : **Four.**

Cylinders arranged : **Vertical in front.**

Cooling : **Water, tubular radiator, fan.**

Ignition : **Jump spark with dynamo and auxiliary storage battery.**

Drive : **Bevel gear.**

Transmission : **Sliding gear.**

Speeds : **Three forward and one re-verse.**

Style of top : **As desired, as extra equipment.**

Descriptive catalogue sent upon application to the above-named company.

THE STANDARD MOTOR CONSTRUCTION CO., JERSEY CITY, N. J.

Price

with top
$3750
without top
$3500
chassis
$3000

Model. **STANDARD.**

Body: **Wood.**

Color: **To order.**

Seating capacity: **Five** persons.

Total weight: **2200** pounds.

Wheel base: **109** inches.

Wheel tread: **54** inches.

Tire dimensions, front: **34 x 4** inches.

Tire dimensions, rear: **34 x 4** inches.

Steering: **Wheel.**

Brakes: **On each rear wheel hub and one on shaft.**

Gasoline capacity: **15** gallons.

Frame: **Pressed steel.**

Horse-power: **25.**

Number of cylinders: **Four.**

Cylinders arranged: **Vertical.**

Cooling: **Water, cellular radiator.**

Ignition: **Make and break with magneto.**

Drive: **Bevel gear.**

Transmission: **Sliding gears, direct drive on top speed.**

Speeds: **Three forward and one reverse.**

Style of top: **Canopy top with glass front and curtains.**

Descriptive catalogue sent upon application to the above-named company.

SMITH & MABLEY, INC., 513 TO 519 7TH AVE., NEW YORK CITY

Price

$6590
chassis
$4600

Model : **PANHARD - LEVASSOR,** **15 horse-power.**

Body: **Labordette side door K. of B.**

Color : **Optional.**

Seating capacity : **Four to five** persons.

Total weight : **Chassis, 2095** pounds.

Wheel base : **113** inches.

Wheel tread : **54** inches.

Tire dimensions, front : **910 x 90** m/m.

Tire dimensions, rear : **910 x 90** m/m.

Steering : **Wheel, worm and sector.**

Brakes : **Two ; pedal operating on differential, emergency on both rear wheels.**

Gasoline capacity : **18-20** gallons.

Frame : **Armored wood, steel reinforced.**

Horse-power : **15.**

Number of cylinders : **Four.**

Cylinders arranged : **Vertical, single.**

Cooling : **Water circulation, centrifugal pump, cellular radiator and fan.**

Ignition : **Jump spark, battery and magneto.**

Drive : **Double chains to both rear wheels.**

Transmission : **Sliding gears.**

Speeds : **Four forward and one reverse.**

Style of top : **Khaki, cape cart.**

Descriptive catalogue sent upon application to the above-named company.

SMITH & MABLEY, INC., 513 TO 519 7TH AVE., NEW YORK CITY

Price

$7000
chassis

$5000

Model: **S. & M. SIMPLEX, 30 horse-power.**

Body: **Extension front brougham.**

Color: **Optional.**

Seating capacity: **Four to five persons.**

Total weight: **Chassis, 2090 pounds.**

Wheel base: **106 inches.**

Wheel tread: **54 inches.**

Tire dimensions, front: **910 x 90 m/m.**

Tire dimensions, rear: **920 x 120 m/m.**

Steering: **Wheel, positive acting worm and sector combination.**

Brakes: **Foot pedal acting on differential. Emergency acting on both rear wheels. All double acting.**

Gasoline capacity: **26½ gallons.**

Frame: **Pressed steel.**

Horse-power: **30.**

Number of cylinders: **Four.**

Cylinders arranged: **Vertical.**

Cooling: **Water circulation, gear-driven centrifugal pump, cellular cooler and fan.**

Ignition: **Jump spark through coil or magneto or both.**

Drive: **Double chain to rear wheels.**

Transmission: **Sliding gear.**

Speeds: **Four forward and one reverse.**

Style of top: **All styles.**

Descriptive catalogue sent upon application to the above-named company.

SMITH & MABLEY, INC., 513 TO 519 7TH AVE., NEW YORK CITY

Price

$7250
chassis

$5400

Model : **RENAULT** 1905, **20-30** horse-power.

Body : **Side door limousine.**

Color : **Optional.**

Seating capacity : **Four to five** persons.

Total weight : **1800 to 2000** pounds.

Wheel base : **2.20 meter chassis, 107 inches ; 2.55 meter chassis, 115 inches.**

Wheel tread : **54** inches.

Tire dimensions, front : **870 x 90** m/m.

Tire dimensions, rear : **870 x 90** m/m.

Steering : **Wheel worm and sector combination.**

Brakes : **Three; expansion, operating on driving shaft and both rear wheels.**

Gasoline capacity : **15** gallons.

Frame : **Pressed steel of new design.**

Horse-power : **20-30.**

Number of cylinders : **Four.**

Cylinders arranged : **Vertical in pairs.**

Cooling : **Water, thermo-syphon system, radiator on dash; self-regulating and air circulation.**

Ignition : **Jump spark ; Simms-Bosch magneto.**

Drive : **Direct bevel gear to rear live axle.**

Transmission : **Sliding and rolling gear.**

Speeds : **Three forward, one reverse.**

Descriptive catalogue sent upon application to the above-named company.

SMITH & MABLEY, INC., 513 TO 519 7TH AVE., NEW YORK CITY

Price

$12,065
chassis

$10,150

Model : **MERCEDES** 1905, 40 - 45 **horse-power.**

Body : **Vedrine, side door K. of B.**

Color : **Optional.**

Seating capacity : **Five** persons.

Total weight : **Chassis, 2112** pounds.

Wheel base : **123** inches.

Wheel tread : **56** inches.

Tire dimensions, front : **910 x 90** m/m.

Tire dimensions, rear : **920 x 120** m/m.

Steering : **Wheel, positive-acting worm and sector combination.**

Brakes : **Three ; on differential, countershaft and expansion on both rear wheels (water cooled).**

Gasoline capacity : **25** gallons.

Frame : **Pressed steel in four lengths.**

Horse-power : **40-50** (also **28-32, 70** and **90**).

Number of cylinders : **Four.**

Cylinders arranged : **Vertical, cast in pairs.**

Cooling : **Water circulation, cellular cooler, air circulation by fan in flywheel.**

Ignition : **Make and break, magneto.**

Drive : **Chains to each rear wheel.**

Transmission : **Sliding gear.**

Speeds : **Four forward and reverse.**

Style of top : **Canopy, glass front and rear.**

Descriptive catalogue sent upon application to the above-named company.

J. STEVENS ARMS & TOOL CO., CHICOPEE FALLS, MASS.

Model: **"L" STEVENS-DURYEA.**

Body: **Wood, folding front seat.**

Color: **Maroon.**

Seating capacity: **Two or four** persons.

Total weight: **1350** pounds.

Wheel base: **69** inches.

Wheel tread: **54** inches.

Tire dimensions, front: **28 x 3** inches.

Tire dimensions, rear: **28 x 3** inches.

Steering: **One spoke of wheel steerer.**

Brakes: **Two.**

Gasoline capacity: **6** gallons.

Frame: **Tubular.**

Horse-power: **7.**

Number of cylinders: **Two.**

Cylinders arranged: **Horizontal.**

Cooling: **Water.**

Ignition: **Jump spark.**

Drive: **Chain.**

Transmission: **Individual clutch system.**

Speeds: **Three forward and reverse.**

Style of top: **Victoria or buggy.**

Descriptive catalogue sent upon application to the above-named company.

J. STEVENS ARMS & TOOL CO., CHICOPEE FALLS, MASS.

Price

with top

$2575

without top

$2500

Model: " R " STEVENS-DURYEA.

Body: Aluminum, tulip style, side entrance.

Color: Body, perfect blue, glazed ; gear, Naples yellow.

Seating capacity: Five persons.

Total weight: 1700 pounds.

Wheel base: 90 inches.

Wheel tread : 56 inches.

Tire dimensions, front : 30 x 3½ inches.

Tire dimensions, rear : 30 x 3½ inches.

Steering: Wheel.

Brakes : Three.

Gasoline capacity : 14 gallons.

Frame : Pressed steel.

Horse-power : 20.

Number of cylinders : Four.

Cylinders arranged : Vertically, in front, individual.

Cooling : Water.

Ignition : Jump spark.

Drive : Bevel gear.

Transmission : Sliding gear.

Speeds : Three forward and reverse.

Style of top : Extension folding.

Descriptive catalogue sent upon application to the above-named company.

THE F. B. STEARNS CO., CLEVELAND, OHIO

Price

$4000

Model : **STEARNS** I905.

Body : **French type, side doors.**

Color : **Optional.**

Seating capacity : **Seven** persons.

Total weight : **2700** pounds.

Wheel base : **118** inches.

Wheel tread : **56** inches.

Tire dimensions, front : **34 x 4½** inches.

Tire dimensions, rear : **34 x 4½** inches.

Steering : **Wheel.**

Brakes : **Hand lever, inner expansion on both rear hubs, foot brake on differential.**

Gasoline capacity : **18** gallons.

Frame : **Pressed steel.**

Horse-power : **32-40.**

Number of cylinders : **Four.**

Cylinders arranged : **Vertical, in pairs, in front.**

Cooling : **Water, special pattern radiator, fan.**

Ignition : **High tension, magneto.**

Drive : **Double side chain.**

Transmission : **Sliding gear.**

Speeds : **Four forward, one reverse.**

Style of top : **As desired.**

Descriptive catalogue sent upon application to the above-named company.

THE F. B. STEARNS CO., CLEVELAND, OHIO

Price
———
with top
$4150

Model : **STEARNS 1905, with top.**

Body : **French type, side doors.**

Color : **Optional.**

Seating capacity : **Seven** persons.

Total weight : **2700** pounds.

Wheel base : **118** inches.

Wheel tread : **56** inches.

Tire dimensions, front : **34 x 4½** inches.

Tire dimensions, rear : **34 x 4½** inches.

Steering : **Wheel.**

Brakes : **Hand lever, inner expansion on both rear hubs ; foot brake on differential.**

Gasoline capacity : **18** gallons.

Frame : **Pressed steel.**

Horse-power : **32-40.**

Number of cylinders : **Four.**

Cylinders arranged : **Vertical, in pairs, in front.**

Cooling : **Water, special pattern radiator and fan.**

Ignition : **High tension, magneto.**

Drive : **Double side chain.**

Transmission : **Sliding gear.**

Speeds : **Four forward, one reverse.**

Style of top : **As desired.**

Descriptive catalogue sent upon application to the above-named company.

E. R. THOMAS MOTOR CO., BUFFALO, N. Y.

Price

with canopy top
$3200
with extension top
$3150
without top
$3000

Model: No. 25.

Body: Touring, side-entrance tonneau, made of metal and patented.

Color: Royal green or automobile
red.

Seating capacity: Five to seven persons.

Total weight: 2400 pounds.

Wheel base: 106 inches.

Wheel tread: Standard.

Tire dimensions, front: 34 x 4 inches.

Tire dimensions, rear: 34 x 4½ inches.

Steering: Irreversible wheel.

Brakes: Two emergency brakes on
hub drums and foot brake on
countershaft.

Gasoline capacity: 19 gallons.

Frame: Pressed cold-rolled steel.

Horse-power: 40.

Number of cylinders: Four.

Cylinders arranged: Vertical under
hood.

Cooling: Water, cellular radiator and
rotary pump.

Ignition: Jump spark, storage and
dry cell batteries.

Drive: Double side chain.

Transmission: Sliding gear, direct
drive on high speed.

Speeds: Three forward and reverse.

Style of top: Either canopy or extension.

Descriptive catalogue sent upon application to the above-named company.

E. R. THOMAS MOTOR CO., BUFFALO, N. Y.

Price
$3500

Model : **No. 26.**

Body : **Side-entrance tonneau, made on patented dust-proof lines.**

Color : **French grey.**

Seating capacity : **Five to seven persons.**

Total weight : **2600** pounds.

Wheel base : **110** inches.

Wheel tread : **Standard.**

Tire dimensions, front : **34 x 4½** inches.

Tire dimensions, rear : **34 x 4½** inches.

Steering : **Irreversible wheel, wheel hard rubber.**

Brakes : **Emergency brake on hub drums and foot brake on counter-shaft.**

Gasoline capacity : **19** gallons.

Frame : **Pressed cold-rolled steel.**

Horse-power : **50.**

Number of cylinders : **Four.**

Cylinders arranged : **Vertical under hood.**

Cooling : **Water, cellular radiator, rotary pump.**

Ignition : **Jump spark, storage and dry cell batteries.**

Drive : **Double side chain.**

Transmission : **Sliding gear, direct drive on high speed.**

Speeds : **Three forward and reverse.**

Style of top : **Victoria top, regular equipment.**

Descriptive catalogue sent upon application to the above-named company.

E. R. THOMAS MOTOR CO., BUFFALO, N. Y.

Price
with top
$4500

Model : **No. 29.**

Body : **Limousine.**

Color : **Optional.**

Seating capacity : **Seven** persons.

Wheel base : **110** inches.

Wheel tread : **Standard.**

Tire dimensions, front : **34 x 4½** inches.

Tire dimensions, rear : **34 x 4½** inches.

Steering : **Irreversible wheel.**

Brakes : **Emergency brake on hub drums and foot brake on countershaft.**

Gasoline capacity : **19** gallons.

Frame : **Pressed cold-rolled steel.**

Horse-power : **50.**

Number of cylinders : **Four.**

Cylinders arranged : **Vertical under hood.**

Cooling : **Water, cellular radiator, rotary pump.**

Ignition : **Jump spark, storage and dry cell batteries.**

Drive : **Double side chain.**

Transmission : **Sliding gear, direct on high speed.**

Speeds : **Three forward and reverse.**

Descriptive catalogue sent upon application to the above-named company.

E. R. THOMAS MOTOR CO., BUFFALO, N. Y.

Model : **No. 27.**

Body :   **Side-entrance tonneau on patent dust-proof lines, or racing.**

Color : **Optional.**

Seating capacity :   **Five to seven persons.**

Total weight : **2800** pounds **with tonneau, 2400** pounds **with racing body.**

Wheel base : **120** inches.

Wheel tread : **Standard.**

Tire dimensions, front : **36 x 4½** inches.

Tire dimensions, rear : **36 x 4½** inches.

Steering : **Irreversible wheel.**

Brakes : **Emergency brake on hub drums and foot brake on countershaft.**

Gasoline capacity : **19** gallons (any size tank made for racer).

Frame : **Pressed cold-rolled steel**

Horse power : **60.**

Number of cylinders : **Six.**

Cylinders arranged : **Vertical under hood.**

Cooling :   **Water, cellular radiator, rotary pump.**

Ignition : **Jump spark, storage and dry cell batteries.**

Drive : **Double side chain.**

Transmission : **Sliding gear, direct on high speed.**

Speeds : **Three forward and reverse.**

Style of top : **Canopy or extension.**

Descriptive catalogue sent upon application to the above-named company.

E. R. THOMAS MOTOR CO., BUFFALO, N. Y.

Price

with top
$7000

Model: **No. 30.**

Body: **Limousine.**

Color: **Optional.**

Seating capacity: **Seven** persons.

Wheel base: **120** inches.

Wheel tread: **Standard.**

Tire dimensions, front: **36 x 4½** inches.

Tire dimensions, rear: **36 x 4½** inches.

Steering: **Irreversible wheel.**

Brakes: **Emergency brake on hub drums and foot brake on counter-shaft.**

Gasoline capacity: **19** gallons.

Frame: **Cold pressed steel.**

Horse-power: **60.**

Number of cylinders: **Six.**

Cylinders arranged: **Vertical under hood.**

Cooling: **Water, cellular radiator, rotary pump.**

Ignition: **Jump spark, storage and dry cell batteries.**

Drive: **Double side chain.**

Transmission: **Sliding gear, direct on high speed.**

Speeds: **Three forward and reverse.**

Descriptive catalogue sent upon application to the above-named company.

WALTHAM MANUFACTURING CO., WALTHAM, MASS.

Price

$375
with top
$397

Model: **ORIENT BUCKBOARD.**

Body: **Wood.**

Color: **Natural oak.**

Seating capacity: **Two persons.**

Total weight: **500 pounds.**

Wheel base: **80 inches.**

Wheel tread: **42 inches.**

Tire dimensions, front: **26 x 2 ½ inches.**

Tire dimensions, rear: **26 x 2 ½ inches.**

Steering: **Tiller.**

Brakes: **One.**

Gasoline capacity: **3 gallons.**

Frame: **Tubular.**

Horse-power: **4.**

Number of cylinders: **One.**

Cylinder arranged: **In rear.**

Cooling: **Air.**

Ignition: **Jump spark.**

Drive: **Spur gear.**

Transmission: **Planetary.**

Speeds: **Two.**

Style of top: **Canopy.**

Descriptive catalogue sent upon application to the above-named company.

WALTHAM MANUFACTURING CO., WALTHAM, MASS.

Price

$1500

Model: " E " TOURING RUN-ABOUT.

Body : Semi-racing model, wood.

Color : Olive green, black striping, red running gear.

Seating capacity : Two persons.

Total weight : 1350 pounds.

Wheel base : 82 inches.

Wheel tread : 56 inches.

Tire dimensions, front : 30 x 3½ inches.

Tire dimensions, rear : 30 x 3½ inches.

Steering : Wheel.

Brakes : Band and emergency.

Gasoline capacity : 7 gallons.

Frame : Pressed steel.

Horse-power : 16.

Number of cylinders : Four.

Cylinders arranged : Vertical tandem in front.

Cooling : Air, with fan.

Ignition : Jump spark, two sets of batteries.

Drive : Direct, bevel gear.

Transmission : Sliding gear.

Speeds : Three forward and one reverse.

Descriptive catalogue sent upon application to the above-named company.

WALTHAM MANUFACTURING CO., WALTHAM, MASS.

Price

$1650

Model: **ORIENT LIGHT TOUR-**
ING CAR.

Body: **Side-entrance tonneau.**

Color: **Quaker green, running gear**
carmine.

Seating capacity: **Four to five persons.**

Total weight: **1450 pounds.**

Wheel base: **82 inches.**

Wheel tread: **56 inches.**

Tire dimensions, front: **30 x 3½ inches.**

Tire dimensions, rear: **30 x 3½ inches.**

Steering: **Wheel.**

Brakes: **Two.**

Gasoline capacity: **7 gallons.**

Frame: **Pressed steel.**

Horse-power: **14-16.**

Number of cylinders: **Four.**

Cylinders arranged: **Vertical in front.**

Cooling: **Air.**

Ignition: **Jump spark; two sets of**
batteries.

Drive: **Direct, bevel gear.**

Transmission: **Sliding gear.**

Speeds: **Three forward and reverse.**

Descriptive catalogue sent upon application to the above-named company.

WALTHAM MANUFACTURING CO., WALTHAM, MASS.

Price

$2250

Model: **DE LUXE TOURING CAR.**

Body : Tonneau, double side entrance.

Color : Body, olive green ; gear, red ;
black striping.

Seating capacity : Five persons.

Total weight : 1650 pounds.

Wheel base : 96 inches.

Wheel tread : 56 inches.

Tire dimensions, front : 32 x 3½ inches.

Tire dimensions, rear : 32 x 3½ inches.

Steering : Wheel.

Brakes : Band and emergency.

Gasoline capacity : 10 gallons.

Frame : Pressed steel.

Horse-power : 20.

Number of cylinders : Four.

Cylinders arranged : Vertical, tandem.

Cooling : Air.

Ignition : Jump spark with two sets of
batteries.

Drive : Direct, bevel gear.

Transmission : Sliding gear.

Speeds : Three forward and one reverse.

Descriptive catalogue sent upon application to the above-named company.

WALTHAM MANUFACTURING CO., WALTHAM, MASS.

Price

$3200

Model : ORIENT LIMOUSINE.

Body : Wood, side door entrance.

Color : Body, olive green; gear, red; black striping.

Seating capacity : Seven persons.

Total weight : 2200 pounds.

Wheel base : 110 inches.

Wheel tread : 56 inches.

Tire dimensions, front : 32 x 4 inches.

Tire dimensions, rear : 32 x 4 inches.

Steering : Wheel.

Brakes : Hand lever on both rear wheels, foot lever on countershaft.

Gasoline capacity : 10 gallons.

Frame : Pressed steel.

Horse-power : 20.

Number of cylinders : Four.

Cylinders arranged : Vertical, tandem.

Cooling : Air.

Ignition : Jump spark, two sets of batteries.

Drive : Direct, bevel gear.

Transmission : Sliding gear.

Speeds : Three forward and one reverse.

Descriptive catalogue sent upon application to the above-named company.

THE WINTON MOTOR CARRIAGE CO., CLEVELAND, OHIO

Price

without top
$1800

Model : "C".

Body : Side-entrance tonneau.

Color : Silver grey or maroon.

Seating capacity : Five persons.

Total weight : 1800 pounds.

Wheel base : 88 inches.

Wheel tread : 56½ inches.

Tire dimensions, front : 30 x 3½ inches.

Tire dimensions, rear : 30 x 3½ inches.

Steering : Screw and nut.

Brakes : Three.

Gasoline capacity : 15 gallons.

Frame : One-piece, channel section, pressed steel.

Horse-power : 16-20.

Number of cylinders : Four.

Cylinders arranged : Vertical under bonnet.

Cooling : Water, centrifugal pump.

Ignition : Jump spark, gear-driven magneto, single non-vibrator coil.

Drive : Longitudinal shaft.

Transmission : Individual clutch.

Speeds : Two forward and reverse.

Descriptive catalogue sent upon application to the above-named company

THE WINTON MOTOR CARRIAGE CO., CLEVELAND, OHIO

Price
without top
$2500

Model : " B."

Body : Side-entrance tonneau.

Color : Optional.

Seating capacity : Six persons.

Total weight : 2100 pounds.

Wheel base : 102 inches.

Wheel tread : 56½ inches.

Tire dimensions, front : 32 x 4 inches.

Tire dimensions, rear : 32 x 4 inches.

Steering : Screw and nut.

Brakes : Three.

Gasoline capacity : 15 gallons.

Frame : One-piece, channel section, pressed steel.

Horse-power : 24-30.

Number of cylinders : Four.

Cylinders arranged : Vertical under bonnet.

Cooling : Water, centrifugal pump.

Ignition : Jump spark, gear-driven magneto, single non-vibrator coil.

Drive : Longitudinal shaft.

Transmission : Individual clutch.

Speeds : Two forward, and reverse.

Descriptive catalogue sent upon application to the above-named company.

THE WINTON MOTOR CARRIAGE CO., CLEVELAND, OHIO

Price

$3500

Model: "B," LIMOUSINE.

Body: Limousine.

Color: Optional.

Seating capacity · Five to eight persons.

Wheel base: 102 inches.

Wheel tread: 56½ inches

Tire dimensions, front: 32 x 4 inches.

Tire dimensions, rear: 32 x 4 inches.

Steering: Screw and nut.

Brakes: Three.

Gasoline capacity: 15 gallons.

Frame: One-piece, channel section, pressed steel.

Horse-power: 24-30.

Number of cylinders: Four.

Cylinders arranged: Vertical under bonnet.

Cooling: Water, centrifugal pump.

Ignition: Jump spark, gear - driven magneto, single non-vibrator coil.

Drive: Longitudinal shaft.

Transmission: Individual clutch.

Speeds: Two forward and reverse.

Style of top: Limousine.

Descriptive catalogue sent upon application to the above-named company.

THE WINTON MOTOR CARRIAGE CO., CLEVELAND, OHIO

Price

without top
$3500

Model: "A."

Body: Side-entrance tonneau.

Color: Optional.

Seating capacity: Six persons.

Total weight: 2400 pounds.

Wheel base: 106 inches.

Wheel tread: 56½ inches.

Tire dimensions, front: 34 x 4½ inches.

Tire dimensions, rear: 34 x 4½ inches.

Steering: Screw and nut.

Brakes: Three.

Gasoline capacity: 15 gallons.

Frame: One piece, channel section, pressed steel.

Horse-power: 40-50.

Number of cylinders: Four.

Cylinders arranged: Vertical under bonnet.

Cooling: Water, centrifugal pump.

Ignition: Jump spark, gear-driven magneto, single non-vibrator coil.

Drive: Longitudinal shaft.

Transmission: Individual clutch.

Speeds: Three forward, and reverse.

Descriptive catalogue sent upon application to the above-named company.

WORTHINGTON AUTOMOBILE CO., 547 FIFTH AVE., NEW YORK

Price

side entrance
$3000
rear entrance
$2500

Model : **BERG.**

Body : **Tonneau, wood or aluminum.**

Color : **Imperial blue with gold striping.**

Seating capacity : **Five** persons.

Total weight : **2200** pounds.

Wheel base : **96** inches.

Wheel tread : **56** inches.

Tire dimensions, front : **34 x 4** inches.

Tire dimensions, rear : **34 x 4** inches.

Steering : **Wheel.**

Brakes : **Hand lever on rear wheels, foot lever on differential.**

Gasoline capacity : **14** gallons.

Frame : **Armored wood.**

Horse-power : **24.**

Number of cylinders : **Four.**

Cylinders arranged : **Vertical in front.**

Cooling : **Water, with tubular cooler and water tank.**

Ignition : **Jump spark.**

Drive : **Double chain.**

Transmission : **Sliding gear.**

Speeds : **Four forward and reverse.**

Style of top : **Canopy top or hood.**

Descriptive catalogue sent upon application to the above-named company.

Hand Book of

Gasoline
Automobiles

[1906]

Hand Book of

Gasoline
Automobiles

For the information of the
public who are interested
in their manufacture
and use

1906

Association of Licensed Automobile
Manufacturers

7 East 42d Street, New York City, U. S. A.

Third Annual Announcement

THE successful results attending the previous issues of this " Hand Book " fully justify its present standardized form as a permanent annual publication for the convenience of the prospective purchaser of an automobile. The products of the principal manufacturers throughout the United States of America and of the importers of gasoline machines are shown by illustrations and specifications. These specifications form a series of the leading questions that arise in the mind of the purchaser, with the answers thereto in red ink. The questions being uniform, the ease of comparison is obvious and the purchaser is enabled to select the machines which are best suited to the service required, to his personal taste, or the means at his command.

It is believed by the several manufacturers who have united in producing this publication that this disinterested method of placing before the purchaser this means of comparison will be found of great advantage.

Each manufacturer or importer conducts his business entirely independently of the other, and, of course, in open competition, but the recognition by the companies represented herein of the basic United States patent No. 549,160, granted to George B. Selden, November 5th, 1895, on gasoline automobiles (which controls broadly all gasoline automobiles which are accepted as commercially practicable), is a guarantee that a purchase through the several companies herein represented, or through any one of their agents, secures to the purchaser freedom from the annoyance and expense of litigation because of infringement of this patent.

Note.—All motors are of the four-cycle type unless otherwise specified.

Organization of Association of Licensed Automobile Manufacturers

▼

Officers

Charles Clifton, *President*	George N. Pierce Company
William E. Metzger, *Vice-President* . .	Cadillac Motor Car Company
L. H. Kittredge, *Secretary* . . .	Peerless Motor Car Company
H. H. Franklin, *Treasurer* .	H. H. Franklin Manufacturing Company

Executive Committee

Charles Clifton	George N. Pierce Company
F. L. Smith	Olds Motor Works
S. T. Davis, Jr.	Locomobile Company of America
E. H. Cutler	Knox Automobile Company
M. J. Budlong	Electric Vehicle Company

Trades Committee

William E. Metzger	Cadillac Motor Car Company
George Pope	Pope Manufacturing Company
G. H. Stilwell	H. H. Franklin Manufacturing Company
C. C. Hildebrand	J. Stevens Arms & Tool Company
Thomas H. Henderson . . .	Winton Motor Carriage Company

Committee on Tires

L. H. Kittredge	Peerless Motor Car Company
Albert L. Pope	Pope Manufacturing Company
S. D. Waldon	Packard Motor Car Company

Hand Book Committee

L. H. Kittredge	Peerless Motor Car Company
William E. Metzger	Cadillac Motor Car Company
Thomas H. Henderson . . .	Winton Motor Carriage Company

Show Committee for 1906

George Pope	Pope Manufacturing Company
Marcus I. Brock	New York Office
C. R. Mabley	Smith & Mabley, Incorporated
M. L. Downs, *Secretary*	New York Office

New York Office

George H. Day . . . . *General Manager*
Marcus I. Brock . . . . . *Assistant General Manager*

Patent Department

Hermann F. Cuntz . . . . *Manager*

Agency Department

Charles A. Wardle . . . . *Manager*

Traffic Department

James S. Marvin . . . . *Manager*

Mechanical Branch

A. L. Riker, *Chairman* . . . Locomobile Company of America
Coker F. Clarkson, *Secretary* . . . . . New York Office
Henry Souther, *Metallurgist* . . . . . Hartford, Conn.

Committee on Tests

A. L. Riker (*Ex-officio*) . . . Locomobile Company of America
H. E. Coffin . . . . Olds Motor Works
H. P. Maxim . . . . Electric Vehicle Company
Charles B. King . . . . . Northern Manufacturing Company
John Wilkinson . . . H. H. Franklin Manufacturing Company
Russell Huff . . . . . . Packard Motor Car Company

Association Patents Company

Directors

Charles Clifton, *President* . . . . George N. Pierce Company
G. H. Stilwell, *Vice-President* . H. H. Franklin Manufacturing Company
Marcus I. Brock, *Secretary* . . . . . New York Office
E. R. Thomas, *Treasurer* . . . E. R. Thomas Motor Company
E. H. Cutler . . . . . . Knox Automobile Company
James H. Becker . . . . Elmore Manufacturing Company
Elwood Haynes . . . . . Haynes Automobile Company

The following manufacturers and importers are licensed under the basic United States patent No. 549,160, granted to George B. Selden, dated November 5th, 1895, and are the owners of about 400 other patents on

Gasoline Automobiles

The Commissioner of Patents in his annual report for the year 1895, said : " Selden, in 1895, received a patent, November 5th, No. 549,160, which may be considered the pioneer invention in the application of the compression gas engine to road or horseless carriage use."

Alphabetical Index

Index of Trade Names

APPERSON BROTHERS AUTOMOBILE COMPANY, KOKOMO, IND.

Price
$3500
With top
$200 extra
Limousine
$5200

Model : **C.**

Body : **Touring or limousine.**

Color : **Optional.**

Seating capacity : **Five persons.**

Total weight : **2500 pounds.**

Wheel base : **104 inches.**

Wheel tread : **56 inches.**

Tire dimensions, front : **32 x 4 inches.**

Tire dimensions, rear : **34 x 4 inches.**

Steering : **Worm and segment.**

Brakes : **Hand emergency and foot.**

Gasoline capacity : **15 gallons.**

Frame : **Pressed steel.**

Horse-power : **30-35.**

Number of cylinders : **Four.**

Cylinders arranged : **Vertically, under hood ; cast separately.**

Cooling : **Water ; pump.**

Ignition : **Jump spark ; storage batteries.**

Drive : **Double side chain.**

Transmission : **Sliding gear.**

Speeds : **Three forward, one reverse.**

Style of top : **Full leather or mackintosh.**

Descriptive catalogue sent upon application to the above-named company.

APPERSON BROTHERS AUTOMOBILE COMPANY, KOKOMO, IND.

Price

$4500
With top
$4700

Model : **B.**

Body : **Touring.**

Color : **Optional.**

Seating capacity : **Seven persons.**

Total weight : **2750 pounds.**

Wheel base : **112 inches.**

Wheel tread : **56 inches.**

Tire dimensions, front: **32 x 4 inches.**

Tire dimensions, rear: **34 x 4½ inches.**

Steering : **Worm and segment.**

Brakes : **Hand emergency and foot.**

Gasoline capacity : **20 gallons.**

Frame : **Pressed steel, reinforced.**

Horse-power : **40-45.**

Number of cylinders : **Four.**

Cylinders arranged : **Vertically, under hood ; cast separately.**

Cooling : **Water ; pump.**

Ignition : **Double system ; jump spark, battery and magneto.**

Drive : **Double side chain.**

Transmission : **Sliding gear.**

Speeds : **Three or four forward (optional), one reverse.**

Style of top : **Full leather, collapsible, for both seats.**

Descriptive catalogue sent upon application to the above-named company.

APPERSON BROTHERS AUTOMOBILE COMPANY, KOKOMO, IND.

Price

$5500
With top
$5700

Model :   **A, SPECIAL.**

Body :   **Touring.**

Color :   **Optional.**

Seating capacity :   **Seven persons.**

Total weight :   **3000 pounds.**

Wheel base :   **116 inches.**

Wheel tread :   **56 inches.**

Tire dimensions, front :   **32 x 4 inches.**

Tire dimensions, rear :   **34 x 4½ inches.**

Steering :   **Worm and segment.**

Brakes :   **Hand emergency and foot.**

Gasoline capacity :   **20 gallons.**

Frame :   **Pressed steel, reinforced.**

Horse-power :   **50-55.**

Number of cylinders :   **Four.**

Cylinders arranged :   **Vertically, under hood ; cast separately.**

Cooling :   **Water ; pump.**

Ignition :   **Double system ; jump spark, battery and magneto.**

Drive :   **Double side chain.**

Transmission :   **Sliding gear.**

Speeds :   **Four forward, one reverse.**

Style of top :   **Full leather, collapsible, for both seats.**

Descriptive catalogue sent upon application to the above-named company.

APPERSON BROTHERS AUTOMOBILE COMPANY, KOKOMO, IND.

Price

$10,500
With top
$10,700

Model : **D.**

Body : **Racing or touring.**

Color : **Special.**

Seating capacity : **Two or seven persons.**

Total weight : **Chassis, 2000 pounds.**

Wheel base : **104 inches.**

Wheel tread : **56 inches.**

Tire dimensions, front : **34 x 4 inches.**

Tire dimensions, rear : **34 x 4½ inches.**

Steering : **Worm and segment.**

Brakes : **Hand emergency and foot.**

Gasoline capacity : **20 gallons.**

Frame : **Pressed steel.**

Horse-power : **95.**

Number of cylinders : **Four.**

Cylinders arranged : **Vertically, under hood ; cast separately.**

Cooling : **Water ; pump.**

Ignition : **Double system, high tension.**

Drive : **Double side chain.**

Transmission : **Sliding gear.**

Speeds : **Four forward, one reverse.**

Style of top : **Optional.**

Descriptive catalogue sent upon application to the above-named company.

AUTO IMPORT COMPANY, 1786 BROADWAY, NEW YORK, N. Y.

Price

$8000

Model: **ROCHET-SCHNEIDER.**

Body: **Double side doors—any style.**

Color: **Optional.**

Seating capacity: **Seven persons.**

Total weight: **2400 pounds.**

Wheel base: **117 inches.**

Wheel tread: **57 inches.**

Tire dimensions, front: **920 x 120 m/m.**

Tire dimensions, rear: **920 x 120 m/m.**

Steering: **Worm and sector.**

Brakes: **Two differential; and two internal expanding emergency on rear wheels.**

Gasoline capacity: **25 gallons.**

Frame: **Pressed steel.**

Horse-power: **30-35 (also 18-22 and 40-50).**

Number of cylinders: **Four.**

Cylinders arranged: **Vertically, under hood.**

Cooling: **Water; honeycomb radiator.**

Ignition: **Make-and-break; magneto.**

Drive: **Double side chain.**

Transmission: **Sliding gear.**

Speeds: **Four, one reverse; direct on high gear.**

Style of top: **Optional.**

Descriptive catalogue sent upon application to the above-named company.

THE   AUTOCAR   COMPANY,   ARDMORE,   PA.

Price

$1000

Model : TYPE X.

Body : Runabout.

Color : Blue.

Seating capacity : Two persons.

Total weight : 1300 pounds.

Wheel base : 76 inches.

Wheel tread : 54 inches.

Tire dimensions, front : 28 x 3 inches.

Tire dimensions, rear : 28 x 3 inches.

Steering : Wheel.

Brakes : External hub on each rear wheel ; one pinion shaft.

Gasoline capacity : 9 gallons.

Frame : Armored wood.

Horse-power : 12.

Number of cylinders : Two.

Cylinders arranged : Horizontally, opposed, under hood.

Cooling : Water ; tubular radiator and centrifugal pump.

Ignition : Jump spark.

Drive : Bevel gear.

Transmission : Sliding gear.

Speeds : Three forward, one reverse.

Descriptive catalogue sent upon application to the above-named company.

THE   AUTOCAR   COMPANY,   ARDMORE,   PA.

Price

$2600

Model : **TYPE XII.**

Body : **Side entrance tonneau—wood.**

Color : **Blue.**

Seating capacity : **Five persons.**

Total weight : **2475 pounds.**

Wheel base : **100 inches.**

Wheel tread : **56 inches.**

Tire dimensions, front : **32 x 4 inches.**

Tire dimensions, rear : **32 x 4 inches.**

Steering : **Wheel.**

Brakes : **External and internal on drums on both rear wheels.**

Gasoline capacity : **16 gallons.**

Frame : **Wood, armored with pressed steel.**

Horse-power : **24.**

Number of cylinders : **Four.**

Cylinders arranged : **Vertically, under hood.**

Cooling : **Water ; tubular radiator, fan and centrifugal pump.**

Ignition : **Jump spark.**

Drive : **Bevel gear.**

Transmission : **Sliding gear.**

Speeds : **Three forward, one reverse.**

Descriptive catalogue sent upon application to the above-named company.

THE   AUTOCAR   COMPANY,   ARDMORE,   PA.

Price

$3500

Model: **TYPE XII.**

Body: **Limousine.**

Color: **Body, green ; running gear, optional.**

Seating capacity : **Five persons.**

Total weight : **2975 pounds.**

Wheel base: **100 inches.**

Wheel tread: **56 inches.**

Tire dimensions, front: **32 x 4 inches.**

Tire dimensions, rear: **32 x 4½ inches.**

Steering : **Wheel.**

Brakes: **External and internal on drums on both rear wheels.**

Gasoline capacity : **16 gallons.**

Frame : **Wood, armored with pressed steel.**

Horse-power : **24.**

Number of cylinders : **Four.**

Cylinders arranged : **Vertically, under hood.**

Cooling: **Water; tubular radiator, fan and centrifugal pump.**

Ignition : **Jump spark.**

Drive : **Bevel gear.**

Transmission : **Sliding gear.**

Speeds : **Three forward, one reverse.**

Descriptive catalogue sent upon application to the above-named company.

SIDNEY B. BOWMAN AUTOMOBILE COMPANY, NEW YORK, N. Y.

Price

$6000
Brougham
$6850

Model : **CLEMENT-BAYARD.**

Body : **Double side entrance, landaulet, brougham or touring.**

Color : **Blue and red, green and yellow, red and red.**

Seating capacity : **Six persons.**

Total weight : **2400 pounds.**

Wheel base : **110 inches.**

Wheel tread : **56 inches.**

Tire dimensions, front : **34 x 3½ inches.**

Tire dimensions, rear : **34 x 4¼ inches.**

Steering : **Wheel, through irreversible worm gear.**

Brakes : **Two internal expansion, double-acting.**

Gasoline capacity : **12 to 18 gallons.**

Frame : **Pressed steel.**

Horse-power : **24.**

Number of cylinders : **Four.**

Cylinders arranged : **Vertically, under hood ; cast separately.**

Cooling : **Water; honeycomb radiator with fan and pump.**

Ignition : **Double; jump spark with high tension magneto and batteries.**

Drive : **Bevel gear.**

Transmission : **Sliding gear ; direct on high gear.**

Speeds : **Four forward, one reverse.**

Style of top : **Cape or canopy.**

Descriptive catalogue sent upon application to the above-named company.

SIDNEY B. BOWMAN AUTOMOBILE COMPANY, NEW YORK, N. Y.

Price.

$9000

With top
$9350

Model : **CLEMENT-BAYARD.**

Body : **Double side entrance, landaulet or brougham.**

Color : **Blue and red, green and yellow, red and red.**

Seating capacity: **Seven persons.**

Total weight : **2900 pounds.**

Wheel base : **120 inches.**

Wheel tread : **56 inches.**

Tire dimensions, front : **36 x 4¼ inches.**

Tire dimensions, rear : **36 x 4¾ inches.**

Steering : **Wheel, through irreversible worm gear.**

Brakes : **Two internal expansion, double-acting.**

Gasoline capacity : **20 gallons.**

Frame : **Pressed steel.**

Horse-power : **45.**

Number of cylinders : **Four.**

Cylinders arranged : **Vertically, under hood ; cast separately.**

Cooling : **Water ; honeycomb radiator with fan and pump.**

Ignition : **Double ; jump spark with high tension magneto and batteries.**

Drive : **Double side chain.**

Transmission : **Sliding gears ; direct on high gear.**

Speeds : **Four forward, one reverse ; selective.**

Style of top : **Cape or canopy.**

Descriptive catalogue sent upon application to the above-named company.

SIDNEY B. BOWMAN AUTOMOBILE COMPANY, NEW YORK, N. Y.

Price

$11,000
With top
$11,150

Model: **CLEMENT-BAYARD.**

Body: **Double side entrance, landaulet or brougham.**

Color: **Blue and red, green and yellow, red and red.**

Seating capacity: **Eight persons.**

Total weight: **3150 pounds.**

Wheel base: **130 inches.**

Wheel tread: **57 inches.**

Tire dimensions, front: **36 x 4¼ inches.**

Tire dimensions, rear: **36 x 4¾ inches.**

Steering: **Wheel, through irreversible worm gear.**

Brakes: **Two internal expansion, double-acting.**

Gasoline capacity: **25 gallons.**

Frame: **Pressed steel.**

Horse-power: **60.**

Number of cylinders: **Four.**

Cylinders arranged: **Vertically, under hood; cast separately.**

Cooling: **Water; honeycomb radiator with fan and pump.**

Ignition: **Double; make - and - break with magneto; and jump spark with batteries.**

Drive: **Double side chain.**

Transmission: **Sliding gear; direct on high gear.**

Speeds: **Four forward, one reverse; selective.**

Style of top: **Cape or canopy.**

Descriptive catalogue sent upon application to the above-named company.

BUICK MOTOR COMPANY, JACKSON, MICHIGAN

Price

$1000
With top
$1080

Model: **G, RUNABOUT.**

Body: **Wood—special design with turtle back.**

Color: **Aluminum or purple lake.**

Seating capacity: **Two persons.**

Total weight: **1400 pounds.**

Wheel base: **87 inches.**

Wheel tread: **56 inches.**

Tire dimensions, front: **30 x 3½ inches.**

Tire dimensions, rear: **30 x 3½ inches.**

Steering: **Bevel gear and sector.**

Brakes: **Hub, internal expanding.**

Gasoline capacity: **15 gallons.**

Frame: **Angle steel.**

Horse-power: **22.**

Number of cylinders: **Two.**

Cylinders arranged: **Horizontally, under body.**

Cooling: **Water.**

Ignition: **Jump spark; storage battery.**

Drive: **Chain.**

Transmission: **Planetary.**

Speeds: **Two forward, one reverse.**

Descriptive catalogue sent upon application to the above-named company.

BUICK MOTOR COMPANY, JACKSON, MICHIGAN

Price

$1250
With top
$1350

Model : **F.**

Body : **Wood—side entrance.**

Color : **Purple lake (deep wine).**

Seating capacity : **Five persons.**

Total weight : **1840 pounds.**

Wheel base : **87 inches.**

Wheel tread : **56 inches.**

Tire dimensions, front : **30 x 3½ inches.**

Tire dimensions, rear : **30 x 3½ inches.**

Steering : **Bevel gear and sector.**

Brakes : **Hub, internal expanding.**

Gasoline capacity : **15 gallons.**

Frame : **Angle steel.**

Horse-power : **22.**

Number of cylinders : **Two.**

Cylinders arranged : **Horizontally, under body.**

Cooling : **Water.**

Ignition : **Jump spark ; storage battery.**

Drive : **Chain.**

Transmission : **Planetary.**

Speeds : **Two forward, one reverse.**

Style of top : **Cape cart.**

Descriptive catalogue sent upon application to the above-named company.

BUICK MOTOR COMPANY, JACKSON, MICHIGAN

Price

$2500

Model: D.

Body: Wood.

Color: Deep blue body, royal blue mouldings.

Seating capacity: Five persons.

Total weight: 2000 pounds.

Wheel base : 102 inches.

Wheel tread: 56 inches.

Tire dimensions, front: 32 x 4 inches.

Tire dimensions, rear: 32 x 4 inches

Steering: Bevel gear and sector.

Brakes: Two; shaft and internal expansion on hubs.

Gasoline capacity: 15 gallons.

Frame: Cold-rolled pressed steel.

Horse-power: 30-35.

Number of cylinders: Four.

Cylinders arranged: Vertically, under hood.

Cooling: Water.

Ignition: Jump spark; storage battery.

Drive: Bevel gear.

Transmission: Sliding gear.

Speeds: Three forward, one reverse.

Style of top: Cape cart.

Descriptive catalogue sent upon application to the above-named company.

CADILLAC MOTOR CAR COMPANY, DETROIT, MICH.

Price
$750
With top
$800

Model : **K, LIGHT RUNABOUT.**

Body : **Wood, runabout.**

Color : **Purple lake, dark carmine running gear.**

Seating capacity : **Two persons.**

Total weight : **1100 pounds.**

Wheel base : **74 inches.**

Wheel tread : **56 or 61 inches.**

Tire dimensions, front : **28 x 3 inches.**

Tire dimensions, rear : **28 x 3 inches.**

Steering : **Wheel, rack and pinion.**

Brakes : **Double-acting, on differential.**

Gasoline capacity : **7 gallons.**

Frame : **Pressed steel.**

Horse-power : **10.**

Number of cylinders : **One.**

Cylinder arranged : **Horizontally, under body.**

Cooling : **Water.**

Ignition : **Jump spark.**

Drive : **Chain.**

Transmission : **Planetary.**

Speeds : **Two forward, one reverse.**

Descriptive catalogue sent upon application to the above-named company.

CADILLAC MOTOR CAR COMPANY, DETROIT, MICH.

Price

$950

With top
$1025

Model: **M, LIGHT TOURING CAR.**

Body: **Wood; double side door entrance.**

Color: **Purple lake, dark carmine running gear.**

Seating capacity: **Four persons.**

Total weight: **1350 pounds.**

Wheel base: **76 inches.**

Wheel tread: **56 or 61 inches.**

Tire dimensions, front: **30 x 3½ inches.**

Tire dimensions, rear: **30 x 3½ inches.**

Steering: **Wheel, rack and pinion.**

Brakes: **Double-acting, on differential.**

Gasoline capacity: **7 gallons.**

Frame: **Pressed steel.**

Horse-power: **10.**

Number of cylinders: **One.**

Cylinder arranged: **Horizontally, under body.**

Cooling: **Water.**

Ignition: **Jump spark.**

Drive: **Chain.**

Transmission: **Planetary.**

Speeds: **Two forward, one reverse.**

Style of top: **Cape cart.**

Descriptive catalogue sent upon application to the above-named company.

CADILLAC MOTOR CAR COMPANY, DETROIT, MICH.

Price (without lamps)
Runabout
$2400
Touring car
$2500
With top (Runabout)
$2450
Touring car
$2625

Model : H.

Body : Wood ; double side door entrance.

Color : Purple lake, dark carmine running gear.

Seating capacity : Five persons.

Total weight : 2400 pounds.

Wheel base : 100 inches.

Wheel tread : 56½ or 61 inches.

Tire dimensions, front : 32 x 4 inches.

Tire dimensions, rear : 32 x 4 inches.

Steering : Wheel, irreversible.

Brakes : Double-acting, contracting
and expanding on rear wheel hub
drums.

Gasoline capacity : 16 gallons.

Frame : Pressed steel.

Horse-power : 30.

Number of cylinders : Four.

Cylinders arranged : Vertically, under
hood.

Cooling : Water.

Ignition : Jump spark.

Drive : Bevel gear.

Transmission : Planetary.

Speeds : Three forward, one reverse.

Style of top : Cape cart on touring car.

Descriptive catalogue sent upon application to the above-named company

CADILLAC MOTOR CAR COMPANY, DETROIT, MICH.

Price

(without lamps)
$3000

Model: **H, COUPE.**

Body: **Wood.**

Color: **Purple lake, dark carmine running gear.**

Seating capacity: **Two persons.**

Total weight: **2500 pounds.**

Wheel base: **100 inches.**

Wheel tread: **56½ inches.**

Tire dimensions, front: **32 x 4 inches.**

Tire dimensions, rear: **32 x 4 inches.**

Steering: **Wheel, irreversible.**

Brakes: **Double-acting, contracting and expanding on rear wheel drums.**

Gasoline capacity: **16 gallons.**

Frame: **Pressed steel.**

Horse-power: **30.**

Number of cylinders: **Four.**

Cylinders arranged: **Vertically, under hood.**

Cooling: **Water.**

Ignition: **Jump spark.**

Drive: **Bevel gear.**

Transmission: **Planetary.**

Speeds: **Three forward, one reverse.**

Descriptive catalogue sent upon application to the above-named company.

CADILLAC MOTOR CAR COMPANY, DETROIT, MICH.

Price

(without lamps)

$3750

With top

$3900

Model: **L.**

Body: **Wood, double side door entrance.**

Color : **Purple lake, dark carmine running gear.**

Seating capacity: **Five to seven persons.**

Total weight : **2850 pounds.**

Wheel base : **110 inches.**

Wheel tread : **56½ inches.**

Tire dimensions, front : **36 x 4 inches.**

Tire dimensions, rear : **36 x 4½ inches.**

Steering : **Wheel, irreversible.**

Brakes : **Double-acting, contracting and expanding on rear wheel drums.**

Gasoline capacity : **18 gallons.**

Frame : **Pressed steel.**

Horse-power : **40.**

Number of cylinders : **Four.**

Cylinders arranged : **Vertically, under hood.**

Cooling : **Water.**

Ignition : **Jump spark.**

Drive : **Bevel gear.**

Transmission : **Planetary.**

Speeds : **Three forward, one reverse.**

Style of top : **Cape cart.**

Descriptive catalogue sent upon application to the above-named company.

CADILLAC MOTOR CAR COMPANY, DETROIT, MICH.

Price

(without lamps)

$5000

Model : **L, LIMOUSINE.**

Body : **Wood.**

Color : **Purple lake, dark carmine running gear.**

Seating capacity : **Seven persons.**

Total weight : **3600 pounds.**

Wheel base : **110 inches.**

Wheel tread : **56½ inches.**

Tire dimensions, front : **36 x 4 inches.**

Tire dimensions, rear : **36 x 4½ inches.**

Steering : **Wheel, irreversible.**

Brakes : **Double-acting, contracting and expanding on rear wheel drums.**

Gasoline capacity : **18 gallons.**

Frame : **Pressed steel.**

Horse-power : **40.**

Number of cylinders : **Four.**

Cylinders arranged : **Vertically, under hood.**

Cooling : **Water.**

Ignition : **Jump spark.**

Drive : **Bevel gear.**

Transmission : **Planetary.**

Speeds : **Three forward, one reverse.**

Descriptive catalogue sent upon application to the above-named company.

CENTRAL AUTOMOBILE COMPANY (^{ARCHER & CO.}_{AGENTS}) NEW YORK, N. Y.

Price

$5000
With top
$5500

Model : **DE LEON**, 1906.

Body : **Double side entrance.**

Color : **Optional.**

Seating capacity : **Five persons.**

Total weight : **Chassis, 2000 pounds.**

Wheel base : **118 inches.**

Wheel tread : **56 inches.**

Tire dimensions, front : **880 x 120 m/m.**

Tire dimensions, rear : **880 x 120 m/m.**

Steering : **Wheel.**

Brakes : **Three ; differential, counter-shaft, and expansion on both rear wheels.**

Gasoline capacity : **18 gallons.**

Frame : **Pressed nickel steel.**

Horse-power : **35 (also 24-30).**

Number of cylinders : **Four.**

Cylinders arranged : **Vertically, under hood ; cast separately.**

Cooling : **Water ; honeycomb radiator, pump and fan.**

Ignition : **Jump spark ; magneto.**

Drive : **Double side chain.**

Transmission : **Sliding gear.**

Speeds : **Three forward, one reverse.**

Style of top : **Demi-limousine.**

Descriptive catalogue sent upon application to the above-named company.

CENTRAL AUTOMOBILE COMPANY ($\left(\begin{smallmatrix}\text{ARCHER & CO.}\\\text{AGENTS}\end{smallmatrix}\right)$) NEW YORK, N. Y.

Price

$6500

With top

$7000

Model: J, 1906 HOTCHKISS.

Body: Double side entrance.

Color : Optional.

Seating capacity : Five persons.

Total weight : Chassis, 2150 pounds.

Wheel base : 120 inches.

Wheel tread : 56 inches.

Tire dimensions, front : 875 x 105 m/m.

Tire dimensions, rear : 880 x 120 m/m.

Steering : Wheel.

Brakes : Three; differential, counter-shaft, and expansion on both rear wheels.

Gasoline capacity : 15 gallons.

Frame : Pressed nickel steel.

Horse-power : 35 (also 25).

Number of cylinders : Four.

Cylinders arranged : Vertically, under hood; cast in pairs.

Cooling : Water ; gear-driven pump and fan.

Ignition : High tension magneto.

Drive : Bevel gear.

Transmission : Sliding gear.

Speeds : Four forward, one reverse.

Style of top : Demi-limousine.

Descriptive catalogue sent upon application to the above-named company.

DARRACQ MOTOR CAR CO., 652 HUDSON ST., NEW YORK CITY

Price

chassis
$4250
Touring body
$5000
Demi-limousine
$5500
Limousine
$6000

Model : **DARRACQ.**

Body : **Double phaeton, demi-limousine or limousine.**

Color : **Royal blue, dark green or red.**

Seating capacity : **Five to seven persons.**

Total weight : **2050 pounds (with touring body).**

Wheel base : **110 inches (long chassis).**

Wheel tread : **52 inches.**

Tire dimensions, front : **810 x 90 m/m.**

Tire dimensions, rear : **810 x 90 m/m.**

Steering : **Worm and segment.**

Brakes : **Internal expansion on shaft, controlled by foot pedal; and on rear wheels, controlled by side hand lever.**

Gasoline capacity : **15 gallons.**

Frame : **Pressed steel.**

Horse-power : **15-20.**

Number of cylinders : **Four.**

Cylinders arranged : **Vertically, under hood; cast in pairs.**

Cooling : **Water; Mercedes honeycomb radiator and gear-driven centrifugal pump.**

Ignition : **Jump spark with coil and accumulator; and make-and-break with low tension magneto.**

Drive : **Bevel gear.**

Transmission : **Sliding gear; direct on high gear.**

Speeds : **Three forward, one reverse, actuated by one lever on quadrant under steering wheel.**

Style of top : **Cape or canopy, sliding glass front and back, as selected.**

Descriptive catalogue sent upon application to the above-named company.

DARRACQ MOTOR CAR CO., 652 HUDSON ST., NEW YORK CITY

Price

chassis

$5250

Touring body

$6000

Demi-limousine

$6450

Limousine

$7000

Model: DARRACQ.

Body: Double phaeton, limousine or demi-limousine.

Color: Royal blue, dark green or red.

Seating capacity: Five to seven persons.

Total weight: 2600 pounds (with touring body).

Wheel base: 120 inches.

Wheel tread: 53 inches.

Tire dimensions, front: 880 x 120 m/m.

Tire dimensions, rear: 880 x 120 m/m.

Steering: Worm and segment.

Brakes: Internal expansion on shaft, controlled by foot pedal; and on rear wheels, controlled by side hand lever.

Gasoline capacity: 15 gallons.

Frame: Pressed steel.

Horse-power: 20-32.

Number of cylinders: Four.

Cylinders arranged: Vertically, under hood; cast in pairs.

Cooling: Water; new type gilled tube radiator and gear-driven centrifugal pump.

Ignition: Jump spark with coil and accumulator; and make-and-break with low tension magneto.

Drive: Bevel gear.

Transmission: Sliding gear; direct on high gear.

Speeds: Three forward, one reverse, actuated by one lever on quadrant under steering wheel.

Style of top: Cape or canopy, sliding glass front and back.

Descriptive catalogue sent upon application to the above-named company.

DE DIETRICH IMPORT COMPANY, 3 WEST 44TH ST., NEW YORK

Price

$10,500

Model : 1906.

Body : Side entrance phaeton.

Color : Optional.

Seating capacity : Seven persons.

Total weight : Chassis, 2800 pounds.

Wheel base : 128 inches.

Wheel tread : 56 inches.

Tire dimensions, front : 870 x 100 m/m.

Tire dimensions, rear : 920 x 125 m/m.

Steering : Wheel, with worm and sector; positive-acting device.

Brakes : One on countershaft; two internal expanding on rear wheels.

Gasoline capacity : 30 gallons.

Frame : Pressed steel.

Horse-power : 40-50.

Number of cylinders : Four.

Cylinders arranged : Vertically, under hood; cast in pairs.

Cooling : Water ; tubular radiator with fan; fan in fly-wheel.

Ignition : Make-and-break; low tension magneto.

Drive : Double side chain.

Transmission : Selective sliding gear.

Speeds : Four forward, one reverse.

Style of top : Cape cart hood.

Descriptive catalogue sent upon application to the above-named company.

DECAUVILLE AUTOMOBILE COMPANY, 136 WEST 38TH ST., N. Y.

Price

chassis
$5850
With body
and top
$7000

Model: **DECAUVILLE TOURING CAR.**

Body: Optional.

Color: Optional.

Seating capacity: According to body.

Total weight: Chassis, 2800 pounds.

Wheel base: 106 to 116 inches.

Wheel tread: Standard.

Tire dimensions, front: 880 x 120 m/m.

Tire dimensions, rear: 880 x 120 m/m.

Steering: **Wheel.**

Brakes: **Expanding on rear hubs; contracting double-acting on drive shaft.**

Gasoline capacity: 20 gallons.

Frame: Pressed steel, with patented steel pan supporting engine and gear case.

Horse-power: 24-28.

Number of cylinders: Four, in pairs.

Cylinders arranged: Vertically, under hood.

Cooling: Water; honeycomb radiator, with fan and gear-driven pump.

Ignition: Two complete systems; high tension magneto; and battery.

Drive: Bevel gear.

Transmission: Sliding gear.

Speeds: Four forward, one reverse.

Descriptive catalogue sent upon application to the above-named company.

DECAUVILLE AUTOMOBILE COMPANY, 136 WEST 38TH ST., N. Y.

Price

chassis
$7000
With body
and top
$9500

Model: **CHARRON, GIRARDOT & VOIGT.**

Body: **Optional.**

Color: **Optional.**

Seating capacity : **According to body.**

Total weight : **Chassis, 2600 pounds.**

Wheel base : **102 to 120 inches, or longer if ordered.**

Wheel tread : **Standard.**

Tire dimensions, front : **920 x 120 m/m.**

Tire dimensions, rear : **920 x 120 m/m.**

Steering : **Wheel.**

Brakes : **Expanding on each rear wheel, as well as on differential shaft.**

Gasoline capacity : **16 gallons.**

Frame : **Nickel steel lined—of hard pressed wood.**

Horse-power : **30-35.**

Number of cylinders : **Four.**

Cylinders arranged : **Vertically, under hood.**

Cooling : **Water ; pump and radiator.**

Ignition : **Jump spark ; accumulator and magneto.**

Drive : **Double side chain.**

Transmission : **Sliding gear.**

Speeds : **Four forward, one reverse.**

Descriptive catalogue sent upon application to the above-named company.

DECAUVILLE AUTOMOBILE COMPANY, 136 WEST 38TH ST., N. Y.

Price

chassis

$7600

With body
and top

$8600

Model: ENGLISH DAIMLER
   TOURING CAR.

Body: Optional.

Color: Optional.

Seating capacity: Five to seven persons.

Total weight : Chassis, 2000 pounds.

Wheel base: 104 to 132 inches.

Wheel tread: Standard.

Tire dimensions, front : 920 x 120 m/m.

Tire dimensions, rear: 920 x 120 m/m.

Steering: Wheel.

Brakes : Two external on cross shaft ;
   two external on hubs.

Gasoline capacity : 14 gallons.

Frame : Pressed steel.

Horse-power : 30-40.

Number of cylinders : Four.

Cylinders arranged : Vertically, under
   hood ; cast in pairs.

Cooling : Water; vertical gilled tubes
   with fan and geared pump.

Ignition: Two systems ; high tension
   magneto ; and jump spark with dis-
   tributor.

Drive : Double side chain.

Transmission : Sliding gear.

Speeds : Four forward, one reverse.

Descriptive catalogue sent upon application to the above-named company.

ELECTRIC VEHICLE COMPANY, HARTFORD, CONN.

Price

$1750
With top
$1850

Model : **COLUMBIA, MARK
XLIV-2.**

Body : **Side entrance.**

Color : Body : **green, gold stripe** ; gear :
green, light green stripe.

Seating capacity : **Five persons.**

Total weight : **1800 pounds.**

Wheel base : **90 inches.**

Wheel tread : **55 inches.**

Tire dimensions, front : **32 x 3½ inches.**

Tire dimensions, rear : **32 x 3½ inches.**

Steering : **Wheel, rack and pinion type.**

Brakes : **Hand brakes, expanding on
both rear hubs ; foot brakes, contracting on both rear hubs ; drums
separated for cooling.**

Gasoline capacity : **10 gallons.**

Frame : **Pressed steel.**

Horse-power : **18-19.**

Number of cylinders : **Two.**

Cylinders arranged : **Horizontally, opposed, under hood.**

Cooling : **Water** ; cellular radiator, fly-
wheel fan.

Ignition : **Jump spark** ; **20 dry cells.**

Drive : **Propeller shaft.**

Transmission : **Sliding gear ; direct on
high gear.**

Speeds : **Three forward, one reverse.**

Style of top : **Cape.**

Descriptive catalogue sent upon application to the above-named company.

ELECTRIC VEHICLE COMPANY, HARTFORD, CONN.

Price
$3000

Model: **COLUMBIA, MARK XLVI.**

Body: **Side entrance.**

Color: **Dark green body, black mouldings; gear: green, black stripe.**

Seating capacity: **Five persons.**

Total weight: **2100 pounds.**

Wheel base: **98 inches.**

Wheel tread: **56 inches.**

Tire dimensions, front: **32 x 3½ inches.**

Tire dimensions, rear: **32 x 4 inches.**

Steering: **Hand wheel, irreversible worm and sector.**

Brakes: **Foot, contracting shoe type; hand, internal expanding shoes in rear wheel drums.**

Gasoline capacity: **12 gallons.**

Frame: **Pressed steel.**

Horse-power: **24-28.**

Number of cylinders: **Four.**

Cylinders arranged: **Vertically, under hood.**

Cooling: **Water; cellular radiator, flywheel fan.**

Ignition: **Make-and-break; low tension magneto.**

Drive: **Bevel gear.**

Transmission: **Sliding gear; direct on high gear.**

Speeds: **Three forward, one reverse.**

Style of top: **Cape.**

Descriptive catalogue sent upon application to the above-named company.

ELECTRIC VEHICLE COMPANY, HARTFORD, CONN.

Price

$4500
With top
$4700

Model: **COLUMBIA, MARK XLVII.**

Body : Side entrance.

Color : Body : dark green, light green stripe ; gear : dark green, light green stripe.

Seating capacity : Seven persons.

Total weight : 3000 pounds.

Wheel base : 108 inches.

Wheel tread : 55 inches.

Tire dimensions, front : 36 x 4 inches.

Tire dimensions, rear : 36 x 4½ inches.

Steering : **Wheel, irreversible worm and sector.**

Brakes : Foot brake, expanding shoes in front sprockets ; hand brake, expanding shoes in rear wheel drums.

Gasoline capacity : 24 gallons.

Frame : Pressed steel.

Horse-power : 40-45.

Number of cylinders : Four.

Cylinders arranged : Vertically, under hood.

Cooling : Water ; cellular radiator with fan.

Ignition : Jump spark ; storage batteries.

Drive : Double side chain.

Transmission : Sliding gear ; direct on high gear.

Speeds : Four forward, one reverse.

Style of top : Cape.

Descriptive catalogue sent upon application to the above-named company.

ELECTRIC VEHICLE COMPANY, HARTFORD, CONN.

Price
$5000

Model: **COLUMBIA, MARK XLVII. (DOUBLE VICTORIA)**.

Body : Double victoria.

Color : Optional.

Seating capacity : Five persons.

Total weight : 3100 pounds.

Wheel base : 112 inches.

Wheel tread : 55 inches.

Tire dimensions, front : 36 x 4 inches.

Tire dimensions, rear : 36 x 4½ inches.

Steering : Wheel, irreversible worm and sector.

Brakes : Foot brake, expanding shoes in front sprockets ; hand brake, expanding shoes in rear wheel drums.

Gasoline capacity : 24 gallons.

Frame : Pressed steel.

Horse-power : 40-45.

Number of cylinders : Four.

Cylinders arranged : Vertically, under hood.

Cooling : Water ; cellular radiator with fan.

Ignition : Jump spark ; storage batteries.

Drive : Double side chain.

Transmission : Sliding gear ; direct on high gear.

Speeds : Four forward, one reverse.

Descriptive catalogue sent upon application to the above-named company.

ELECTRIC VEHICLE COMPANY, HARTFORD, CONN.

Price

$5500

Model: **COLUMBIA, MARK XLVII.
(LIMOUSINE).**

Body: **Limousine.**

Color: **Optional.**

Seating capacity: **Seven persons.**

Total weight: **3400 pounds.**

Wheel base: **112 inches.**

Wheel tread: **55 inches.**

Tire dimensions, front: **36 x 4 inches.**

Tire dimensions, rear: **36 x 4½ inches.**

Steering: **Wheel, irreversible worm and sector.**

Brakes: **Foot, expanding shoes in front sprockets; hand, expanding shoes in rear wheel drums.**

Gasoline capacity: **24 gallons.**

Frame: **Pressed steel.**

Horse-power: **40-45.**

Number of cylinders: **Four.**

Cylinders arranged: **Vertically, under hood.**

Cooling: **Water; cellular radiator with fan.**

Ignition: **Jump spark; storage batteries.**

Drive: **Double side chain.**

Transmission: **Sliding gear; direct on high gear.**

Speeds: **Four forward, one reverse.**

Descriptive catalogue sent upon application to the above-named company.

ELMORE MANUFACTURING COMPANY, CLYDE, OHIO

Price

$1500

Model : 14.

Body : Detachable side entrance tonneau.

Color : Dark red.

Seating capacity : Four persons.

Total weight : 1750 pounds.

Wheel base : 92 inches.

Wheel tread : 56 inches.

Tire dimensions, front : 32 x 3½ inches.

Tire dimensions, rear : 32 x 3½ inches.

Steering : Wheel.

Brakes : Two on hubs, rear wheels ;
one on propeller shaft.

Gasoline capacity : 15 gallons.

Frame : Pressed cold-rolled steel.

Horse-power : 24.

Number of cylinders : Three. two-cycle.

Cylinders arranged : Vertically, under
hood.

Cooling : Water.

Ignition : Jump spark.

Drive : Bevel gear.

Transmission : Planetary.

Speeds : Two forward, one reverse.

Descriptive catalogue sent upon application to the above-named company.

ELMORE MANUFACTURING COMPANY, CLYDE, OHIO

Price

    $2500
    With top
    $2650

Model : I5.

Body : Tonneau.

Color : Elmore blue.

Seating capacity : Five persons.

Total weight : 2200 pounds.

Wheel base : 104 inches.

Wheel tread : 56 inches.

Tire dimensions, front : 34 x 4 inches.

Tire dimensions, rear : 34 x 4 inches.

Steering : Wheel.

Brakes : Two on hubs, rear wheels ; one on propeller shaft.

Gasoline capacity : 20 gallons.

Frame : Pressed cold-rolled steel.

Horse-power : 35.

Number of cylinders : Four. **two-cycle.**

Cylinders arranged : Vertically, under hood.

Cooling : Water.

Ignition : Jump spark.

Drive : Bevel gear.

Transmission : Sliding gear.

Speeds : Three forward, one reverse.

Style of top : Cape cart.

Descriptive catalogue sent upon application to the above-named company.

H. H. FRANKLIN MANUFACTURING CO., SYRACUSE, N. Y.

Price

$1400

Model: **E.**

Body: **Stanhope.**

Color: **Royal blue and yellow, light brilliant green and yellow, Franklin green, Franklin red, royal blue.**

Seating capacity: **Two persons.**

Total weight: **1100 pounds.**

Wheel base: **81 inches.**

Wheel tread: **54 inches.**

Tire dimensions, front: **28 x 3 inches.**

Tire dimensions, rear: **28 x 3 inches.**

Steering: **Wheel, irreversible.**

Brakes: **Two equalizing bands on rear wheels.**

Gasoline capacity: **7 gallons.**

Frame: **Wood.**

Horse-power: **12.**

Number of cylinders: **Four.**

Cylinders arranged: **Vertically, under hood.**

Cooling: **Air.**

Ignition: **Jump spark.**

Drive: **Chain.**

Transmission: **Planetary.**

Speeds: **Two forward, one reverse.**

Descriptive catalogue sent upon application to the above-named company.

H. H. FRANKLIN MANUFACTURING CO., SYRACUSE, N. Y.

Price
$1800

Model: **G.**

Body: **Aluminum, with side entrance, detachable tonneau, divided front seats.**

Color: **Black and red, Holland blue and yellow, dark blue, Franklin red.**

Seating capacity: **Four persons.**

Total weight: **1400 pounds.**

Wheel base: **88 inches.**

Wheel tread: **54 inches.**

Tire dimensions, front: **760 x 90 m/m.**

Tire dimensions, rear: **760 x 90 m/m.**

Steering: **Wheel, irreversible.**

Brakes: **One on countershaft and two equalizing bands on rear wheels.**

Gasoline capacity: **7 gallons.**

Frame: **Wood.**

Horse-power: **12.**

Number of cylinders: **Four.**

Cylinders arranged: **Vertically, under hood.**

Cooling: **Air.**

Ignition: **Jump spark.**

Drive: **Bevel gear.**

Transmission: **Sliding gear.**

Speeds: **Three forward, one reverse.**

Descriptive catalogue sent upon application to the above-named company.

H. H. FRANKLIN MANUFACTURING CO., SYRACUSE, N. Y.

Price
$2800

Model : D.

Body : Aluminum, with side entrance, detachable tonneau, divided front seats.

Color : Dark blue, Franklin red, black and red, light brilliant green, Holland blue and yellow.

Seating capacity : Five persons.

Total weight : 1800 pounds.

Wheel base : 100 inches.

Wheel tread : 54 inches.

Tire dimensions, front : 32 x 3½ inches.

Tire dimensions, rear : 32 x 3½ inches.

Steering : Wheel, irreversible.

Brakes : One on countershaft and two equalizing bands on rear wheels.

Gasoline capacity : 12 gallons.

Frame : Wood.

Horse-power : 20.

Number of cylinders : Four.

Cylinders arranged : Vertically, under hood.

Cooling : Air.

Ignition : Jump spark.

Drive : Bevel gear.

Transmission : Sliding gear.

Speeds : Three forward, one reverse.

Descriptive catalogue sent upon application to the above-named company.

H. H. FRANKLIN MANUFACTURING CO., SYRACUSE, N. Y.

Price
$4000

Model: H.

Body: Aluminum, with side entrance, detachable tonneau, divided front seats.

Color: Dark blue, Franklin red, black and red, light brilliant green, Holland blue and yellow.

Seating capacity: Five persons.

Total weight: 2200 pounds.

Wheel base: 119 inches.

Wheel tread: 54 inches.

Tire dimensions, front: 34 x 4 inches.

Tire dimensions, rear: 34 x 4 inches.

Steering: Wheel, irreversible.

Brakes: One on countershaft and two equalizing bands on rear wheels.

Gasoline capacity: 16 gallons.

Frame: Wood.

Horse-power: 30.

Number of cylinders: Six.

Cylinders arranged: Vertically, under hood.

Cooling: Air.

Ignition: Jump spark.

Drive: Bevel gear.

Transmission: Sliding gear.

Speeds: Three forward, one reverse

Descriptive catalogue sent upon application to the above-named company.

THE HAYNES AUTOMOBILE COMPANY, KOKOMO, INDIANA

Price
$2250
With top
$2375

Model: **O.**

Body: **Wood and aluminum.**

Color: **Royal green, maroon or black.**

Seating capacity: **Five persons.**

Total weight: **2250 pounds.**

Wheel base: **97 inches.**

Wheel tread: **56 inches.**

Tire dimensions, front: **32 x 4 inches.**

Tire dimensions, rear: **32 x 4 inches.**

Steering: **Wheel.**

Brakes: **Double bands on 10-inch drums on rear wheels; internal expanding, controlled by hand lever; external contracting, controlled by foot pedal.**

Gasoline capacity: **18 gallons.**

Frame: **Pressed steel, reinforced with wood.**

Horse-power: **30.**

Number of cylinders: **Four.**

Cylinders arranged: **Vertically, under hood.**

Cooling: **Water; gear-driven pump.**

Ignition: **Jump spark; one storage battery, one set dry cells.**

Drive: **Bevel gear.**

Transmission: **Sliding gear.**

Speeds: **Three forward, one reverse.**

Style of top: **Folding extension.**

Descriptive catalogue sent upon application to the above-named company.

THE HAYNES AUTOMOBILE COMPANY, KOKOMO, INDIANA

Price

$3500
With top
$3625

Model: R.

Body: Aluminum and wood.

Color: Royal green, maroon or black.

Seating capacity: Five persons; two extra seats may be added at small additional cost.

Total weight: 2750 pounds.

Wheel base: 108 inches.

Wheel tread: 56 inches.

Tire dimensions, front: 34 x 4½ inches.

Tire dimensions, rear: 34 x 4½ inches.

Steering: Wheel.

Brakes: Double bands on 10-inch drums on rear wheels; internal expanding, controlled by hand lever; external contracting, controlled by foot pedal.

Gasoline capacity: 20 gallons.

Frame: Pressed steel, reinforced with wood.

Horse-power: 50.

Number of cylinders: Four.

Cylinders arranged: Vertically, under hood.

Cooling: Water; gear-driven pump.

Ignition: Jump spark; one storage battery, one set dry cells.

Drive: Bevel gear.

Transmission: Sliding gear.

Speeds: Three forward, one reverse.

Style of top: Folding extension.

Descriptive catalogue sent upon application to the above-named company.

HEWITT MOTOR COMPANY, 6 EAST 31st ST., NEW YORK

Price

$1500

Model: **RUNABOUT.**

Body: **Two individual seats.**

Color: **Optional.**

Seating capacity: **Two persons.**

Total weight: **1300 pounds.**

Wheel base: **72 inches.**

Wheel tread: **54½ inches.**

Tire dimensions, front: **760 x 90 m/m.**

Tire dimensions, rear: **760 x 90 m/m.**

Steering: **Wheel and worm.**

Brakes: **Internal expanding on rear wheels and differential.**

Gasoline capacity: **6½ gallons.**

Frame: **Pressed steel.**

Horse-power: **10.**

Number of cylinders: **One.**

Cylinder arranged: **Horizontally, under body.**

Cooling: **Water; pump.**

Ignition: **Low tension magneto; jump spark with battery.**

Drive: **Chain.**

Transmission: **Planetary.**

Speeds: **Two forward, one reverse.**

Style of top: **Leather.**

Descriptive catalogue sent upon application to the above-named company.

HEWITT MOTOR COMPANY, 6 EAST 31st ST., NEW YORK

Price

$1600

Model: **LIGHT DELIVERY.**

Body: **Closed.**

Color: **Optional.**

Carrying capacity: **1000 pounds.**

Total weight: **1700 pounds.**

Wheel base: **84 inches.**

Wheel tread: **54½ inches.**

Tire dimensions, front: **30 x 3 inches, solid.**

Tire dimensions, rear: **30 x 4 inches, solid.**

Steering: **Wheel and worm.**

Brakes: **Internal expanding on rear wheels and differential.**

Gasoline capacity: **7 gallons.**

Frame: **Pressed steel.**

Horse-power: **10.**

Number of cylinders: **One.**

Cylinder arranged: **Horizontally, under body.**

Cooling: **Water; pump.**

Ignition: **Wipe spark with magneto and jump spark with battery.**

Drive: **Chain.**

Transmission: **Planetary.**

Speeds: **Two forward, one reverse.**

Style of top: **Closed, wooden.**

Descriptive catalogue sent upon application to the above-named company.

HEWITT' MOTOR COMPANY, 6 EAST 31st ST., NEW YORK

Price

$2600

Model: **LIMOUSINE OR LAN-DAULET.**

Body: **Limousine or landaulet.**

Color: **Optional.**

Seating capacity: **Five persons.**

Total weight: **2000 pounds.**

Wheel base: **84 inches.**

Wheel tread: **54½ inches.**

Tire dimensions, front: **760 x 90 m/m.**

Tire dimensions, rear: **765 x 105 m/m.**

Steering: **Wheel and worm.**

Brakes: **Internal expanding on rear wheels and differential.**

Gasoline capacity: **7 gallons.**

Frame: **Pressed steel.**

Horse-power: **10.**

Number of cylinders: **One.**

Cylinder arranged: **Horizontally, under body.**

Cooling: **Water; pump.**

Ignition: **Low tension magneto; jump spark with battery.**

Drive: **Chain, with countershaft.**

Transmission: **Planetary.**

Speeds: **Two forward, one reverse.**

Descriptive catalogue sent upon application to the above-named company.

HEWITT   MOTOR   COMPANY,   6   EAST   31st   ST.,   NEW   YORK

Price

$4000
Limousine
$4500

Model : **TOURING CAR.**

Body : **Tonneau, side entrance ; or limousine.**

Color : **Optional.**

Seating capacity : **Five persons.**

Total weight : **2600 pounds.**

Wheel base : **110 inches.**

Wheel tread : **54½ inches.**

Tire dimensions, front : **875 x 105 m/m.**

Tire dimensions, rear : **875 x 105 m/m.**

Steering : **Wheel and worm.**

Brakes : **Internal expanding on rear wheels and differential.**

Gasoline capacity : **20 gallons.**

Frame : **Pressed steel.**

Horse-power : **20-30.**

Number of cylinders : **Four.**

Cylinders arranged : **Vertically, under hood ; cast in pairs.**

Cooling : **Water ; pump.**

Ignition : **Low tension magneto ; jump spark with battery.**

Drive : **Bevel gear.**

Transmission : **Sliding gear or planetary.**

Speeds : **Three forward, one reverse ; or two forward, one reverse.**

Descriptive catalogue sent upon application to the above-named company.

HEWITT MOTOR COMPANY, 6 EAST 31st ST., NEW YORK

Price

chassis
$4000

Model: **TRUCK.**

Body: **Optional.**

Color: **Optional.**

Carrying capacity: **8000 pounds.**

Total weight: **4700 pounds.**

Wheel base: **144 inches.**

Wheel tread: **66 inches.**

Tire dimensions, front: **36 x 6 inches.**

Tire dimensions, rear: **36 x 3½ inches** (two tires on each wheel).

Steering: **Wheel, rack and pinion.**

Brakes: **Internal expanding on rear wheels and differential.**

Gasoline capacity: **40 gallons;** two separate tanks.

Frame: **Pressed steel.**

Horse power: **25.**

Number of cylinders: **Four.**

Cylinders arranged: **Vertically, under hood; cast in pairs.**

Cooling: **Water; pump.**

Ignition: **Low tension magneto; jump spark with battery.**

Drive: **Double side chain.**

Transmission: **Planetary, or sliding gear.**

Speeds: **Two forward, one reverse; or three forward, one reverse.**

Descriptive catalogue sent upon application to the above-named company.

THE HOL-TAN COMPANY, BROADWAY, Cor. 56th St., NEW YORK

Price

$7000
any folding
top included

Model: F I A T.

Body: Optional.

Color: Optional.

Seating capacity: Five, seven or nine persons.

Total weight: 2600 pounds.

Wheel base: 111, 119 and 129 inches.

Wheel tread: 54 inches.

Tire dimensions, front: 910 x 90 m/m.

Tire dimensions, rear: 920 x 120 m/m.

Steering: Wheel, with worm and sector.

Brakes: Internal expanding, water cooled.

Gasoline capacity: 30 gallons.

Frame: Pressed steel.

Horse-power: 20.

Number of cylinders: Four.

Cylinders arranged: Vertically, under hood; cast in pairs.

Cooling: Water; Daimler radiator.

Ignition: Make-and-break; low tension Simms-Bosch magneto.

Drive: Double side chain.

Transmission: Selective sliding gear.

Speeds: Four forward, one reverse.

Style of top: Optional.

Descriptive catalogue sent upon application to the above-named company.

THE HOL-TAN COMPANY, BROADWAY, Cor. 56TH St., NEW YORK

Price

$9000
any folding
top included

Model: F I A T.

Body: Optional.

Color: Optional.

Seating capacity: Five, seven or nine persons.

Total weight: 3000 pounds.

Wheel base: 114, 122 and 131 inches.

Wheel tread: 54 inches.

Tire dimensions, front: 910 x 90 m/m.

Tire dimensions, rear: 920 x 120 m/m.

Steering: Wheel, with worm and sector.

Brakes: Internal expanding, water cooled.

Gasoline capacity: 30 gallons.

Frame: Pressed steel.

Horse-power: 35.

Number of cylinders: Four.

Cylinders arranged: Vertically, under hood; cast in pairs.

Cooling: Water; Daimler radiator.

Ignition: Make-and-break; low tension Simms-Bosch magneto.

Drive: Double side chain.

Transmission: Selective sliding gear.

Speeds: Four forward, one reverse.

Style of top: Optional.

Descriptive catalogue sent upon application to the above-named company.

THE HOL-TAN COMPANY, BROADWAY, Cor. 56th St., NEW YORK

Price

$12,000
any folding
top included

Model: **F I A T.**

Body: **Optional.**

Color: **Optional.**

Seating capacity: **Five, seven or nine persons.**

Total weight: **3300 pounds.**

Wheel base: **116, 124 and 134 inches.**

Wheel tread: **54 inches.**

Tire dimensions, front: **910 x 90 m/m.**

Tire dimensions, rear: **920 x 120 m/m.**

Steering: **Wheel, with worm and sector.**

Brakes: **Internal expanding, water cooled.**

Gasoline capacity: **30 gallons.**

Frame: **Pressed steel.**

Horse-power: **50.**

Number of cylinders: **Four.**

Cylinders arranged: **Vertically, under hood; cast in pairs.**

Cooling: **Water; Daimler radiator.**

Ignition: **Make-and-break; low tension Simms-Bosch magneto.**

Drive: **Double side chain.**

Transmission: **Selective sliding gear.**

Speeds: **Four forward, one reverse.**

Style of top: **Optional.**

Descriptive catalogue sent upon application to the above-named company.

KNOX AUTOMOBILE COMPANY, SPRINGFIELD, MASS.

Price

$1400
With top
$1450

Model : **F-4, TOURIST.**

Body : **As shown.**

Color : **Green.**

Seating capacity : **Two persons.**

Total weight : **1600 pounds.**

Wheel base : **81 inches.**

Wheel tread : **56 inches.**

Tire dimensions, front : **30 x 3½ inches.**

Tire dimensions, rear : **30 x 3½ inches.**

Steering : **Wheel.**

Brakes : **Two foot and one hand.**

Gasoline capacity : **8 gallons.**

Frame : **Angle steel.**

Horse-power : **14-16.**

Number of cylinders : **Two.**

Cylinders arranged : **Horizontally, opposed, under center of body.**

Cooling : **Air.**

Ignition : **Jump spark ; dry cells.**

Drive : **Chain.**

Transmission : **Planetary.**

Speeds : **Two forward, one reverse.**

Style of top : **Cloth.**

Descriptive catalogue sent upon application to the above-named company.

59

KNOX AUTOMOBILE COMPANY, SPRINGFIELD, MASS.

Price

$1800

Model: 4I.

Body: **Delivery wagon.**

Color: **Red or green.**

Carrying capacity: **1500 pounds.**

Total weight: **2700 pounds.**

Wheel base: **78 inches.**

Wheel tread: **56 inches**

Tire dimensions, front: **32 x 3½ inches.**

Tire dimensions, rear: **32 x 3½ inches.**

Steering: **Irreversible lever; Lemp check.**

Brakes: **Two foot; one hand.**

Gasoline capacity: **13 gallons.**

Frame: **Angle steel.**

Horse-power: **8-10.**

Number of cylinders: **One.**

Cylinder arranged: **Horizontally, under center of body.**

Cooling: **Air.**

Ignition: **Jump spark; dry cells.**

Drive: **Chain.**

Transmission: **Planetary.**

Speeds: **Two forward, one reverse.**

Style of top: **Metal grill.**

Descriptive catalogue sent upon application to the above-named company.

KNOX AUTOMOBILE COMPANY, SPRINGFIELD, MASS.

Model : **F, TONNEAU.**

Body : **Side entrance.**

Color : **Green.**

Seating capacity : **Five persons.**

Total weight : **2000 pounds.**

Wheel base : **90 inches.**

Wheel tread : **56 inches.**

Tire dimensions, front : **30 x 4 inches.**

Tire dimensions, rear : **30 x 4 inches.**

Steering : **Wheel or lever ; Lemp check.**

Brakes : **Two foot ; one hand.**

Gasoline capacity : **16 gallons.**

Frame : **Angle steel.**

Horse-power : **14-16.**

Number of cylinders : **Two.**

Cylinders arranged : **Horizontally, opposed, under center of body.**

Cooling : **Air.**

Ignition : **Jump spark ; dry cells.**

Drive : **Chain.**

Transmission : **Planetary.**

Speeds : **Two forward, one reverse.**

Style of top : **Cloth, extension.**

Descriptive catalogue sent upon application to the above-named company.

KNOX AUTOMOBILE COMPANY, SPRINGFIELD, MASS.

Price

$3700

With top
$3900

Model : 102.

Body : **Slat truck.**

Color : **Optional.**

Carrying capacity : **6000 pounds.**

Total weight : **5000 pounds.**

Wheel base : **111 inches.**

Wheel tread : **62 inches.**

Tire dimensions, front : **36 x 4 inches, solid.**

Tire dimensions, rear : **36 x 6 inches, solid.**

Steering : **Wheel.**

Brakes : **Two foot ; one hand.**

Gasoline capacity : **15 gallons.**

Frame : **Channel steel.**

Horse-power : **16-20.**

Number of cylinders : **Two.**

Cylinders arranged : **Horizontally, opposed, under center of body.**

Cooling : **Air.**

Ignition : **Jump spark ; dry cells.**

Drive : **Double side chain.**

Transmission : **Planetary.**

Speeds : **Two forward, one reverse.**

Style of top : **Permanent.**

Descriptive catalogue sent upon application to the above-named company.

KNOX AUTOMOBILE COMPANY, SPRINGFIELD, MASS.

Price

$4000

With top
$4200

Model: **G, TONNEAU.**

Body: **Straight line or K. of B.; side entrance.**

Color: **Optional.**

Seating capacity: **Seven persons.**

Total weight: **2800 pounds.**

Wheel base: **112 inches.**

Wheel tread: **56 inches.**

Tire dimensions, front: **34 x 4 inches.**

Tire dimensions, rear: **34 x 4½ inches.**

Steering: **Wheel, screw and nut type.**

Brakes: **Foot, on differential; hand, internal expanding, on both rear wheels—all double acting; metal to metal.**

Gasoline capacity: **20 gallons.**

Frame: **Pressed steel, without bend.**

Horse-power: **35-40.**

Number of cylinders: **Four.**

Cylinders arranged: **Vertically, under hood.**

Cooling: **Air.**

Ignition: **Jump spark; magneto and battery.**

Drive: **Double side chain.**

Transmission: **Sliding gear.**

Speeds: **Four forward, one reverse.**

Style of top: **Waterproof cloth, extension.**

Descriptive catalogue sent upon application to the above-named company.

KNOX AUTOMOBILE COMPANY, SPRINGFIELD, MASS.

Price
$5000

Model : **G, LIMOUSINE.**

Body : **Limousine, side entrance.**

Color : **Optional.**

Seating capacity : **Six persons.**

Total weight : **3200 pounds.**

Wheel base : **112 inches.**

Wheel tread : **56 inches.**

Tire dimensions, front : **34 x 4 inches.**

Tire dimensions, rear : **34 x 4½ inches.**

Steering : **Wheel, screw and nut type.**

Brakes : **Foot, on differential ; hand, internal expanding, on both rear wheels—all double acting ; metal to metal.**

Gasoline capacity : **20 gallons.**

Frame : **Pressed steel, without bend.**

Horse-power : **35-40.**

Number of cylinders : **Four.**

Cylinders arranged : **Vertically, under hood.**

Cooling : **Air.**

Ignition : **Jump spark ; magneto and battery.**

Drive : **Double side chain.**

Transmission : **Sliding gear.**

Speeds : **Four forward, one reverse.**

Style of top : **As shown.**

Descriptive catalogue sent upon application to the above-named company.

THE LOCOMOBILE COMPANY OF AMERICA, BRIDGEPORT, CONN.

Price

$2900

Model : E.

Body : Fish-tail runabout.

Color : Optional.

Seating capacity : Two persons.

Total weight : 1700 pounds.

Wheel base : 93 inches.

Wheel tread : 50 inches.

Tire dimensions, front : 32 x 4 inches.

Tire dimensions, rear : 32 x 4 inches.

Steering : Irreversible worm gear mechanism, brass column, hard rubber grip.

Brakes : Metal running brake ; internal expansion metal emergency brakes.

Gasoline capacity : 17 gallons.

Frame : Pressed steel.

Horse-power : 15-20.

Number of cylinders : Four.

Cylinders arranged : Vertically, under hood.

Cooling : Water ; cellular radiator, with gear-driven centrifugal pump.

Ignition : Made-and-break ; iridium contacts ; Locomobile magneto.

Drive : Double side chain.

Transmission : Sliding gear.

Speeds : Three forward, one reverse.

Descriptive catalogue sent upon application to the above-named company.

THE LOCOMOBILE COMPANY OF AMERICA, BRIDGEPORT, CONN.

Price

$3000

With top
$3130

Model: E.

Body: Side entrance; top irons.

Color: Optional.

Seating capacity: Five persons.

Total weight: 2000 pounds.

Wheel base: 93 inches.

Wheel tread: 50 inches.

Tire dimensions, front: 32 x 4 inches.

Tire dimensions, rear: 32 x 4 inches.

Steering: Irreversible worm gear mechanism, brass column, hard rubber grip.

Brakes: Metal running brake; internal expansion metal emergency brakes.

Gasoline capacity: 17 gallons.

Frame: Pressed steel.

Horse-power: 15-20.

Number of cylinders: Four.

Cylinders arranged: Vertically, under hood.

Cooling: Water; cellular radiator, with gear-driven centrifugal pump.

Ignition: Make-and-break; iridium contacts; Locomobile magneto.

Drive: Double side chain.

Transmission: Sliding gear.

Speeds: Three forward, one reverse.

Style of top: Cape cart hood.

Descriptive catalogue sent upon application to the above-named company.

THE LOCOMOBILE COMPANY OF AMERICA, BRIDGEPORT, CONN.

Price
$3750

Model : E.

Body : Limousine.

Color : Optional.

Seating capacity : Five persons.

Total weight : 2500 pounds.

Wheel base : 97 inches.

Wheel tread : 50 inches.

Tire dimensions, front : 32 x 4 inches.

Tire dimensions, rear : 32 x 4 inches.

Steering : Irreversible worm gear mechanism, brass column, hard rubber grip.

Brakes : Metal running brake ; internal expansion metal emergency brakes.

Gasoline capacity : 17 gallons.

Frame : Pressed steel.

Horse-power : 15-20.

Number of cylinders : Four.

Cylinders arranged . Vertically, under hood.

Cooling : Water ; cellular radiator, with gear-driven centrifugal pump

Ignition : Make-and-break ; iridium contacts ; Locomobile magneto.

Drive : Double side chain.

Transmission : Sliding gear.

Speeds : Three forward, one reverse.

Descriptive catalogue sent upon application to the above-named company.

THE LOCOMOBILE COMPANY OF AMERICA, BRIDGEPORT, CONN.

Price

$5000

Model : **H.**

Body : **Side entrance.**

Color : **Optional.**

Seating capacity: **Five to seven persons.**

Total weight : **2600 pounds.**

Wheel base : **106 inches.**

Wheel tread : **54 inches.**

Tire dimensions, front : **34 x 4½ inches.**

Tire dimensions, rear : **34 x 4½ inches.**

Steering : **Irreversible worm gear mechanism, brass column, hard rubber grip.**

Brakes : **Metal running brake; internal expansion metal emergency brakes.**

Gasoline capacity: **23 gallons.**

Frame : **Pressed steel.**

Horse-power : **30-35.**

Number of cylinders : **Four.**

Cylinders arranged : **Vertically, under hood.**

Cooling : **Water; cellular radiator, with gear-driven centrifugal pump.**

Ignition : **Make - and - break ; iridium contacts ; Locomobile magneto.**

Drive : **Double side chain.**

Transmission : **Sliding gear.**

Speeds : **Three forward, one reverse.**

Descriptive catalogue sent upon application to the above-named company.

THE LOCOMOBILE COMPANY OF AMERICA, BRIDGEPORT, CONN.

Price

$6200

Model: **H.**

Body: **Limousine.**

Color: **Optional.**

Seating capacity: **Five to seven persons.**

Total weight: **3100 pounds.**

Wheel base: **106 inches.**

Wheel tread: **54 inches.**

Tire dimensions, front: **34 x 4½ inches.**

Tire dimensions, rear: **34 x 4½ inches.**

Steering: **Irreversible worm gear mechanism, brass column, hard rubber grip.**

Brakes: **Metal running brake; internal expansion metal emergency brakes.**

Gasoline capacity: **23 gallons.**

Frame: **Pressed steel.**

Horse-power: **30-35.**

Number of cylinders: **Four.**

Cylinders arranged: **Vertically, under hood.**

Cooling: **Water; cellular radiator, with gear-driven centrifugal pump.**

Ignition: **Make-and-break; iridium contacts; Locomobile magneto.**

Drive: **Double side chain.**

Transmission: **Sliding gear.**

Speeds: **Three forward, one reverse.**

Style of top: **Limousine.**

Descriptive catalogue sent upon application to the above-named company.

THE LOCOMOBILE COMPANY OF AMERICA, BRIDGEPORT, CONN.

Price

$18,000

Model : **CUP RACER.**

Body : **Racing.**

Color : **Red.**

Seating capacity : **Two persons.**

Total weight : **2204 pounds.**

Wheel base : **110 inches.**

Wheel tread : **54 inches.**

Tire dimensions, front : **34 x 3½ inches.**

Tire dimensions, rear : **34 x 4½ inches.**

Steering: **Wheel and worm ; hard rubber grip.**

Brakes : **Metal running brake ; internal expansion metal emergency brakes.**

Gasoline capacity **33 gallons.**

Frame : **Pressed steel.**

Horse-power . **90.**

Number of cylinders . **Four.**

Cylinders arranged : **Vertically, under hood.**

Cooling : **Water, cellular radiator, with gear-driven centrifugal pump.**

Ignition : **Make-and-break ; iridium contacts ; Locomobile magneto.**

Drive : **Double side chain.**

Transmission : **Sliding gear.**

Speeds : **Three forward, one reverse.**

Descriptive catalogue sent upon application to the above-named company

LOZIER MOTOR COMPANY, BROADWAY AT 55TH ST., NEW YORK

Price
$5500
With top
$5700

Model : **D.**

Body : **Touring.**

Color : **French gray, red running gear ; or other colors.**

Seating capacity : **Seven persons.**

Total weight : **2850 pounds.**

Wheel base : **117 inches.**

Wheel tread : **56 inches.**

Tire dimensions, front : **36 x 4 inches.**

Tire dimensions, rear : **36 x 4½ inches.**

Steering : **Wheel, worm and sector.**

Brakes : **Two running, contracting on differential ; two emergency, expanding on rear wheel drums.**

Gasoline capacity : **30 gallons.**

Frame : **Pressed steel.**

Horse-power : **40.**

Number of cylinders : **Four.**

Cylinders arranged : **Vertically, under hood ; cast in pairs.**

Cooling : **Water ; fan and centrifugal pump.**

Ignition : **Double system ; jump spark ; storage battery and magneto.**

Drive : **Double side chain.**

Transmission : **Selective sliding gear ; direct on high gear.**

Speeds : **Four forward, one reverse.**

Descriptive catalogue sent upon application to the above-named company.

LOZIER MOTOR COMPANY, BROADWAY AT 55TH ST., NEW YORK

Price

$6500

Model : **D, LIMOUSINE.**

Body : **Limousine.**

Color : **Optional.**

Seating capacity : **Seven persons.**

Total weight : **3200 pounds.**

Wheel base : **117 inches.**

Wheel tread : **56 inches.**

Tire dimensions, front : **36 x 4 inches.**

Tire dimensions, rear : **36 x 4½ inches.**

Steering : **Wheel, worm and sector.**

Brakes : **Two running, contracting on differential ; two emergency, expanding on rear wheel drums.**

Gasoline capacity : **30 gallons.**

Frame : **Pressed steel.**

Horse-power : **40.**

Number of cylinders : **Four.**

Cylinders arranged : **Vertically, under hood ; cast in pairs.**

Cooling : **Water ; fan and centrifugal pump.**

Ignition : **Double system ; jump spark ; storage battery and magneto.**

Drive : **Double side chain.**

Transmission : **Selective sliding gear ; direct on high gear.**

Speeds : **Four forward, one reverse.**

Descriptive catalogue sent upon application to the above-named company.

MATHESON MOTOR CAR COMPANY, WILKESBARRE, PA.

Price
$5000

Model : **RUNABOUT.**

Body : **Aluminum.**

Color : **Optional.**

Seating capacity : **Two persons.**

Total weight : **2300 pounds.**

Wheel base : **112 inches.**

Wheel tread : **56 inches.**

Tire dimensions, front : **36 x 4 inches.**

Tire dimensions, rear : **36 x 4½ inches.**

Steering : **Wheel, irreversible.**

Brakes : **Four; two expanding clutch on rear hubs; and two band on differential sprockets, water-cooled.**

Gasoline capacity : **20 gallons.**

Frame : **Cold-pressed nickel steel.**

Horse-power : **40-45 (also 60-65).**

Number of cylinders : **Four.**

Cylinders arranged : **Vertically, under hood.**

Cooling : **Water; honeycomb radiator.**

Ignition : **Make-and-break; magneto.**

Drive : **Double side chain.**

Transmission : **Sliding gear.**

Speeds : **Three or four forward (optional), one reverse.**

Descriptive catalogue sent upon application to the above-named company.

MATHESON MOTOR CAR COMPANY, WILKESBARRE, PA.

Price

with top and
glass front
$6000

Model: **TOURING CAR.**

Body: **Aluminum, side entrance.**

Color: **Optional.**

Seating capacity: **Seven persons.**

Total weight: **2960 pounds.**

Wheel base: **112 inches.**

Wheel tread: **56 inches.**

Tire dimensions, front: **36 x 4 inches.**

Tire dimensions, rear: **36 x 4½ inches.**

Steering: **Wheel, irreversible.**

Brakes: **Four; two expanding clutch on rear hubs; and two band on differential sprockets, water-cooled.**

Gasoline capacity: **20 gallons.**

Frame: **Cold-pressed nickel steel.**

Horse-power: **40-45.**

Number of cylinders: **Four.**

Cylinders arranged: **Vertically, in front.**

Cooling: **Water; honeycomb radiator.**

Ignition: **Make-and-break; magneto.**

Drive: **Double side chain.**

Transmission: **Sliding gear.**

Speeds: **Three or four forward (optional), one reverse.**

Style of top: **Cape cart, waterproof.**

Descriptive catalogue sent upon application to the above-named company.

MATHESON   MOTOR   CAR   COMPANY,   WILKESBARRE, PA.

Price
$6500

Model: **LIMOUSINE.**

Body: **Aluminum.**

Color: **Optional.**

Seating capacity: **Seven persons.**

Total weight: **3250 pounds.**

Wheel base: **112 inches.**

Wheel tread: **56 inches.**

Tire dimensions, front: **36 x 4 inches.**

Tire dimensions, rear: **36 x 4½ inches.**

Steering: **Wheel, irreversible.**

Brakes: **Four; two expanding clutch on rear hubs ; and two band on differential sprockets, water-cooled.**

Gasoline capacity: **20 gallons.**

Frame: **Cold-pressed nickel steel.**

Horse-power: **40-45 (also 60-65).**

Number of cylinders: **Four.**

Cylinders arranged: **Vertically, in front.**

Cooling: **Water; honeycomb radiator.**

Ignition: **Make-and-break ; magneto.**

Drive: **Double side chain.**

Transmission: **Sliding gear.**

Speeds: **Three or four forward (optional), one reverse.**

Descriptive catalogue sent upon application to the above-named company.

MATHESON MOTOR CAR COMPANY, WILKESBARRE, PA.

Price

with top

$7500

Model : **TOURING CAR.**

Body : Aluminum, side entrance.

Color : Optional.

Seating capacity : Seven persons.

Total weight : 3160 pounds.

Wheel base : 118 inches.

Wheel tread : 56 inches.

Tire dimensions, front : 36 x 4 inches.

Tire dimensions, rear : 36 x 4½ inches.

Steering : Wheel, irreversible.

Brakes : Four; two expanding clutch on rear hubs ; and two band on differential sprockets, water-cooled.

Gasoline capacity : 20 gallons.

Frame : Cold-pressed nickel steel.

Horse-power : 60-65.

Number of cylinders : Four.

Cylinders arranged : Vertically, in front.

Cooling : Water; honeycomb radiator.

Ignition : Make-and-break ; magneto.

Drive : Double side chain.

Transmission : Sliding gear.

Speeds : Three or four forward (optional), one reverse.

Style of top : Cape cart, waterproof.

Descriptive catalogue sent upon application to the above-named company.

NORTHERN MANUFACTURING COMPANY, DETROIT, MICHIGAN

Price

$650

With top
$700

Model: 1906 NORTHERN RUN-
ABOUT.

Body: Wood.

Color: Carmine.

Seating capacity: Two, or four with
dos-a-dos seat.

Total weight: 1100 pounds.

Wheel base: 70 inches.

Wheel tread: 56 or 60 inches.

Tire dimensions, front: 28 x 3 inches.

Tire dimensions, rear: 28 x 3 inches.

Steering: Center lever.

Brakes: On rear axle differential and
transmission reverse.

Gasoline capacity: 7½ gallons.

Frame: Angle steel.

Horse-power: 7.

Number of cylinders: One.

Cylinder arranged: Horizontally, under
body.

Cooling: Water; 18-tube radiator and
rotary pump.

Ignition: Jump spark; batteries.

Drive: Chain.

Transmission: Planetary.

Speeds: Two forward, one reverse.

Style of top: Full leather carriage top
with front storm shield.

Descriptive catalogue sent upon application to the above-named company.

NORTHERN MANUFACTURING COMPANY, DETROIT, MICHIGAN

Price

$1700

With top
$1775

Model : **C, TWO - PASSENGER NORTHERN TOURING CAR.**

Body : **Wood.**

Color : **Body, Northern green ; gear, cream yellow.**

Seating capacity : **Two persons.**

Total weight : **1700 pounds.**

Wheel base : **88, 100 or 106 inches.**

Wheel tread : **56 inches.**

Tire dimensions, front : **30 x 4 inches.**

Tire dimensions, rear : **30 x 4 inches.**

Steering : **Wheel ; adjustable gear.**

Brakes : **Hub and transmission.**

Gasoline capacity : **10 gallons.**

Frame : **Angle steel.**

Horse-power : **20.**

Number of cylinders : **Two.**

Cylinders arranged : **Double opposed, under hood.**

Cooling : **Water ; radiator and rotary pump.**

Ignition : **Jump spark ; batteries.**

Drive : **Bevel gear.**

Transmission : **Planetary.**

Speeds : **Two forward, one reverse.**

Style of top : **Optional.**

Descriptive catalogue sent upon application to the above-named company.

NORTHERN MANUFACTURING COMPANY, DETROIT, MICHIGAN

Price

$1800
With top
$1900

Model : C, FIVE - PASSENGER NORTHERN TOURING CAR.

Body : Wood.

Color : Body, Northern green ; gear, cream yellow.

Seating capacity : Five persons.

Total weight : 2100 pounds.

Wheel base : 106 inches.

Wheel tread : 56 inches.

Tire dimensions, front : 30 x 4 inches.

Tire dimensions, rear : 30 x 4 inches.

Steering : Wheel ; adjustable gear.

Brakes : Hub and transmission.

Gasoline capacity : 10 gallons.

Frame : Angle steel.

Horse-power : 20.

Number of cylinders : Two.

Cylinders arranged : Double opposed, under hood.

Cooling : Water ; radiator and rotary pump.

Ignition : Jump spark ; batteries.

Drive : Bevel gear.

Transmission : Planetary.

Speeds : Two forward, one reverse.

Style of top : Optional.

Descriptive catalogue sent upon application to the above-named company.

NORTHERN MANUFACTURING COMPANY, DETROIT, MICHIGAN

Price

$2800

Model : **C, NORTHERN LIMOU-
SINE.**

Body : **Wood.**

Color : **Optional.**

Seating capacity : **Four or five persons.**

Total weight : **2300 pounds.**

Wheel base : **106 inches.**

Wheel tread : **56 inches.**

Tire dimensions, front : **30 x 4 inches.**

Tire dimensions, rear : **30 x 4 inches.**

Steering : **Wheel ; adjustable gear.**

Brakes : **Hubs and transmission.**

Gasoline capacity : **10 gallons.**

Frame : **Angle steel.**

Horse-power : **20.**

Number of cylinders : **Two.**

Cylinders arranged : **Double opposed,
under hood.**

Cooling : **Water ; radiator and rotary
pump.**

Ignition : **Jump spark ; batteries.**

Drive : **Bevel gear.**

Transmission : **Planetary.**

Speeds : **Two forward, one reverse.**

Descriptive catalogue sent upon application to the above-named company.

NORTHERN MANUFACTURING COMPANY, DETROIT, MICHIGAN

Price
$3000
With top
$3200

Model: **K, NORTHERN TOUR-ING CAR.**

Body: **Wood.**

Color: **Optional.**

Seating capacity: **Five or six persons.**

Total weight: **2200 pounds.**

Wheel base: **112 inches.**

Wheel tread: **56 inches.**

Tire dimensions, front: **32 x 4 inches.**

Tire dimensions, rear: **32 x 4 inches.**

Steering: **Wheel; irreversible adjustable gear.**

Brakes: **Two independent sets; one air-controlled, the other foot-controlled.**

Gasoline capacity: **18 gallons.**

Frame: **Angle steel.**

Horse-power: **30.**

Number of cylinders: **Four.**

Cylinders arranged: **Vertically, under hood.**

Cooling: **Water; radiator and gear pump.**

Ignition: **Jump spark; with storage and dry batteries.**

Drive: **Bevel gear.**

Transmission: **Sliding gear (in rear axle housing).**

Speeds: **Three forward, one reverse.**

Style of top: **Optional.**

Descriptive catalogue sent upon application to the above-named company.

OLDS   MOTOR   WORKS,   LANSING,   MICHIGAN

Price

$650

Model : **B, STRAIGHT DASH.**

Body : **Wood, piano box.**

Color : **Black with red trimmings.**

Seating capacity : **Two persons.**

Total weight : **1100 pounds.**

Wheel base : **66 inches.**

Wheel tread : **55 inches.**

Tire dimensions, front : **28 x 3 inches.**

Tire dimensions, rear : **28 x 3 inches.**

Steering : **Tiller.**

Brakes : **Transmission and rear hub, operated by pedal.**

Gasoline capacity : **5 gallons.**

Frame : **Angle steel.**

Horse-power : **7.**

Number of cylinders : **One.**

Cylinder arranged : **Horizontally, under body.**

Cooling : **Water; gear pump and copper disk radiator.**

Ignition : **Jump spark; dry cells.**

Drive : **Chain.**

Transmission : **Planetary.**

Speeds : **Two forward, one reverse.**

Style of top : **Carriage.**

Descriptive catalogue sent upon application to the above-named company.

OLDS MOTOR WORKS, LANSING, MICHIGAN

Price

$650

Model: **B, CURVED DASH.**

Body: **Wood.**

Color: **Black** with red trimmings.

Seating capacity: **Two** persons.

Total weight: **1100** pounds.

Wheel base: **66** inches.

Wheel tread: **55** inches.

Tire dimensions, front: **28 x 3** inches.

Tire dimensions, rear: **28 x 3** inches.

Steering: **Tiller.**

Brakes: **Transmission** and **rear** hub, operated by pedal.

Gasoline capacity: **5** gallons.

Frame: **Angle steel.**

Horse-power: **7.**

Number of cylinders: **One.**

Cylinder arranged: **Horizontally, under** body.

Cooling: **Water;** gear pump and copper disk radiator.

Ignition: **Jump spark;** dry cells.

Drive: **Chain.**

Transmission: **Planetary.**

Speeds: **Two forward, one reverse.**

Style of top: **Carriage.**

Descriptive catalogue sent upon application to the above-named company.

OLDS MOTOR WORKS, LANSING, MICHIGAN

Price

$1250

Model: L, THE DOUBLE-ACTION OLDS.

Body: Wood; removable rear seats; beetle baggage compartment.

Color: Gray or dark green.

Seating capacity: Four persons.

Total weight: 2100 pounds.

Wheel base: 102 inches.

Wheel tread: 55 inches.

Tire dimensions, front: 30 x 3½ inches.

Tire dimensions, rear: 30 x 3½ inches.

Steering: Wheel, irreversible; worm and nut type.

Brakes: Two; cardan shaft, operated by pedal; rear hub, operated by lever.

Gasoline capacity: 15 gallons.

Frame: Pressed steel, channel section.

Horse-power: 20-24.

Number of cylinders: Two, of the two-cycle type.

Cylinders arranged: Vertically, under hood.

Cooling: Water; gear pump and flat tube radiator.

Ignition: Jump spark; dry cells and storage cell.

Drive: Bevel gear.

Transmission: Selective sliding gear.

Speeds: Three forward, one reverse.

Style of top: Canopy or extension top furnished on special order.

Descriptive catalogue sent upon application to the above-named company.

OLDS MOTOR WORKS, LANSING, MICHIGAN

Price
$2250

Model : S.

Body : Wood, side door in both front and rear seats.

Color : Gray or dark green.

Seating capacity : Five persons.

Total weight : 2300 pounds.

Wheel base : 106 inches.

Wheel tread : 55 inches.

Tire dimensions, front : 32 x 3½ inches.

Tire dimensions, rear : 32 x 4 inches.

Steering : Wheel, irreversible ; worm and nut type.

Brakes : Two ; cardan shaft, operated by pedal ; rear hub, operated by lever.

Gasoline capacity : 15 gallons.

Frame : Pressed steel, channel section.

Horse-power : 26-28.

Number of cylinders : Four.

Cylinders arranged : Vertically, under hood.

Cooling : Water ; gear pump and flat tube radiator.

Ignition : Jump spark ; dry cells and storage cell.

Drive : Bevel gear.

Transmission : Selective sliding gear.

Speeds : Three forward, one reverse.

Style of top : Canopy or extension top furnished on special order.

Descriptive catalogue sent upon application to the above-named company.

OLDS   MOTOR   WORKS,   LANSING,   MICHIGAN

Price

with top
$2250

Model: **WAGONETTE TYPE.**

Body: **Wood.**

Color: **Optional.**

Seating capacity: **18 persons.**

Total weight: **3000 pounds.**

Wheel base: **110 inches.**

Wheel tread: **56 inches.**

Tire dimensions, front: **34 x 4 inches, solid.**

Tire dimensions, rear: **34 x 4 inches, solid.**

Steering: **Wheel, irreversible.**

Brakes: **Transmission, controlled by pedal; internal hub, controlled by hand lever.**

Gasoline capacity: **12 gallons.**

Frame: **Pressed steel.**

Horse-power: **16.**

Number of cylinders: **Two.**

Cylinders arranged: **Vertically, under seat.**

Cooling: **Water; gear pump, and radiator on front of dash.**

Ignition: **Jump spark; dry cells and storage battery.**

Drive: **Double side chain.**

Transmission: **Planetary, mounted on countershaft.**

Speeds: **Two forward, one reverse.**

Style of top: **Canopy.**

Descriptive catalogue sent upon application to the above-named company.

OLDS   MOTOR   WORKS,   LANSING,   MICHIGAN

Price
$2350

Model: **OLDSMOBILE DELIVERY.**

Body : **Wood, delivery, built to order.**

Color : **Optional.**

Carrying capacity : **3000 pounds.**

Total weight : **3000 pounds.**

Wheel base : **110 inches.**

Wheel tread : **56 inches.**

Tire dimensions, front : **34 x 4 inches, solid.**

Tire dimensions, rear : **34 x 4 inches, solid.**

Steering : **Wheel, irreversible.**

Brakes : **Transmission, controlled by pedal ; internal hub, controlled by hand lever.**

Gasoline capacity : **12 gallons.**

Frame : **Pressed steel.**

Horse-power : **16.**

Number of cylinders : **Two.**

Cylinders arranged : **Vertically, under seat.**

Cooling : **Water ; gear pump, and radiator on front of dash.**

Ignition : **Jump spark ; dry cells and storage battery.**

Drive : **Double side chain.**

Transmission : **Planetary, mounted on countershaft.**

Speeds : **Two forward, one reverse.**

Style of top : **Built to order.**

Descriptive catalogue sent upon application to the above-named company.

PACKARD MOTOR CAR COMPANY, DETROIT, MICHIGAN

Price

$4000
With top
$4100

Model: PACKARD RUNABOUT.

Body: Two-passenger.

Color: Body and frame, Richelieu blue, with black moulding ; running gear, cream yellow.

Seating capacity : Two persons.

Total weight : 2425 pounds.

Wheel base : 108 inches.

Wheel tread : 56½ inches.

Tire dimensions, front : 34 x 3½ inches.

Tire dimensions, rear : 34 x 4 inches.

Steering: Wheel, with worm and sector.

Brakes: Four, two expanding and two contracting, all acting directly on the rear wheels.

Gasoline capacity : 10 gallons.

Frame : Pressed cold-rolled steel with integral gussets.

Horse-power : 24.

Number of cylinders : Four.

Cylinders arranged : Vertically, under hood ; cast in pairs.

Cooling : Water ; tubular radiator, forced circulation.

Ignition : Jump spark ; low tension magneto and storage battery.

Drive : Bevel gear.

Transmission : Sliding gear.

Speeds : Three forward, one reverse.

Style of top : Cape cart.

Descriptive catalogue sent upon application to the above-named company.

PACKARD MOTOR CAR COMPANY, DETROIT, MICHIGAN

Price

$4000
With top
$4180

Model: **PACKARD** 24 (with extension cape cart top).

Body: **Double side entrance phaeton.**

Color: **Body and frame, Richelieu blue, with black moulding; running gear, cream yellow.**

Seating capacity: **Five persons.**

Total weight: **2820 pounds.**

Wheel base: **119 inches.**

Wheel tread: **56½ inches.**

Tire dimensions, front: **34 x 4 inches.**

Tire dimensions, rear: **34 x 4½ inches.**

Steering: **Wheel, with worm and sector.**

Brakes: **Four, two expanding and two contracting, all acting directly on the rear wheels.**

Gasoline capacity: **20 gallons.**

Frame: **Pressed cold-rolled steel with integral gussets.**

Horse-power: **24.**

Number of cylinders: **Four.**

Cylinders arranged: **Vertically, under hood; cast in pairs.**

Cooling: **Water; tubular radiator, forced circulation.**

Ignition: **Jump spark; low tension magneto and storage batteries.**

Drive: **Bevel gear.**

Transmission: **Sliding gear.**

Speeds: **Three forward, one reverse.**

Style of top: **Extension cape cart.**

Descriptive catalogue sent upon application to the above-named company.

PACKARD MOTOR CAR COMPANY, DETROIT, MICHIGAN

Price

$4000
With top
$4180 to
$4375

Model: **PACKARD** 24.

Body: Double side entrance phaeton.

Color: Body and frame, Richelieu blue, with black moulding; running gear, cream yellow.

Seating capacity: Five persons.

Total weight: 2740 pounds.

Wheel base: 119 inches.

Wheel tread: 56½ inches.

Tire dimensions, front: 34 x 4 inches.

Tire dimensions, rear: 34 x 4½ inches.

Steering: Wheel, with worm and sector.

Brakes: Four, two expanding and two contracting, all acting directly on the rear wheels.

Gasoline capacity: 20 gallons.

Frame: Pressed cold-rolled steel with integral gussets.

Horse-power: 24.

Number of cylinders: Four.

Cylinders arranged: Vertically, under hood; cast in pairs.

Cooling: Water; tubular radiator, forced circulation.

Ignition: Jump spark; low tension magneto and storage batteries.

Drive: Bevel gear.

Transmission: Sliding gear.

Speeds: Three forward, one reverse.

Style of top: Extension cape cart, victoria, canopy or touring canopy.

Descriptive catalogue sent upon application to the above-named company.

PACKARD MOTOR CAR COMPANY, DETROIT, MICHIGAN

Price

$4187.50

Model: **PACKARD 24, VICTORIA**

Body: Double phaeton.

Color: Body, Richelieu blue; gear, cream yellow.

Seating capacity: Five persons.

Total weight: 2850 pounds.

Wheel base: 119 inches.

Wheel tread: 56½ inches.

Tire dimensions, front: 34 x 4 inches.

Tire dimensions, rear: 34 x 4½ inches.

Steering: Wheel, with worm and sector.

Brakes: Four double acting, on rear wheels.

Gasoline capacity: 20 gallons.

Frame: Pressed cold-rolled steel, with integral gussets.

Horse-power: 24.

Number of cylinders: Four.

Cylinders arranged: Vertically, under hood; cast in pairs.

Cooling: Water; positive circulating tubular radiator.

Ignition: Low tension magneto and storage battery.

Drive: Bevel gear.

Transmission: Sliding gear.

Speeds: Three forward, one reverse.

Style of top: Victoria.

Descriptive catalogue sent upon application to the above-named company.

PACKARD MOTOR CAR COMPANY, DETROIT, MICHIGAN

Price

$5200

Model : **PACKARD 24, LIMOU-SINE.**

Body : Limousine.

Color : Richelieu blue, with black top and panels.

Seating capacity : Six persons.

Total weight : 3000 pounds.

Wheel base : 119 inches.

Wheel tread : 56½ inches.

Tire dimensions, front : 34 x 4 inches.

Tire dimensions, rear : 34 x 4½ inches.

Steering : Wheel, with worm and sector.

Brakes : Four, two expanding and two contracting, all acting directly on the rear wheels.

Gasoline capacity : 20 gallons.

Frame : Cold-rolled steel with integral gussets.

Horse-power : 24.

Number of cylinders : Four.

Cylinders arranged : Vertically, under hood; cast in pairs.

Cooling : Water; tubular radiator, forced circulation.

Ignition : Jump spark ; magneto and storage battery.

Drive : Bevel gear.

Transmission : Sliding gear.

Speeds : Three forward, one reverse.

Descriptive catalogue sent upon application to the above-named company.

PACKARD MOTOR CAR COMPANY, DETROIT, MICHIGAN

Price

$5225

Model: **PACKARD 24, LANDAU-LET.**

Body: Collapsible landaulet.

Color: Richelieu blue, with black top and panels.

Seating capacity: Six persons.

Total weight: 3050 pounds.

Wheel base: 119 inches.

Wheel tread: 56½ inches.

Tire dimensions, front: 34 x 4 inches.

Tire dimensions, rear: 34 x 4½ inches.

Steering: Wheel, with worm and sector.

Brakes: Four, two expanding and two contracting, all acting directly on the rear wheels.

Gasoline capacity: 20 gallons.

Frame: Pressed cold-rolled steel with integral gussets.

Horse-power: 24.

Number of cylinders: Four.

Cylinders arranged: Vertically, under hood; cast in pairs.

Cooling: Water; tubular radiator, forced circulation.

Ignition: Jump spark; magneto and storage battery.

Drive: Bevel gear.

Transmission: Sliding gear.

Speeds: Three forward, one reverse.

Descriptive catalogue sent upon application to the above-named company.

THE PEERLESS MOTOR CAR COMPANY, CLEVELAND, OHIO

Price

$3750

Model: **14 PEERLESS ROADSTER.**

Body: **Runabout.**

Color: **Optional.**

Seating capacity: **Five persons.**

Total weight: **2500 pounds.**

Wheel base: **107 inches.**

Wheel tread: **56 inches.**

Tire dimensions, front: **34 x 3½ inches.**

Tire dimensions, rear: **34 x 4½ inches.**

Steering: **Wheel.**

Brakes: **Foot and hand, on rear wheels.**

Gasoline capacity: **18 gallons.**

Frame: **Pressed steel.**

Horse-power: **30.**

Number of cylinders: **Four.**

Cylinders arranged: **Vertically, under hood.**

Cooling: **Water.**

Ignition: **Jump spark; batteries.**

Drive: **Bevel gear.**

Transmission: **Selective sliding gear.**

Speeds: **Four forward, one reverse.**

Descriptive catalogue sent upon application to the above-named company.

THE PEERLESS MOTOR CAR COMPANY, CLEVELAND, OHIO

Price

$3750
With cape cart top
$3900
Canopy or victoria
$4000

Model: 14.

Body: King of Belgians.

Color: Optional.

Seating capacity: Five persons.

Total weight: 2600 pounds.

Wheel base: 107 inches.

Wheel tread: 56 inches.

Tire dimensions, front: 34 x 3½ inches.

Tire dimensions, rear: 34 x 4½ inches.

Steering: Wheel.

Brakes: Foot and hand, on rear wheels.

Gasoline capacity: 18 gallons.

Frame: Pressed steel.

Horse-power: 30.

Number of cylinders: Four.

Cylinders arranged: Vertically, under hood.

Cooling: Water.

Ignition: Jump spark; batteries.

Drive: Bevel gear.

Transmission: Selective sliding gear.

Speeds: Four forward, one reverse.

Style of top: Cape cart, canopy or victoria.

Descriptive catalogue sent upon application to the above-named company.

THE PEERLESS MOTOR CAR COMPANY, CLEVELAND, OHIO

Price

$4500

Model: 14.

Body: Limousine.

Color: Optional.

Seating capacity : Five persons.

Wheel base : 107 inches.

Wheel tread : 56 inches.

Tire dimensions, front : 34 x 3½ inches.

Tire dimensions, rear : 34 x 4½ inches.

Steering : Wheel.

Brakes : Foot and hand, on rear wheels.

Gasoline capacity : 18 gallons.

Frame : Pressed steel.

Horse-power : 30.

Number of cylinders : Four.

Cylinders arranged : Vertically, under hood.

Cooling : Water.

Ignition : Jump spark ; batteries.

Drive : Bevel gear.

Transmission : Selective sliding gear.

Speeds : Four forward, one reverse.

Descriptive catalogue sent upon application to the above-named company.

THE PEERLESS MOTOR CAR COMPANY, CLEVELAND, OHIO

Price

$5000
With cape cart top
$5150
Canopy or victoria
$5250

Model : 15.

Body : King of Belgians.

Color : Optional.

Seating capacity : Five persons.

Total weight : 2800 pounds.

Wheel base : 114 inches.

Wheel tread : 56 inches.

Tire dimensions, front : 34 x 4 inches.

Tire dimensions, rear : 34 x 4½ inches.

Steering : Wheel.

Brakes : Foot and hand, on rear wheels.

Gasoline capacity : 18 gallons.

Frame : Pressed steel.

Horse-power : 45.

Number of cylinders : Four.

Cylinders arranged : Vertically, under hood.

Cooling : Water.

Ignition : Jump spark ; batteries.

Drive : Bevel gear.

Transmission : Selective sliding gear.

Speeds : Four forward, one reverse.

Style of top : Cape cart, canopy or victoria.

Descriptive catalogue sent upon application to the above-named company.

THE GEORGE N. PIERCE COMPANY, BUFFALO, N. Y.

Price

$900
With top
$985 and
$1000

Model: PIERCE STANHOPE.

Body: Stanhope, with folding front seat.

Color: Quaker green.

Seating capacity: Four persons.

Total weight: 1250 pounds.

Wheel base: 70 inches.

Wheel tread: 54 inches.

Tire dimensions, front: 30 x 3 inches.

Tire dimensions, rear: 30 x 3 inches.

Steering: Wheel.

Brakes: Hub.

Gasoline capacity: 5 gallons.

Frame: Shelby tubular steel.

Horse-power: 8.

Number of cylinders: One.

Cylinder arranged: Vertically.

Cooling: Water.

Ignition: Jump spark.

Drive: Spur gear.

Transmission: Planetary.

Speeds: Two forward, one reverse.

Style of top: Buggy or victoria.

Descriptive catalogue sent upon application to the above-named company.

THE GEORGE N. PIERCE COMPANY, BUFFALO, N. Y.

Price

$4000
With cape top
$4200
Victoria
$4150
Semi-enclosed top
$4350

Model : **PIERCE GREAT ARROW.**

Body : **Victoria tonneau or straight-line tonneau.**

Color : **Dark blue.**

Seating capacity : **Five persons.**

Total weight : **2700 pounds.**

Wheel base : **107 inches.**

Wheel tread : **56 inches.**

Tire dimensions, front : **34 x 4 inches.**

Tire dimensions, rear : **34 x 4½ inches.**

Steering : **Wheel.**

Brakes : **Internal and external on drums on both rear wheels.**

Gasoline capacity : **18 gallons.**

Frame : **Pressed special carbon steel, channel section.**

Horse-power : **28-32.**

Number of cylinders : **Four.**

Cylinders arranged : **Vertically, under hood.**

Cooling : **Water ; pump, radiator and fan.**

Ignition : **Jump spark.**

Drive : **Bevel gear.**

Transmission : **Sliding gear ; direct on high gear.**

Speeds : **Three forward, one reverse.**

Style of top : **Cape, victoria or canopy semi-enclosed rear.**

Descriptive catalogue sent upon application to the above-named company.

THE GEORGE N. PIERCE COMPANY, BUFFALO, N. Y.

Price

$5000
With cape top
$5200
Victoria
$5150
Semi-enclosed top
$5350

Model : **PIERCE GREAT ARROW.**

Body : **Victoria tonneau or straight-line tonneau.**

Color : **Dark Brewster green.**

Seating capacity : **Seven persons.**

Total weight : **3100 pounds.**

Wheel base : **109 inches.**

Wheel tread : **56 inches.**

Tire dimensions, front : **36 x 4½ inches.**

Tire dimensions, rear : **36 x 5 inches.**

Steering : **Wheel.**

Brakes : **Internal and external on drums on both rear wheels.**

Gasoline capacity : **20 gallons.**

Frame : **Pressed special carbon steel, channel section.**

Horse-power : **40-45.**

Number of cylinders : **Four.**

Cylinders arranged : **Vertically, under hood.**

Cooling : **Water ; pump, radiator and fan.**

Ignition : **Jump spark.**

Drive : **Bevel gear.**

Transmission : **Sliding gear ; direct on high gear.**

Speeds : **Three forward, one reverse.**

Style of top : **Cape, victoria or canopy semi-enclosed rear.**

Descriptive catalogue sent upon application to the above-named company.

THE GEORGE N. PIERCE COMPANY, BUFFALO, N. Y.

Price

$5000
With 40-45
horse-power
$6000

Model : **GREAT ARROW OPERA COACH.**

Body : **Sheet aluminum.**

Color : **Optional.**

Seating capacity : **Eight persons.**

Wheel base : **107 inches.**

Wheel tread : **56 inches.**

Tire dimensions, front : **34 x 4 inches.**

Tire dimensions, rear : **34 x 4½ inches.**

Steering : **Wheel.**

Brakes : **Internal and external on drums on both rear wheels.**

Gasoline capacity : **18 gallons.**

Frame : **Pressed special carbon steel, channel section.**

Horse-power : **28-32.**

Number of cylinders : **Four.**

Cylinders arranged : **Vertically, under hood.**

Cooling : **Water ; pump, radiator and fan.**

Ignition : **Jump spark.**

Drive : **Bevel gear.**

Transmission : **Sliding gear ; direct on high gear.**

Speeds : **Three forward, one reverse.**

Style of top : **Enclosed.**

Descriptive catalogue sent upon application to the above-named company.

THE GEORGE N. PIERCE COMPANY, BUFFALO, N. Y.

Price

$5000
With 40-45
horse-power
$6000

Model: **GREAT ARROW SUBUR-BAN.**

Body: **Cast aluminum.**

Color: **Optional.**

Seating capacity: **Seven persons.**

Wheel base : **107 inches.**

Wheel tread : **56 inches.**

Tire dimensions, front: **34 x 4 inches.**

Tire dimensions, rear: **34 x 4½ inches.**

Steering: **Wheel.**

Brakes: **Internal and external on drums on both rear wheels.**

Gasoline capacity: **18 gallons.**

Frame: **Pressed special carbon steel, channel section.**

Horse-power: **28-32.**

Number of cylinders: **Four.**

Cylinders arranged: **Vertically, under hood.**

Cooling: **Water; pump, radiator and fan.**

Ignition: **Jump spark.**

Drive: **Bevel gear.**

Transmission: **Sliding gear; direct on high gear.**

Speeds: **Three forward, one reverse.**

Style of top: **Enclosed.**

Descriptive catalogue sent upon application to the above-named company.

THE GEORGE N. PIERCE COMPANY, BUFFALO, N. Y

Price

$5250
With 40-45
horse-power
$6250

**Model: GREAT ARROW LAN-
DAULET.**

Body: Sheet aluminum.

Color: Optional.

Seating capacity: Seven persons.

Wheel base: 107 inches.

Wheel tread: 56 inches.

Tire dimensions, front: 34 x 4 inches.

Tire dimensions, rear: 34 x 4½ inches.

Steering: Wheel.

Brakes: Internal and external on
drums on both rear wheels.

Gasoline capacity: 18 gallons.

Frame: Pressed special carbon steel,
channel section.

Horse-power: 28-32.

Number of cylinders: Four.

Cylinders arranged: Vertically, under
hood.

Cooling: Water; pump, radiator and
fan.

Ignition: Jump spark.

Drive: Bevel gear.

Transmission: Sliding gear; direct on
high gear.

Speeds: Three forward, one reverse.

Style of top: Enclosed.

Descriptive catalogue sent upon application to the above-named company.

POPE MANUFACTURING COMPANY, HARTFORD, CONN.

Price

$1600

With top
$1700

Model: P O P E - H A R T F O R D,
M O D E L   G.

Body: Double side entrance.

Color: Brewster green.

Seating capacity: Five persons.

Total weight: 2000 pounds.

Wheel base: 88 inches.

Wheel tread: 56 inches.

Tire dimensions, front: 30 x 3½ inches.

Tire dimensions, rear: 30 x 3½ inches.

Steering: Wheel, worm and sector.

Brakes: Two on rear wheel drums;
one on propeller shaft.

Gasoline capacity: 11½ gallons.

Frame: Armored wood.

Horse-power: 18.

Number of cylinders Two.

Cylinders arranged: Horizontally, opposed, under hood.

Cooling: Water; pump, driven from
secondary shaft.

Ignition: Jump spark; two sets of dry
cell batteries.

Drive: Bevel gear.

Transmission: Sliding gear.

Speeds: Three forward, one reverse.

Style of top: Extension.

Descriptive catalogue sent upon application to the above-named company.

POPE MANUFACTURING COMPANY, HARTFORD, CONN.

Price

$2500
With top
$2625

Model: **POPE-HARTFORD, MODEL F.**

Body: **Double side entrance.**

Color: **Purple lake.**

Seating capacity: **Five persons.**

Total weight: **2250 pounds.**

Wheel base: **98 inches.**

Wheel tread: **56 inches.**

Tire dimensions, front: **32 x 4 inches.**

Tire dimensions, rear: **32 x 4 inches.**

Steering: **Wheel, worm and sector.**

Brakes: **Two on rear wheel drums; one on propeller shaft.**

Gasoline capacity: **15 gallons.**

Frame: **Armored wood.**

Horse-power: **28-30.**

Number of cylinders: **Four.**

Cylinders arranged: **Vertically, under hood.**

Cooling: **Water; pump, driven from secondary shaft.**

Ignition: **Jump spark.**

Drive: **Bevel gear.**

Transmission: **Sliding gear.**

Speeds: **Three forward, one reverse.**

Style of top: **Extension.**

Descriptive catalogue sent upon application to the above-named company.

POPE MANUFACTURING COMPANY, HARTFORD, CONN.

Price

$900

Model : POPE-TRIBUNE, MODEL V.

Body : Double side entrance tonneau.

Color : Tribune brown, gold striping.

Seating capacity : Four persons.

Total weight : 1500 pounds.

Wheel base : 85 inches.

Wheel tread : 56 inches.

Tire dimensions, front : 30 x 3½ inches.

Tire dimensions, rear : 30 x 3½ inches.

Steering : Hand wheel, through worm.

Brakes : Two on drum attached to rear wheels ; one on propeller shaft.

Gasoline capacity : 8 gallons.

Frame : Angle steel.

Horse-power : 14.

Number of cylinders : Two.

Cylinders arranged : Vertically, under hood.

Cooling : Water ; centrifugal pump, gear-driven from timing gear.

Ignition : Jump spark.

Drive : Bevel gear.

Transmission : Sliding gear.

Speeds : Three forward, one reverse.

Style of top : Extension when ordered, $100 extra.

Descriptive catalogue sent upon application to the above-named company.

POPE MOTOR CAR COMPANY, TOLEDO, OHIO

Price

$2800

With top

$3000

Model: **POPE-TOLEDO, TYPE X.**

Body: **Double side entrance.**

Color: **To specifications.**

Seating capacity: **Five persons.**

Total weight: **1800 pounds.**

Wheel base: **88 inches.**

Wheel tread: **54 inches.**

Tire dimensions, front: **32 x 3½ inches.**

Tire dimensions, rear: **32 x 3½ inches.**

Steering: **Wheel, irreversible; worm and segment type.**

Brakes: **Main brake on drive shaft; two band brakes on rear wheels.**

Gasoline capacity: **15 gallons.**

Frame: **Channel steel.**

Horse-power: **24.**

Number of cylinders: **Four.**

Cylinders arranged: **Vertically, under hood.**

Cooling: **Water, "planetic."**

Ignition: **Jump spark.**

Drive: **Double side chain.**

Transmission: **Sliding gear (six-pitch teeth).**

Speeds: **Three forward, one reverse.**

Style of top: **Extension cape cart, victoria or canopy.**

Descriptive catalogue sent upon application to the above-named company.

POPE MOTOR CAR COMPANY, TOLEDO, OHIO

Price

$3500

With top
$3700

Model : **POPE - TOLEDO, TYPE
XII.**

Body : **Double side entrance.**

Color : **To specifications.**

Seating capacity : **Seven persons.**

Total weight : **2500 pounds.**

Wheel base : **104 inches.**

Wheel tread : **54 inches.**

Tire dimensions, front : **34 x 4 inches.**

Tire dimensions, rear : **34 x 4 inches.**

Steering : **Irreversible ; worm and segment type.**

Brakes : **Hand lever emergency brake
and foot brake, internal expanding
type, engaging wide drum attached
to each rear wheel.**

Gasoline capacity : **17 gallons.**

Frame : **Channel steel of new design,
straight sided.**

Horse-power : **35-40.**

Number of cylinders : **Four.**

Cylinders arranged : **Vertically, under
hood.**

Cooling : **Water, "planetic."**

Ignition : **Jump spark ; coils and batteries. Provision made for magneto.**

Drive : **Double side chain.**

Transmission : **Sliding gear (six-pitch
teeth).**

Speeds : **Three forward, one reverse.**

Style of top : **Extension cape cart, victoria or canopy.**

Descriptive catalogue sent upon application to the above-named company.

POPE MOTOR CAR COMPANY, TOLEDO, OHIO

Price
$5000

Model: **POPE - TOLEDO, TYPE XII, LIMOUSINE.**

Body: **Double side entrance.**

Color: **To specifications.**

Seating capacity: **Seven persons.**

Total weight: **2900 pounds**

Wheel base: **104 inches.**

Wheel tread: **54 inches.**

Tire dimensions, front: **34 x 4 inches.**

Tire dimensions, rear: **34 x 4 inches.**

Steering: **Irreversible ; worm and segment type.**

Brakes: **Hand lever emergency brake and foot brake, internal expanding type, engaging wide drum attached to each rear wheel.**

Gasoline capacity: **17 gallons.**

Frame: **Channel steel of new design, straight sided.**

Horse-power: **35-40.**

Number of cylinders : **Four.**

Cylinders arranged: **Vertically.**

Cooling: **Water, "planetic."**

Ignition: **Jump spark; coils and batteries. Provision made for magneto.**

Drive: **Double side chain.**

Transmission: **Sliding gear (six-pitch teeth).**

Speeds: **Three forward, one reverse.**

Style of top: **Limousine.**

Descriptive catalogue sent upon application to the above-named company.

THE ROYAL MOTOR CAR COMPANY, CLEVELAND, OHIO

Price

$3500

Model : **N.**

Body : **Runabout.**

Color : **Optional.**

Seating capacity : **Two persons.**

Total weight : **2500 pounds.**

Wheel base : **110 inches.**

Wheel tread : **56 inches.**

Tire dimensions, front : **34 x 4½ inches.**

Tire dimensions, rear : **34 x 4½ inches.**

Steering : **Worm and segment.**

Brakes : **Internal expanding on rear wheels and on transmission.**

Gasoline capacity : **22 gallons.**

Frame : **Pressed steel.**

Horse-power : **40.**

Number of cylinders : **Four.**

Cylinders arranged : **Vertically, under hood ; cast in pairs.**

Cooling : **Cellular radiator.**

Ignition : **Jump spark ; storage battery.**

Drive : **Bevel gear.**

Transmission : **Sliding gear.**

Speeds : **Three forward, one reverse.**

Style of top : **Optional.**

Descriptive catalogue sent upon application to the above-named company.

THE   ROYAL   MOTOR   CAR   COMPANY,   CLEVELAND,   OHIO

Price

$3500

Model: G.

Body: King of Belgians.

Color: Standard Royal blue, or to order.

Seating capacity : Five persons.

Total weight : 2650 pounds.

Wheel base : 110 inches.

Wheel tread : 56 inches.

Tire dimensions, front : 34 x 4½ inches.

Tire dimensions, rear : 34 x 4½ inches.

Steering : Worm and segment.

Brakes : Internal expanding on rear wheels and on transmission.

Gasoline capacity : 22 gallons.

Frame : Pressed steel.

Horse-power : 40.

Number of cylinders : Four.

Cylinders arranged : Vertically, under hood ; cast in pairs.

Cooling : Cellular radiator.

Ignition : Jump spark ; storage battery.

Drive : Bevel gear.

Transmission : Sliding gear.

Speeds : Three forward, one reverse.

Style of top : Optional.

Descriptive catalogue sent upon application to the above-named company.

THE ROYAL MOTOR CAR COMPANY, CLEVELAND, OHIO

Price
$4750

Model: **H.**

Body: **Small limousine.**

Color: **Optional.**

Seating capacity: **Seven persons.**

Total weight: **2900 pounds.**

Wheel base: **110 inches.**

Wheel tread: **56 inches.**

Tire dimensions, front: **34 x 4½ inches.**

Tire dimensions, rear: **34 x 4½ inches.**

Steering: **Worm and segment.**

Brakes: **Internal expanding on rear wheels and on transmission.**

Gasoline capacity: **22 gallons.**

Frame: **Pressed steel.**

Horse-power: **40.**

Number of cylinders: **Four.**

Cylinders arranged: **Vertically, under hood; cast in pairs.**

Cooling: **Cellular radiator.**

Ignition: **Jump spark; storage battery.**

Drive: **Bevel gear.**

Transmission: **Sliding gear.**

Speeds: **Three forward, one reverse.**

Descriptive catalogue sent upon application to the above-named company.

THE ROYAL MOTOR CAR COMPANY, CLEVELAND, OHIO

Price

$5000

Model: **J.**

Body: **Large limousine.**

Color: **Optional.**

Seating capacity: **Seven persons.**

Total weight : **3000 pounds.**

Wheel base : **110 inches.**

Wheel tread: **56 inches.**

Tire dimensions, front : **34 x 4½ inches.**

Tire dimensions, rear : **34 x 4½ inches**

Steering : **Worm and segment.**

Brakes : **Internal expanding on rear wheels and on transmission.**

Gasoline capacity: **22 gallons.**

Frame : **Pressed steel.**

Horse-power : **40.**

Number of cylinders : **Four.**

Cylinders arranged : **Vertically, under hood ; cast in pairs.**

Cooling : **Cellular radiator.**

Ignition : **Jump spark ; storage battery.**

Drive : **Bevel gear.**

Transmission : **Sliding gear.**

Speeds : **Three forward, one reverse.**

Descriptive catalogue sent upon application to the above-named company.

THE ROYAL MOTOR CAR COMPANY, CLEVELAND, OHIO

Price
$4000

Model : M.

Body : Demi-limousine.

Color : Optional.

Seating capacity : Five persons.

Total weight : 2750 pounds.

Wheel base : 110 inches.

Wheel tread : 56 inches.

Tire dimensions, front . 34 x 4½ inches.

Tire dimensions, rear : 34 x 4½ inches.

Steering : Worm and segment.

Brakes : Internal expanding on rear wheels and on transmission.

Gasoline capacity : 22 gallons.

Frame : Pressed steel.

Horse-power : 50.

Number of cylinders : Four.

Cylinders arranged : Vertically, under hood ; cast in pairs.

Cooling : Cellular radiator.

Ignition : Jump spark ; storage battery.

Drive : Bevel gear.

Transmission : Sliding gear.

Speeds : Three forward, one reverse.

Style of top : Optional.

Descriptive catalogue sent upon application to the above-named company.

SMITH & MABLEY, INC., 1763 BROADWAY (57TH ST.), NEW YORK

Price

chassis
$5000
Body
$750 to
$2000

Model: **SMITH & MABLEY SIM-PLEX** 1906.

Body: **Optional.**

Color: **Optional.**

Seating capacity: **5 to 7 persons.**

Total weight: **Chassis, 2100 pounds.**

Wheel base: **106 to 112 inches.**

Wheel tread: **56 inches.**

Tire dimensions, front: **910 x 90 m/m.**

Tire dimensions, rear: **920 x 120 m/m.**

Steering: **Wheel, positive worm and sector.**

Brakes: **Foot, on differential; emergency, on both rear wheels.**

Gasoline capacity: **25 to 28 gallons.**

Frame: **Pressed steel.**

Horse-power: **30.**

Number of cylinders: **Four.**

Cylinders arranged: **Vertically, under hood; cast in pairs.**

Cooling: **Water; centrifugal pump, radiator and fan.**

Ignition: **Jump spark; coil or magneto, or both.**

Drive: **Double side chain.**

Transmission: **Sliding gear.**

Speeds: **Four forward, one reverse.**

Style of top: **Optional.**

Descriptive catalogue sent upon application to the above-named company.

SMITH & MABLEY, INC., 1763 BROADWAY (57TH ST.), NEW YORK

Price
chassis
$8400
Body
**$750 to
$2000**

Model : **MERCEDES, 1906.**

Body : **Optional.**

Color : **Optional.**

Seating capacity : **5 to 7 persons.**

Total weight : **2100 to 2300 pounds.**

Wheel base : **125 inches.**

Wheel tread : **56 inches.**

Tire dimensions, front : **910 x 90 m/m.**

Tire dimensions, rear : **920 x 120 m/m.**

Steering : **Wheel, positive worm and sector.**

Brakes : **Foot, on differential and on countershaft; emergency, on rear wheels.**

Gasoline capacity : **25 to 28 gallons.**

Frame : **Pressed steel.**

Horse-power : **35 (also 45).**

Number of cylinders : **Four.**

Cylinders arranged : **Vertically, under hood; cast in pairs.**

Cooling : **Water; centrifugal pump, radiator and fan.**

Ignition : **Make-and-break; magneto.**

Drive : **Double side chain.**

Transmission : **Sliding gear.**

Speeds : **Four forward, one reverse.**

Style of top : **Optional.**

Descriptive catalogue sent upon application to the above-named company.

SMITH & MABLEY, INC., 1763 BROADWAY (57TH ST.), NEW YORK

Price

chassis

$6000

Body

**$750 to
$2000**

Model: **PANHARD-LEVASSOR.**

Body: **Optional.**

Color: **Optional.**

Seating capacity: **Five to seven persons**

Total weight: **3000 pounds.**

Wheel base: **109 inches.**

Wheel tread: **56 inches.**

Tire dimensions, front: **910 x 90 m/m.**

Tire dimensions, rear: **910 x 90 m/m.**

Steering: **Wheel, worm and sector.**

Brakes: **On differential, and on rear wheels.**

Gasoline capacity. **25 gallons.**

Frame: **Armored wood, steel reinforced.**

Horse-power: **24 (also 15, 18, 35 and 50).**

Number of cylinders: **Four.**

Cylinders arranged: **Vertically, under hood; cast separately.**

Cooling: **Water; centrifugal pump, radiator and fan.**

Ignition: **Jump spark; battery and magneto.**

Drive: **Double side chain.**

Transmission: **Sliding gear.**

Speeds: **Four forward, one reverse.**

Style of top: **Optional.**

Descriptive catalogue sent upon application to the above-named company.

SMITH & MABLEY, INC., 1763 BROADWAY (57TH ST.), NEW YORK

Price

chassis
$5400
Body
$750 to
$2000

Model: **RENAULT.**

Body: Optional.

Color: Optional.

Seating capacity: Five to seven persons

Total weight: 3400 pounds.

Wheel base: 115 inches.

Wheel tread: 54 inches.

Tire dimensions, front: 870 x 90 m/m.

Tire dimensions, rear: 875 x 105 m/m.

Steering: Wheel, worm and sector.

Brakes: On driving shaft and rear wheels.

Gasoline capacity: 20 gallons.

Frame: Pressed steel.

Horse-power: 20-30 (also 10-14, 14-20 and 35-45).

Number of cylinders: Four.

Cylinders arranged: Vertically, under hood; cast in pairs.

Cooling: Water; thermo-syphon system; radiator on dash.

Ignition: Jump spark; magneto.

Drive: Bevel gear.

Transmission: Sliding and drop gear.

Speeds: Three forward, one reverse.

Style of top: Optional.

Descriptive catalogue sent upon application to the above-named company.

THE F. B. STEARNS COMPANY, CLEVELAND, OHIO

Price
$4250

Model: **STEARNS, 40-45.**

Body: **Cast aluminum, French type, double side door.**

Color: **Optional.**

Seating capacity: **Five to seven persons.**

Total weight: **3000 pounds.**

Wheel base: **118 inches.**

Wheel tread: **56 inches.**

Tire dimensions, front: **36 x 4 inches.**

Tire dimensions, rear: **36 x 4½ inches.**

Steering: **Wheel.**

Brakes: **Expanding on rear hubs, foot on differential.**

Gasoline capacity: **25 gallons.**

Frame: **Pressed steel.**

Horse-power: **40-45.**

Number of cylinders: **Four.**

Cylinders arranged: **Vertically, under hood; cast in pairs.**

Cooling: **Water.**

Ignition: **High tension magneto.**

Drive: **Double side chain.**

Transmission: **Sliding gear.**

Speeds: **Four forward, one reverse.**

Style of top: **Optional.**

Descriptive catalogue sent upon application to the above-named company.

THE F. B. STEARNS COMPANY, CLEVELAND, OHIO

Price

$4600

Model : **STEARNS, 40-45.**

Body : **Cast aluminum, French type, double side door.**

Color : **Optional.**

Seating capacity : **Five to seven persons.**

Total weight : **3000 pounds.**

Wheel base : **118 inches.**

Wheel tread : **56 inches.**

Tire dimensions, front : **36 x 4 inches.**

Tire dimensions, rear : **36 x 4½ inches.**

Steering : **Wheel.**

Brakes : **Expanding on rear hubs, foot on differential.**

Gasoline capacity : **25 gallons.**

Frame : **Pressed steel.**

Horse-power : **40-45.**

Number of cylinders : **Four.**

Cylinders arranged : **Vertically, under hood ; cast in pairs.**

Cooling : **Water.**

Ignition : **High tension magneto.**

Drive : **Double side chain.**

Transmission : **Sliding gear.**

Speeds : **Four forward, one reverse.**

Style of top : **Optional.**

Descriptive catalogue sent upon application to the above-named company.

THE F. B. STEARNS COMPANY, CLEVELAND, OHIO

Price
$5200

Model: **STEARNS, 40-45.**

Body: **Cast aluminum, French type, double side door.**

Color: **Optional.**

Seating capacity: **Five to seven persons.**

Total weight: **3000 pounds.**

Wheel base: **118 inches.**

Wheel tread: **56 inches.**

Tire dimensions, front: **36 x 4 inches.**

Tire dimensions, rear: **36 x 4½ inches.**

Steering: **Wheel.**

Brakes: **Expanding on rear hubs, foot on differential.**

Gasoline capacity: **25 gallons.**

Frame: **Pressed steel.**

Horse-power: **40-45.**

Number of cylinders: **Four.**

Cylinders arranged: **Vertically, under hood; cast in pairs.**

Cooling: **Water.**

Ignition: **High tension magneto.**

Drive: **Double side chain.**

Transmission: **Sliding gear.**

Speeds: **Four forward, one reverse.**

Style of top: **Optional.**

Descriptive catalogue sent upon application to the above-named company.

J. STEVENS ARMS & TOOL CO., CHICOPEE FALLS, MASS.

Price

$1250
With top
$1300

Model: **L, STEVENS-DURYEA.**

Body: **Wood ; folding front seat.**

Color: **Maroon.**

Seating capacity : **Two or four persons.**

Total weight : **1350 pounds.**

Wheel base : **69 inches.**

Wheel tread : **54 inches.**

Tire dimensions, front : **28 x 3 inches.**

Tire dimensions, rear : **28 x 3½ inches.**

Steering: **One spoke of steering-wheel.**

Brakes : **Two.**

Gasoline capacity : **6 gallons.**

Frame : **Tubular.**

Horse-power : **7.**

Number of cylinders : **Two.**

Cylinders arranged : **Horizontally, op-posed, under body.**

Cooling : **Water.**

Ignition : **Jump spark.**

Drive : **Chain.**

Transmission : **Individual clutch.**

Speeds : **Three forward, one reverse.**

Style of top : **Victoria or buggy.**

Descriptive catalogue sent upon application to the above-named company.

J. STEVENS ARMS & TOOL CO., CHICOPEE FALLS, MASS.

Price

$2400

Model : **R, STEVENS - DURYEA FOUR-CYLINDER RUNABOUT.**

Body : **Aluminum, tulip style.**

Color : **Brewster green.**

Seating capacity : **Two persons.**

Total weight : **1650 pounds.**

Wheel base : **90 inches.**

Wheel tread : **56 inches.**

Tire dimensions, front : **30 x 3½ inches.**

Tire dimensions, rear : **30 x 3½ inches.**

Steering : **Wheel.**

Brakes : **Two.**

Gasoline capacity : **14 gallons.**

Frame : **Pressed steel.**

Horse-power : **20.**

Number of cylinders : **Four.**

Cylinders arranged : **Vertically, under hood ; cast separately.**

Cooling : **Water.**

Ignition : **Jump spark.**

Drive : **Bevel gear.**

Transmission : **Sliding gear.**

Speeds : **Three forward, one reverse.**

Style of top : **Extension folding.**

Descriptive catalogue sent upon application to the above-named company.

J. STEVENS ARMS & TOOL CO., CHICOPEE FALLS, MASS.

Price

$2500
With top
$2600

Model: **R, STEVENS-DURYEA.**

Body: **Aluminum, tulip style ; side entrance.**

Color: **Brewster green.**

Seating capacity : **Five persons.**

Total weight : **1700 pounds.**

Wheel base : **90 inches.**

Wheel tread : **56 inches.**

Tire dimensions, front : **30 x 3½ inches.**

Tire dimensions, rear : **30 x 3½ inches.**

Steering : **Wheel.**

Brakes : **Two.**

Gasoline capacity : **14 gallons.**

Frame : **Pressed steel.**

Horse-power : **20.**

Number of cylinders : **Four.**

Cylinders arranged : **Vertically, under hood ; cast separately.**

Cooling : **Water.**

Ignition : **Jump spark.**

Drive : **Bevel gear.**

Transmission : **Sliding gear.**

Speeds : **Three forward, one reverse.**

Style of top : **Extension folding.**

Descriptive catalogue sent upon application to the above-named company.

J. STEVENS ARMS & TOOL CO., CHICOPEE FALLS, MASS.

Price
$3300

Model : **R, STEVENS - DURYEA LIMOUSINE.**

Body : **Limousine.**

Color : **Optional.**

Seating capacity : **Four persons.**

Total weight : **2000 pounds.**

Wheel base : **90 inches.**

Wheel tread : **56 inches.**

Tire dimensions, front : **31 x 4 inches.**

Tire dimensions, rear : **31 x 4 inches.**

Steering : **Wheel.**

Brakes : **Two.**

Gasoline capacity : **14 gallons.**

Frame : **Pressed steel.**

Horse-power : **20.**

Number of cylinders : **Four.**

Cylinders arranged · **Vertically, under hood ; cast separately.**

Cooling : **Water.**

Ignition : **Jump spark.**

Drive : **Bevel gear.**

Transmission : **Sliding gear.**

Speeds : **Three forward, one reverse.**

Style of top : **Limousine.**

Descriptive catalogue sent upon application to the above-named company.

J. STEVENS ARMS & TOOL CO., CHICOPEE FALLS, MASS.

Price
with top
$5000

Model: **STEVENS-DURYEA BIG 6** (unit power plant).

Body: **Side entrance.**

Color: **Optional.**

Seating capacity: **Seven persons.**

Total weight: **2900 pounds.**

Wheel base: **122 inches.**

Wheel tread: **56 inches.**

Tire dimensions, front: **34 x 4½ inches.**

Tire dimensions, rear: **34 x 4½ inches.**

Steering: **Wheel.**

Brakes: **Two; both rear axle.**

Gasoline capacity: **22 gallons.**

Frame: **Pressed steel, channel; high carbon.**

Horse-power · **50.**

Number of cylinders: **Six.**

Cylinders arranged: **Vertically, under hood.**

Cooling: **Water.**

Ignition: **Jump spark.**

Drive: **Bevel gear.**

Transmission: **Sliding gear; direct on high gear.**

Speeds: **Three forward, one reverse.**

Style of top: **Extension folding.**

Descriptive catalogue sent upon application to the above-named company.

STUDEBAKER AUTOMOBILE COMPANY, SOUTH BEND, INDIANA

Price

$2600

Model: **STUDEBAKER E-20.**

Body: **Studebaker light construction, with special reinforcements.**

Color: **Dark blue, maroon, dark green or pearl gray.**

Seating capacity: **Five persons.**

Total weight: **2400 pounds.**

Wheel base: **98 inches.**

Wheel tread: **54 inches.**

Tire dimensions, front: **32 x 4 inches.**

Tire dimensions, rear: **32 x 4 inches.**

Steering: **Irreversible wheel.**

Brakes: **Foot, on propeller shaft; hand, on drums on both rear wheels.**

Gasoline capacity: **14 gallons.**

Frame: **Pressed steel.**

Horse-power: **20.**

Number of cylinders: **Four.**

Cylinders arranged: **Vertically, under hood.**

Cooling: **Water; gear-driven centrifugal pump, cellular radiator and fan.**

Ignition: **Jump spark; storage batteries.**

Drive: **Bevel gear.**

Transmission: **Sliding gear; direct on high gear.**

Speeds: **Three forward, one reverse.**

Style of top: **Optional.**

Descriptive catalogue sent upon application to the above-named company.

STUDEBAKER AUTOMOBILE COMPANY, SOUTH·BEND, INDIANA

Price
$3000

Model: **STUDEBAKER F-28.**

Body: **Studebaker light construction, with special reinforcements.**

Color: **Dark blue, maroon, dark green or pearl gray.**

Seating capacity: **Five persons.**

Total weight: **2700 pounds.**

Wheel base: **104 inches.**

Wheel tread: **54 inches.**

Tire dimensions, front: **34 x 4 inches.**

Tire dimensions, rear: **34 x 4 inches.**

Steering: **Wheel, irreversible.**

Brakes: **Internal and external on both rear wheels.**

Gasoline capacity: **14 gallons.**

Frame: **Pressed steel.**

Horse-power: **28.**

Number of cylinders: **Four.**

Cylinders arranged: **Vertically, under hood.**

Cooling: **Water; gear-driven pump, radiator and fan.**

Ignition: **Jump spark; storage batteries.**

Drive: **Bevel gear.**

Transmission: **Sliding gear; direct on high gear.**

Speeds: **Three forward, one reverse.**

Style of top: **Optional.**

Descriptive catalogue sent upon application to the above-named company.

STUDEBAKER AUTOMOBILE COMPANY, SOUTH BEND, INDIANA

Price
$3700

Model : **STUDEBAKER G-30.**

Body : **Studebaker light construction, with special reinforcements.**

Color : **Dark blue, maroon, dark green or pearl gray.**

Seating capacity : **Five persons.**

Total weight : **2700 pounds.**

Wheel base : **104 inches.**

Wheel tread : **56 inches.**

Tire dimensions, front : **34 x 4 inches.**

Tire dimensions, rear : **34 x 4 inches.**

Steering : **Wheel, irreversible.**

Brakes : **Foot, on propeller shaft ; hand, on drums on both rear wheels.**

Gasoline capacity : **14 gallons.**

Frame : **Pressed steel.**

Horse-power : **30.**

Number of cylinders : **Four.**

Cylinders arranged : **Vertically, under hood.**

Cooling : **Water ; gear-driven pump, radiator and fan.**

Ignition : **Make-and-break ; magneto.**

Drive : **Bevel gear.**

Transmission : **Sliding gear ; direct on high gear.**

Speeds : **Three forward, one reverse.**

Style of top : **Optional.**

Descriptive catalogue sent upon application to the above-named company.

STUDEBAKER AUTOMOBILE COMPANY, SOUTH BEND, INDIANA

Price

$4000

Model: **STUDEBAKER E-20 TOWN CAR.**

Body: **Studebaker light construction, with special reinforcements.**

Color: **Optional.**

Seating capacity: **Five persons.**

Total weight: **2750 pounds.**

Wheel base: **98 inches.**

Wheel tread: **54 inches.**

Tire dimensions, front: **32 x 4½ inches.**

Tire dimensions, rear: **32 x 4½ inches.**

Steering: **Wheel, irreversible.**

Brakes: **Foot, on propeller shaft; hand, on drums on both rear wheels.**

Gasoline capacity: **14 gallons.**

Frame: **Pressed steel.**

Horse-power: **20.**

Number of cylinders: **Four.**

Cylinders arranged: **Vertically, under hood.**

Cooling: **Water; gear-driven centrifugal pump, cellular radiator and fan.**

Ignition: **Jump spark; storage batteries.**

Drive: **Bevel gear.**

Transmission: **Sliding gear; direct on high gear.**

Speeds: **Three forward, one reverse.**

Descriptive catalogue sent upon application to the above-named company.

E. R. THOMAS MOTOR COMPANY, BUFFALO, N. Y.

Price

$3500
With top and
glass front

$3700

Model : 3I, **THOMAS FLYER.**

Body : **Touring.**

Color : **Optional.**

Seating capacity : **Seven persons.**

Total weight : **3200 pounds.**

Wheel base : **118 inches.**

Wheel tread : **56½ inches.**

Tire dimensions, front : **34 x 4½ inches.**

Tire dimensions, rear : **34 x 4½ inches.**

Steering : **Wheel, with worm and sector.**

Brakes : **Two internal expanding, two external contracting, ratchet and pawl safety device, all on rear hubs.**

Gasoline capacity : **20 gallons.**

Frame : **Cold-pressed steel, reinforced and trussed.**

Horse-power : **50.**

Number of cylinders : **Four.**

Cylinders arranged : **Vertically, under hood.**

Cooling : **Water ; fan.**

Ignition : **Jump spark ; single coil ; storage battery or magneto.**

Drive : **Double side chain.**

Transmission : **Selective sliding gear.**

Speeds : **Four forward, one reverse.**

Style of top : **Cape or extension.**

Descriptive catalogue sent upon application to the above-named company.

E. R. THOMAS MOTOR COMPANY, BUFFALO, N. Y.

Price
$4000

Model: 34.

Body: Semi-limousine.

Color: Optional.

Seating capacity: Seven persons.

Total weight: 3300 pounds.

Wheel base: 118 inches.

Wheel tread: 56½ inches.

Tire dimensions, front: 34 x 4½ inches.

Tire dimensions, rear: 34 x 4½ inches.

Steering: Wheel, with worm and sector.

Brakes: Two internal expanding, two external contracting, ratchet and pawl safety device, all on rear hubs.

Gasoline capacity: 20 gallons.

Frame: Cold-pressed steel, reinforced and trussed,

Horse-power: 50.

Number of cylinders: Four.

Cylinders arranged: Vertically, under hood.

Cooling: Water; fan.

Ignition: Jump spark; single coil; storage battery or magneto.

Drive: Double side chain.

Transmission: Selective sliding gear.

Speeds: Four forward, one reverse.

Descriptive catalogue sent upon application to the above-named company.

E. R. THOMAS MOTOR COMPANY, BUFFALO, N. Y.

Price.

$4500

Model : 32.

Body : **Limousine.**

Color : **Optional.**

Seating capacity : **Seven persons.**

Total weight : **3500 pounds.**

Wheel base : **118 inches.**

Wheel tread : **56½ inches.**

Tire dimensions, front : **34 x 4½ inches.**

Tire dimensions, rear : **34 x 5 inches.**

Steering : **Wheel, with worm and sector.**

Brakes : **Two internal expanding, two external contracting, ratchet and pawl safety device, all on rear hubs.**

Gasoline capacity : **20 gallons.**

Frame : **Cold-pressed steel, reinforced and trussed.**

Horse-power : **50.**

Number of cylinders : **Four.**

Cylinders arranged : **Vertically, under hood.**

Cooling : **Water; fan.**

Ignition : **Jump spark; single coil; storage battery or magneto.**

Drive : **Double side chain.**

Transmission : **Selective sliding gear.**

Speeds : **Four forward, one reverse.**

Descriptive catalogue sent upon application to the above-named company.

E. R. THOMAS MOTOR COMPANY, BUFFALO. N. Y.

Price

$4600

Model : **33.**

Body : **Landaulet.**

Color : **Optional.**

Seating capacity : **Seven persons.**

Total weight : **3500 pounds.**

Wheel base : **118 inches.**

Wheel tread : **56½ inches.**

Tire dimensions, front : **34 x 4½ inches.**

Tire dimensions, rear : **34 x 5 inches.**

Steering : **Wheel, with worm and sector.**

Brakes : **Two internal expanding, two external contracting, ratchet and pawl safety device, all on rear hubs.**

Gasoline capacity : **20 gallons.**

Frame : **Cold-pressed steel, reinforced and trussed.**

Horse-power : **50.**

Number of cylinders : **Four.**

Cylinders arranged : **Vertically, under hood.**

Cooling : **Water ; fan.**

Ignition : **Jump spark ; single coil ; storage battery or magneto.**

Drive : **Double side chain.**

Transmission : **Selective sliding gear.**

Speeds : **Four forward, one reverse.**

Descriptive catalogue sent upon application to the above-named company.

WALTER AUTOMOBILE COMPANY, 49–51 WEST 66TH ST., NEW YORK

Price

$4000

With limousine body

$4700

Model: **WALTER, SIDE ENTRANCE PHAETON.**

Body: **Aluminum.**

Color: **Optional.**

Seating capacity: **Five to seven persons.**

Total weight: **2800 pounds.**

Wheel base: **110 to 122 inches.**

Wheel tread: **56 inches.**

Tire dimensions, front: **34 x 4½ inches.**

Tire dimensions, rear: **34 x 4½ inches.**

Steering: **Wheel, worm and segment.**

Brakes: **Two internal expansion, on rear hubs; foot, on differential.**

Gasoline capacity: **30 gallons.**

Frame: **Pressed steel.**

Horse-power: **40.**

Number of cylinders: **Four.**

Cylinders arranged: **Vertically, under hood; cast in pairs.**

Cooling: **Water; honeycomb radiator.**

Ignition: **Jump spark; storage battery and magneto.**

Drive: **Bevel gear.**

Transmission **Double sliding gear; direct on high gear.**

Speeds: **Three forward, one reverse.**

Style of top: **None furnished—body fitted for one.**

Descriptive catalogue sent upon application to the above-named company.

WALTHAM MANUFACTURING COMPANY, WALTHAM, MASS.

Price

$400

With top

$412

Model: **ORIENT, BB.**

Body: **Wood.**

Color: **Natural wood; carmine running gear.**

Seating capacity: **Two persons.**

Total weight: **600 pounds.**

Wheel base: **80 inches.**

Wheel tread: **42 inches (or 56, extra).**

Tire dimensions, front: **26 x 2½ inches.**

Tire dimensions, rear: **26 x 2½ inches.**

Steering: **Tiller.**

Brakes: **External bands on both rear hubs, with foot lever.**

Gasoline capacity: **3½ gallons.**

Frame: **Ash.**

Horse-power: **4.**

Number of cylinders: **One.**

Cylinder arranged: **In rear of car.**

Cooling: **Air.**

Ignition: **Jump spark; dry batteries.**

Drive: **Double side chain.**

Transmission: **Friction discs.**

Speeds: **Innumerable, forward and reverse.**

Style of top: **Canopy.**

Descriptive catalogue sent upon application to the above-named company.

WALTHAM   MANUFACTURING   COMPANY,   WALTHAM,   MASS.

Price

$1600
With top
$1700

Model: **K, WALTHAM-ORIENT.**

Body: **Wood.**

Color: **Quaker green; carmine running gear.**

Seating capacity: **Two persons.**

Total weight: **1300 pounds.**

Wheel base: **82 inches.**

Wheel tread: **56 inches.**

Tire dimensions, front: **30 x 3½ inches.**

Tire dimensions, rear: **30 x 3½ inches.**

Steering: **Wheel.**

Brakes: **Foot, on transmission shaft; hand, external bands on rear hubs.**

Gasoline capacity: **7 gallons.**

Frame: **Pressed steel.**

Horse-power: **16.**

Number of cylinders: **Four.**

Cylinders arranged: **Vertically, under hood.**

Cooling: **Air.**

Ignition: **Jump spark; storage and dry batteries.**

Drive: **Bevel gear.**

Transmission: **Sliding gear.**

Speeds: **Three forward, one reverse.**

Style of top: **Buggy or victoria.**

Descriptive catalogue sent upon application to the above-named company.

WALTHAM MANUFACTURING COMPANY, WALTHAM, MASS.

Price

$1750

With top

$1850

Model : **M, WALTHAM-ORIENT.**

Body : **Wood.**

Color : **Quaker green ; carmine running gear.**

Seating capacity : **Four persons.**

Total weight : **1450 pounds.**

Wheel base : **82 inches.**

Wheel tread : **56 inches.**

Tire dimensions, front : **30 x 3½ inches.**

Tire dimensions, rear : **30 x 3½ inches.**

Steering : **Wheel.**

Brakes : **Foot, on transmission shaft ; hand, external bands on rear hubs.**

Gasoline capacity : **7 gallons.**

Frame : **Pressed steel.**

Horse-power : **16.**

Number of cylinders : **Four.**

Cylinders arranged : **Vertically, under hood.**

Cooling · **Air.**

Ignition : **Jump spark ; storage and dry batteries.**

Drive : **Bevel gear.**

Transmission : **Sliding gear.**

Speeds : **Three forward, one reverse.**

Style of top : **Cape cart.**

Descriptive catalogue sent upon application to the above-named company.

WALTHAM   MANUFACTURING   COMPANY,   WALTHAM,   MASS.

Price

$1750
With top
$1850

Model: **L, WALTHAM-ORIENT.**

Body: **Wood.**

Color: **Quaker green ; carmine running gear.**

Seating capacity: **Five persons.**

Total weight: **1450 pounds.**

Wheel base: **82 inches.**

Wheel tread: **56 inches.**

Tire dimensions, front: **30 x 3½ inches.**

Tire dimensions, rear: **30 x 3½ inches.**

Steering: **Wheel.**

Brakes: **Foot, on transmission shaft ; hand, external bands on rear hubs.**

Gasoline capacity: **8 gallons.**

Frame : **Pressed steel.**

Horse-power : **16.**

Number of cylinders : **Four.**

Cylinders arranged : **Vertically, under hood.**

Cooling : **Air.**

Ignition : **Jump spark ; storage and dry batteries.**

Drive : **Bevel gear.**

Transmission : **Sliding gear.**

Speeds : **Three forward, one reverse.**

Style of top : **Cape cart.**

Descriptive catalogue sent upon application to the above-named company.

WALTHAM MANUFACTURING COMPANY, WALTHAM, MASS.

Price

$2000
With top
$2125

Model: **N, WALTHAM-ORIENT.**

Body : **Wood.**

Color : **Quaker green ; carmine running gear.**

Seating capacity : **Five persons.**

Total weight : **1800 pounds.**

Wheel base : **96 inches.**

Wheel tread : **56 inches.**

Tire dimensions, front : **32 x 3½ inches.**

Tire dimensions, rear : **32 x 3½ inches.**

Steering : **Wheel.**

Brakes : **Foot, on transmission shaft ; hand, external bands on rear hubs.**

Gasoline capacity : **10 gallons.**

Frame : **Pressed steel.**

Horse-power : **20.**

Number of cylinders : **Four.**

Cylinders arranged : **Vertically, under hood.**

Cooling : **Air.**

Ignition : **Jump spark ; storage and dry batteries.**

Drive : **Bevel gear.**

Transmission : **Sliding gear.**

Speeds : **Three forward, one reverse.**

Style of top : **Cape cart.**

Descriptive catalogue sent upon application to the above-named company.

WALTHAM   MANUFACTURING   COMPANY,   WALTHAM,   MASS.

Price

$2250
With top
$2375

Model: **R, WALTHAM-ORIENT.**

Body: **Wood.**

Color: **Brewster green; carmine running gear.**

Seating capacity : **Five persons.**

Total weight : **1850 pounds.**

Wheel base : **96 inches.**

Wheel tread: **56 inches.**

Tire dimensions, front : **32 x 3½ inches.**

Tire dimensions, rear : **32 x 3½ inches.**

Steering : **Wheel.**

Brakes : **Foot, on transmission shaft ; hand, external bands on rear hubs.**

Gasoline capacity : **10 gallons.**

Frame : **Pressed steel.**

Horse-power : **20.**

Number of cylinders : **Four.**

Cylinders arranged : **Vertically, under hood.**

Cooling : **Air.**

Ignition : **Jump spark ; storage and dry batteries.**

Drive : **Bevel gear.**

Transmission : **Sliding gear.**

Speeds : **Three forward, one reverse.**

Style of top : **Cape cart.**

Descriptive catalogue sent upon application to the above-named company.

THE WINTON MOTOR CARRIAGE CO., CLEVELAND, O.

Price

$2500
With top full leather
$2700

Model: **K.**

Body: **Touring car.**

Color: **Option of four.**

Seating capacity: **Five persons.**

Wheel base: **102 inches.**

Wheel tread: **56½ inches.**

Tire dimensions, front: **34 x 4 inches.**

Tire dimensions, rear: **34 x 4 inches.**

Steering: **Wheel.**

Brakes: **Three.**

Gasoline capacity: **15 gallons.**

Frame: **Pressed steel.**

Horse-power: **30.**

Number of cylinders: **Four.**

Cylinders arranged: **Vertically, under hood.**

Cooling: **Water; centrifugal pump.**

Ignition: **Jump spark; unit coil, dry and storage batteries.**

Drive: **Bevel gear.**

Transmission: **Individual clutch.**

Speeds: **Two forward, one reverse.**

Style of top: **Full leathei, imitation leather, khaki or pantasote.**

Descriptive catalogue sent upon application to the above-named company.

THE WINTON MOTOR CARRIAGE CO., CLEVELAND, O.

Price

$3500

Model : **K, LIMOUSINE.**

Body : **Limousine.**

Color : **Optional.**

Seating capacity : **Seven persons.**

Wheel base : **102 inches.**

Wheel tread : **56½ inches.**

Tire dimensions, front : **34 x 4 inches.**

Tire dimensions, rear : **34 x 4 inches.**

Steering : **Wheel.**

Brakes : **Three.**

Gasoline capacity : **15 gallons.**

Frame : **Pressed steel.**

Horse-power : **30.**

Number of cylinders : **Four.**

Cylinders arranged : **Vertically, under hood.**

Cooling : **Water ; centrifugal pump.**

Ignition : **Jump spark ; unit coil, dry and storage batteries.**

Drive : **Bevel gear.**

Transmission : **Individual clutch.**

Speeds : **Two forward, one reverse.**

Style of top : **Limousine.**

Descriptive catalogue sent upon application to the above-named company.

A CATALOGUE OF SELECTED DOVER BOOKS
IN ALL FIELDS OF INTEREST

A CATALOGUE OF SELECTED DOVER BOOKS
IN ALL FIELDS OF INTEREST

WHAT IS SCIENCE?, *N. Campbell*
The role of experiment and measurement, the function of mathematics, the nature of scientific laws, the difference between laws and theories, the limitations of science, and many similarly provocative topics are treated clearly and without technicalities by an eminent scientist. "Still an excellent introduction to scientific philosophy," H. Margenau in *Physics Today.* "A first-rate primer . . . deserves a wide audience," *Scientific American.* 192pp. 5⅜ x 8.

S43   Paperbound $1.25

THE NATURE OF LIGHT AND COLOUR IN THE OPEN AIR, *M. Minnaert*
Why are shadows sometimes blue, sometimes green, or other colors depending on the light and surroundings? What causes mirages? Why do multiple suns and moons appear in the sky? Professor Minnaert explains these unusual phenomena and hundreds of others in simple, easy-to-understand terms based on optical laws and the properties of light and color. No mathematics is required but artists, scientists, students, and everyone fascinated by these "tricks" of nature will find thousands of useful and amazing pieces of information. Hundreds of observational experiments are suggested which require no special equipment. 200 illustrations; 42 photos. xvi + 362pp. 5⅜ x 8.

T196   Paperbound $2.00

THE STRANGE STORY OF THE QUANTUM, AN ACCOUNT FOR THE GENERAL READER OF THE GROWTH OF IDEAS UNDERLYING OUR PRESENT ATOMIC KNOWLEDGE, *B. Hoffmann*
Presents lucidly and expertly, with barest amount of mathematics, the problems and theories which led to modern quantum physics. Dr. Hoffmann begins with the closing years of the 19th century, when certain trifling discrepancies were noticed, and with illuminating analogies and examples takes you through the brilliant concepts of Planck, Einstein, Pauli, Broglie, Bohr, Schroedinger, Heisenberg, Dirac, Sommerfeld, Feynman, etc. This edition includes a new, long postscript carrying the story through 1958. "Of the books attempting an account of the history and contents of our modern atomic physics which have come to my attention, this is the best," H. Margenau, Yale University, in *American Journal of Physics.* 32 tables and line illustrations. Index. 275pp. 5⅜ x 8.   T518   Paperbound $2.00

GREAT IDEAS OF MODERN MATHEMATICS: THEIR NATURE AND USE, *Jagjit Singh*
Reader with only high school math will understand main mathematical ideas of modern physics, astronomy, genetics, psychology, evolution, etc. better than many who use them as tools, but comprehend little of their basic structure. Author uses his wide knowledge of non-mathematical fields in brilliant exposition of differential equations, matrices, group theory, logic, statistics, problems of mathematical foundations, imaginary numbers, vectors, etc. Original publication. 2 appendixes. 2 indexes. 65 ills. 322pp. 5⅜ x 8.

T587   Paperbound $2.00

A SHORT ACCOUNT OF THE HISTORY OF MATHEMATICS,
W. W. Rouse Ball
Last previous edition (1908) hailed by mathematicians and laymen for lucid overview of math as living science, for understandable presentation of individual contributions of great mathematicians. Treats lives, discoveries of every important school and figure from Egypt, Phoenicia to late nineteenth century. Greek schools of Ionia, Cyzicus, Alexandria, Byzantium, Pythagoras; primitive arithmetic; Middle Ages and Renaissance, including European and Asiatic contributions; modern math of Descartes, Pascal, Wallis, Huygens, Newton, Euler, Lambert, Laplace, scores more. More emphasis on historical development, exposition of ideas than other books on subject. Non-technical, readable text can be followed with no more preparation than high-school algebra. Index. 544pp. 5⅜ x 8. Paperbound $2.25

GREAT IDEAS AND THEORIES OF MODERN COSMOLOGY, *Jagjit Singh*
Companion volume to author's popular "Great Ideas of Modern Mathematics" (Dover, $2.00). The best non-technical survey of post-Einstein attempts to answer perhaps unanswerable questions of origin, age of Universe, possibility of life on other worlds, etc. Fundamental theories of cosmology and cosmogony recounted, explained, evaluated in light of most recent data: Einstein's concepts of relativity, space-time; Milne's a priori world-system; astrophysical theories of Jeans, Eddington; Hoyle's "continuous creation;" contributions of dozens more scientists. A faithful, comprehensive critical summary of complex material presented in an extremely well-written text intended for laymen. Original publication. Index. xii + 276pp. 5⅜ x 8½. Paperbound $2.00

THE RESTLESS UNIVERSE, *Max Born*
A remarkably lucid account by a Nobel Laureate of recent theories of wave mechanics, behavior of gases, electrons and ions, waves and particles, electronic structure of the atom, nuclear physics, and similar topics. "Much more thorough and deeper than most attempts . . . easy and delightful," *Chemical and Engineering News*. Special feature: 7 animated sequences of 60 figures each showing such phenomena as gas molecules in motion, the scattering of alpha particles, etc. 11 full-page plates of photographs. Total of nearly 600 illustrations. 351pp. 6⅛ x 9¼. Paperbound $2.00

PLANETS, STARS AND GALAXIES: DESCRIPTIVE ASTRONOMY FOR BEGINNERS,
A. E. Fanning
What causes the progression of the seasons? Phases of the moon? The Aurora Borealis? How much does the sun weigh? What are the chances of life on our sister planets? Absorbing introduction to astronomy, incorporating the latest discoveries and theories: the solar wind, the surface temperature of Venus, the pock-marked face of Mars, quasars, and much more. Places you on the frontiers of one of the most vital sciences of our time. Revised (1966). Introduction by Donald H. Menzel, Harvard University. References. Index. 45 illustrations. 189pp. 5¼ x 8¼. Paperbound $1.50

GREAT IDEAS IN INFORMATION THEORY, LANGUAGE AND CYBERNETICS,
Jagjit Singh
Non-mathematical, but profound study of information, language, the codes used by men and machines to communicate, the principles of analog and digital computers, work of McCulloch, Pitts, von Neumann, Turing, and Uttley, correspondences between intricate mechanical network of "thinking machines" and more intricate neurophysiological mechanism of human brain. Indexes. 118 figures. 50 tables. ix + 338pp. 5⅜ x 8½. Paperbound $2.00

THE MUSIC OF THE SPHERES: THE MATERIAL UNIVERSE—FROM ATOM TO QUASAR, SIMPLY EXPLAINED, *Guy Murchie*
Vast compendium of fact, modern concept and theory, observed and calculated data, historical background guides intelligent layman through the material universe. Brilliant exposition of earth's construction, explanations for moon's craters, atmospheric components of Venus and Mars (with data from recent fly-by's), sun spots, sequences of star birth and death, neighboring galaxies, contributions of Galileo, Tycho Brahe, Kepler, etc.; and (Vol. 2) construction of the atom (describing newly discovered sigma and xi subatomic particles), theories of sound, color and light, space and time, including relativity theory, quantum theory, wave theory, probability theory, work of Newton, Maxwell, Faraday, Einstein, de Broglie, etc. "Best presentation yet offered to the intelligent general reader," *Saturday Review*. Revised (1967). Index. 319 illustrations by the author. Total of xx + 644pp. 5⅜ x 8½.
Vol. 1 Paperbound $2.00, Vol. 2 Paperbound $2.00,
The set $4.00

FOUR LECTURES ON RELATIVITY AND SPACE, *Charles Proteus Steinmetz*
Lecture series, given by great mathematician and electrical engineer, generally considered one of the best popular-level expositions of special and general relativity theories and related questions. Steinmetz translates complex mathematical reasoning into language accessible to laymen through analogy, example and comparison. Among topics covered are relativity of motion, location, time; of mass; acceleration; 4-dimensional time-space; geometry of the gravitational field; curvature and bending of space; non-Euclidean geometry. Index. 40 illustrations. x + 142pp. 5⅜ x 8½.   Paperbound $1.35

HOW TO KNOW THE WILD FLOWERS, *Mrs. William Starr Dana*
Classic nature book that has introduced thousands to wonders of American wild flowers. Color-season principle of organization is easy to use, even by those with no botanical training, and the genial, refreshing discussions of history, folklore, uses of over 1,000 native and escape flowers, foliage plants are informative as well as fun to read. Over 170 full-page plates, collected from several editions, may be colored in to make permanent records of finds. Revised to conform with 1950 edition of Gray's Manual of Botany. xlii + 438pp. 5⅜ x 8½.   Paperbound $2.00

MANUAL OF THE TREES OF NORTH AMERICA, *Charles Sprague Sargent*
Still unsurpassed as most comprehensive, reliable study of North American tree characteristics, precise locations and distribution. By dean of American dendrologists. Every tree native to U.S., Canada, Alaska; 185 genera, 717 species, described in detail—leaves, flowers, fruit, winterbuds, bark, wood, growth habits, etc. plus discussion of varieties and local variants, immaturity variations. Over 100 keys, including unusual 11-page analytical key to genera, aid in identification. 783 clear illustrations of flowers, fruit, leaves. An unmatched permanent reference work for all nature lovers. Second enlarged (1926) edition. Synopsis of families. Analytical key to genera. Glossary of technical terms. Index. 783 illustrations, 1 map. Total of 982pp. 5⅜ x 8.
Vol. 1 Paperbound $2.25, Vol. 2 Paperbound $2.25,
The set $4.50

IT'S FUN TO MAKE THINGS FROM SCRAP MATERIALS,
Evelyn Glantz Hershoff
What use are empty spools, tin cans, bottle tops? What can be made from
rubber bands, clothes pins, paper clips, and buttons? This book provides
simply worded instructions and large diagrams showing you how to make
cookie cutters, toy trucks, paper turkeys, Halloween masks, telephone sets,
aprons, linoleum block- and spatter prints — in all 399 projects! Many are easy
enough for young children to figure out for themselves; some challenging
enough to entertain adults; all are remarkably ingenious ways to make things
from materials that cost pennies or less! Formerly "Scrap Fun for Everyone."
Index. 214 illustrations. 373pp. 5⅜ x 8½.   Paperbound $1.50

SYMBOLIC LOGIC and THE GAME OF LOGIC, *Lewis Carroll*
"Symbolic Logic" is not concerned with modern symbolic logic, but is instead
a collection of over 380 problems posed with charm and imagination, using
the syllogism and a fascinating diagrammatic method of drawing conclusions.
In "The Game of Logic" Carroll's whimsical imagination devises a logical game
played with 2 diagrams and counters (included) to manipulate hundreds of
tricky syllogisms. The final section, "Hit or Miss" is a lagniappe of 101 additional puzzles in the delightful Carroll manner. Until this reprint edition,
both of these books were rarities costing up to $15 each. Symbolic Logic:
Index. xxxi + 199pp. The Game of Logic: 96pp. 2 vols. bound as one. 5⅜ x 8.
                                                             Paperbound $2.00

MATHEMATICAL PUZZLES OF SAM LOYD, PART I
selected and edited by M. Gardner
Choice puzzles by the greatest American puzzle creator and innovator. Selected
from his famous collection, "Cyclopedia of Puzzles," they retain the unique
style and historical flavor of the originals. There are posers based on arithmetic,
algebra, probability, game theory, route tracing, topology, counter and sliding
block, operations research, geometrical dissection. Includes the famous "14-15"
puzzle which was a national craze, and his "Horse of a Different Color" which
sold millions of copies. 117 of his most ingenious puzzles in all. 120 line
drawings and diagrams. Solutions. Selected references. xx + 167pp. 5⅜ x 8.
                                                             Paperbound $1.00

STRING FIGURES AND HOW TO MAKE THEM, *Caroline Furness Jayne*
107 string figures plus variations selected from the best primitive and modern
examples developed by Navajo, Apache, pygmies of Africa, Eskimo, in Europe,
Australia, China, etc. The most readily understandable, easy-to-follow book in
English on perennially popular recreation. Crystal-clear exposition; step-by-
step diagrams. Everyone from kindergarten children to adults looking for
unusual diversion will be endlessly amused. Index. Bibliography. Introduction
by A. C. Haddon. 17 full-page plates, 960 illustrations. xxiii + 401pp. 5⅜ x 8½.
                                                             Paperbound $2.00

PAPER FOLDING FOR BEGINNERS, *W. D. Murray and F. J. Rigney*
A delightful introduction to the varied and entertaining Japanese art of
origami (paper folding), with a full, crystal-clear text that anticipates every
difficulty; over 275 clearly labeled diagrams of all important stages in creation.
You get results at each stage, since complex figures are logically developed
from simpler ones. 43 different pieces are explained: sailboats, frogs, roosters,
etc. 6 photographic plates. 279 diagrams. 95pp. 5⅜ x 8⅜. Paperbound $1.00

PRINCIPLES OF ART HISTORY,
H. Wölfflin
Analyzing such terms as "baroque," "classic," "neoclassic," "primitive," "picturesque," and 164 different works by artists like Botticelli, van Cleve, Dürer, Hobbema, Holbein, Hals, Rembrandt, Titian, Brueghel, Vermeer, and many others, the author establishes the classifications of art history and style on a firm, concrete basis. This classic of art criticism shows what really occurred between the 14th-century primitives and the sophistication of the 18th century in terms of basic attitudes and philosophies. "A remarkable lesson in the art of seeing," *Sat. Rev. of Literature*. Translated from the 7th German edition. 150 illustrations. 254pp. 6⅛ x 9¼. Paperbound $2.00

PRIMITIVE ART,
Franz Boas
This authoritative and exhaustive work by a great American anthropologist covers the entire gamut of primitive art. Pottery, leatherwork, metal work, stone work, wood, basketry, are treated in detail. Theories of primitive art, historical depth in art history, technical virtuosity, unconscious levels of patterning, symbolism, styles, literature, music, dance, etc. A must book for the interested layman, the anthropologist, artist, handicrafter (hundreds of unusual motifs), and the historian. Over 900 illustrations (50 ceramic vessels, 12 totem poles, etc.). 376pp. 5⅜ x 8. Paperbound $2.25

THE GENTLEMAN AND CABINET MAKER'S DIRECTOR,
Thomas Chippendale
A reprint of the 1762 catalogue of furniture designs that went on to influence generations of English and Colonial and Early Republic American furniture makers. The 200 plates, most of them full-page sized, show Chippendale's designs for French (Louis XV), Gothic, and Chinese-manner chairs, sofas, canopy and dome beds, cornices, chamber organs, cabinets, shaving tables, commodes, picture frames, frets, candle stands, chimney pieces, decorations, etc. The drawings are all elegant and highly detailed; many include construction diagrams and elevations. A supplement of 24 photographs shows surviving pieces of original and Chippendale-style pieces of furniture. Brief biography of Chippendale by N. I. Bienenstock, editor of *Furniture World*. Reproduced from the 1762 edition. 200 plates, plus 19 photographic plates. vi + 249pp. 9⅛ x 12¼. Paperbound $3.50

AMERICAN ANTIQUE FURNITURE: A BOOK FOR AMATEURS,
Edgar G. Miller, Jr.
Standard introduction and practical guide to identification of valuable American antique furniture. 2115 illustrations, mostly photographs taken by the author in 148 private homes, are arranged in chronological order in extensive chapters on chairs, sofas, chests, desks, bedsteads, mirrors, tables, clocks, and other articles. Focus is on furniture accessible to the collector, including simpler pieces and a larger than usual coverage of Empire style. Introductory chapters identify structural elements, characteristics of various styles, how to avoid fakes, etc. "We are frequently asked to name some book on American furniture that will meet the requirements of the novice collector, the beginning dealer, and . . . the general public. . . . We believe Mr. Miller's two volumes more completely satisfy this specification than any other work," *Antiques*. Appendix. Index. Total of vi + 1106pp. 7⅞ x 10¾.
Two volume set, paperbound $7.50

THE BAD CHILD'S BOOK OF BEASTS, MORE BEASTS FOR WORSE CHILDREN, and A MORAL ALPHABET, H. *Belloc*
Hardly and anthology of humorous verse has appeared in the last 50 years without at least a couple of these famous nonsense verses. But one must see the entire volumes — with all the delightful original illustrations by Sir Basil Blackwood — to appreciate fully Belloc's charming and witty verses that play so subacidly on the platitudes of life and morals that beset his day — and ours. A great humor classic. Three books in one. Total of 157pp. 5⅜ x 8.
Paperbound $1.00

THE DEVIL'S DICTIONARY, *Ambrose Bierce*
Sardonic and irreverent barbs puncturing the pomposities and absurdities of American politics, business, religion, literature, and arts, by the country's greatest satirist in the classic tradition. Epigrammatic as Shaw, piercing as Swift, American as Mark Twain, Will Rogers, and Fred Allen, Bierce will always remain the favorite of a small coterie of enthusiasts, and of writers and speakers whom he supplies with "some of the most gorgeous witticisms of the English language" (H. L. Mencken). Over 1000 entries in alphabetical order. 144pp. 5⅜ x 8.
Paperbound $1.00

THE COMPLETE NONSENSE OF EDWARD LEAR.
This is the only complete edition of this master of gentle madness available at a popular price. *A Book of Nonsense, Nonsense Songs, More Nonsense Songs and Stories* in their entirety with all the old favorites that have delighted children and adults for years. The Dong With A Luminous Nose, The Jumblies, The Owl and the Pussycat, and hundreds of other bits of wonderful nonsense. 214 limericks, 3 sets of Nonsense Botany, 5 Nonsense Alphabets, 546 drawings by Lear himself, and much more. 320pp. 5⅜ x 8.
Paperbound $1.00

THE WIT AND HUMOR OF OSCAR WILDE, *ed. by Alvin Redman*
Wilde at his most brilliant, in 1000 epigrams exposing weaknesses and hypocrisies of "civilized" society. Divided into 49 categories—sin, wealth, women, America, etc.—to aid writers, speakers. Includes excerpts from his trials, books, plays, criticism. Formerly "The Epigrams of Oscar Wilde." Introduction by Vyvyan Holland, Wilde's only living son. Introductory essay by editor. 260pp. 5⅜ x 8.
Paperbound $1.00

A CHILD'S PRIMER OF NATURAL HISTORY, *Oliver Herford*
Scarcely an anthology of whimsy and humor has appeared in the last 50 years without a contribution from Oliver Herford. Yet the works from which these examples are drawn have been almost impossible to obtain! Here at last are Herford's improbable definitions of a menagerie of familiar and weird animals, each verse illustrated by the author's own drawings. 24 drawings in 2 colors; 24 additional drawings. vii + 95pp. 6½ x 6.
Paperbound $1.00

THE BROWNIES: THEIR BOOK, *Palmer Cox*
The book that made the Brownies a household word. Generations of readers have enjoyed the antics, predicaments and adventures of these jovial sprites, who emerge from the forest at night to play or to come to the aid of a deserving human. Delightful illustrations by the author decorate nearly every page. 24 short verse tales with 266 illustrations. 155pp. 6⅝ x 9¼.
Paperbound $1.50

THE PRINCIPLES OF PSYCHOLOGY,
William James
The full long-course, unabridged, of one of the great classics of Western literature and science. Wonderfully lucid descriptions of human mental activity, the stream of thought, consciousness, time perception, memory, imagination, emotions, reason, abnormal phenomena, and similar topics. Original contributions are integrated with the work of such men as Berkeley, Binet, Mills, Darwin, Hume, Kant, Royce, Schopenhauer, Spinoza, Locke, Descartes, Galton, Wundt, Lotze, Herbart, Fechner, and scores of others. All contrasting interpretations of mental phenomena are examined in detail—introspective analysis, philosophical interpretation, and experimental research. "A classic," *Journal of Consulting Psychology.* "The main lines are as valid as ever," *Psychoanalytical Quarterly.* "Standard reading...a classic of interpretation," *Psychiatric Quarterly.* 94 illustrations. 1408pp. 5⅜ x 8.

Vol. 1 Paperbound $2.50, Vol. 2 Paperbound $2.50,
The set $5.00

VISUAL ILLUSIONS: THEIR CAUSES, CHARACTERISTICS AND APPLICATIONS,
M. Luckiesh
"Seeing is deceiving," asserts the author of this introduction to virtually every type of optical illusion known. The text both describes and explains the principles involved in color illusions, figure-ground, distance illusions, etc. 100 photographs, drawings and diagrams prove how easy it is to fool the sense: circles that aren't round, parallel lines that seem to bend, stationary figures that seem to move as you stare at them — illustration after illustration strains our credulity at what we see. Fascinating book from many points of view, from applications for artists, in camouflage, etc. to the psychology of vision. New introduction by William Ittleson, Dept. of Psychology, Queens College. Index. Bibliography. xxi + 252pp. 5⅜ x 8½.   Paperbound $1.50

FADS AND FALLACIES IN THE NAME OF SCIENCE,
Martin Gardner
This is the standard account of various cults, quack systems, and delusions which have masqueraded as science: hollow earth fanatics. Reich and orgone sex energy, dianetics, Atlantis, multiple moons, Forteanism, flying saucers, medical fallacies like iridiagnosis, zone therapy, etc. A new chapter has been added on Bridey Murphy, psionics, and other recent manifestations in this field. This is a fair, reasoned appraisal of eccentric theory which provides excellent inoculation against cleverly masked nonsense. "Should be read by everyone, scientist and non-scientist alike," R. T. Birge, Prof. Emeritus of Physics, Univ. of California; Former President, American Physical Society. Index. x + 365pp. 5⅜ x 8.   Paperbound $1.85

ILLUSIONS AND DELUSIONS OF THE SUPERNATURAL AND THE OCCULT,
D. H. Rawcliffe
Holds up to rational examination hundreds of persistent delusions including crystal gazing, automatic writing, table turning, mediumistic trances, mental healing, stigmata, lycanthropy, live burial, the Indian Rope Trick, spiritualism, dowsing, telepathy, clairvoyance, ghosts, ESP, etc. The author explains and exposes the mental and physical deceptions involved, making this not only an exposé of supernatural phenomena, but a valuable exposition of characteristic types of abnormal psychology. Originally titled "The Psychology of the Occult." 14 illustrations. Index. 551pp. 5⅜ x 8.   Paperbound $2.25

FAIRY TALE COLLECTIONS, *edited by Andrew Lang*
Andrew Lang's fairy tale collections make up the richest shelf-full of traditional children's stories anywhere available. Lang supervised the translation of stories from all over the world—familiar European tales collected by Grimm, animal stories from Negro Africa, myths of primitive Australia, stories from Russia, Hungary, Iceland, Japan, and many other countries. Lang's selection of translations are unusually high; many authorities consider that the most familiar tales find their best versions in these volumes. All collections are richly decorated and illustrated by H. J. Ford and other artists.

THE BLUE FAIRY BOOK. 37 stories. 138 illustrations. ix + 390pp. 5⅜ x 8½.
Paperbound $1.50

THE GREEN FAIRY BOOK. 42 stories. 100 illustrations. xiii + 366pp. 5⅜ x 8½.
Paperbound $1.50

THE BROWN FAIRY BOOK. 32 stories. 50 illustrations, 8 in color. xii + 350pp. 5⅜ x 8½.
Paperbound $1.50

THE BEST TALES OF HOFFMANN, *edited by E. F. Bleiler*
10 stories by E. T. A. Hoffmann, one of the greatest of all writers of fantasy. The tales include "The Golden Flower Pot," "Automata," "A New Year's Eve Adventure," "Nutcracker and the King of Mice," "Sand-Man," and others. Vigorous characterizations of highly eccentric personalities, remarkably imaginative situations, and intensely fast pacing has made these tales popular all over the world for 150 years. Editor's introduction. 7 drawings by Hoffmann. xxxiii + 419pp. 5⅜ x 8½.
Paperbound $2.00

GHOST AND HORROR STORIES OF AMBROSE BIERCE,
edited by E. F. Bleiler
Morbid, eerie, horrifying tales of possessed poets, shabby aristocrats, revived corpses, and haunted malefactors. Widely acknowledged as the best of their kind between Poe and the moderns, reflecting their author's inner torment and bitter view of life. Includes "Damned Thing," "The Middle Toe of the Right Foot," "The Eyes of the Panther," "Visions of the Night," "Moxon's Master," and over a dozen others. Editor's introduction. xxii + 199pp. 5⅜ x 8½.
Paperbound $1.25

THREE GOTHIC NOVELS, *edited by E. F. Bleiler*
Originators of the still popular Gothic novel form, influential in ushering in early 19th-century Romanticism. Horace Walpole's *Castle of Otranto*, William Beckford's *Vathek*, John Polidori's *The Vampyre*, and a *Fragment* by Lord Byron are enjoyable as exciting reading or as documents in the history of English literature. Editor's introduction. xi + 291pp. 5⅜ x 8½.
Paperbound $2.00

BEST GHOST STORIES OF LEFANU, *edited by E. F. Bleiler*
Though admired by such critics as V. S. Pritchett, Charles Dickens and Henry James, ghost stories by the Irish novelist Joseph Sheridan LeFanu have never become as widely known as his detective fiction. About half of the 16 stories in this collection have never before been available in America. Collection includes "Carmilla" (perhaps the best vampire story ever written), "The Haunted Baronet," "The Fortunes of Sir Robert Ardagh," and the classic "Green Tea." Editor's introduction. 7 contemporary illustrations. Portrait of LeFanu. xii + 467pp. 5⅜ x 8.
Paperbound $2.00

EASY-TO-DO ENTERTAINMENTS AND DIVERSIONS WITH COINS, CARDS, STRING, PAPER AND MATCHES, *R. M. Abraham*
Over 300 tricks, games and puzzles will provide young readers with absorbing fun. Sections on card games; paper-folding; tricks with coins, matches and pieces of string; games for the agile; toy-making from common household objects; mathematical recreations; and 50 miscellaneous pastimes. Anyone in charge of groups of youngsters, including hard-pressed parents, and in need of suggestions on how to keep children sensibly amused and quietly content will find this book indispensable. Clear, simple text, copious number of delightful line drawings and illustrative diagrams. Originally titled "Winter Nights' Entertainments." Introduction by Lord Baden Powell. 329 illustrations. v + 186pp. 5⅜ x 8½. Paperbound $1.00

AN INTRODUCTION TO CHESS MOVES AND TACTICS SIMPLY EXPLAINED, *Leonard Barden*
Beginner's introduction to the royal game. Names, possible moves of the pieces, definitions of essential terms, how games are won, etc. explained in 30-odd pages. With this background you'll be able to sit right down and play. Balance of book teaches strategy — openings, middle game, typical endgame play, and suggestions for improving your game. A sample game is fully analyzed. True middle-level introduction, teaching you all the essentials without oversimplifying or losing you in a maze of detail. 58 figures. 102pp. 5⅜ x 8½. Paperbound $1.00

LASKER'S MANUAL OF CHESS, *Dr. Emanuel Lasker*
Probably the greatest chess player of modern times, Dr. Emanuel Lasker held the world championship 28 years, independent of passing schools or fashions. This unmatched study of the game, chiefly for intermediate to skilled players, analyzes basic methods, combinations, position play, the aesthetics of chess, dozens of different openings, etc., with constant reference to great modern games. Contains a brilliant exposition of Steinitz's important theories. Introduction by Fred Reinfeld. Tables of Lasker's tournament record. 3 indices. 308 diagrams. 1 photograph. xxx + 349pp. 5⅜ x 8. Paperbound $2.25

COMBINATIONS: THE HEART OF CHESS, *Irving Chernev*
Step-by-step from simple combinations to complex, this book, by a well-known chess writer, shows you the intricacies of pins, counter-pins, knight forks, and smothered mates. Other chapters show alternate lines of play to those taken in actual championship games; boomerang combinations; classic examples of brilliant combination play by Nimzovich, Rubinstein, Tarrasch, Botvinnik, Alekhine and Capablanca. Index. 356 diagrams. ix + 245pp. 5⅜ x 8½. Paperbound $1.85

HOW TO SOLVE CHESS PROBLEMS, *K. S. Howard*
Full of practical suggestions for the fan or the beginner — who knows only the moves of the chessmen. Contains preliminary section and 58 two-move, 46 three-move, and 8 four-move problems composed by 27 outstanding American problem creators in the last 30 years. Explanation of all terms and exhaustive index. "Just what is wanted for the student," Brian Harley. 112 problems, solutions. vi + 171pp. 5⅜ x 8. Paperbound $1.35

SOCIAL THOUGHT FROM LORE TO SCIENCE,
H. E. Barnes and H. Becker
An immense survey of sociological thought and ways of viewing, studying, planning, and reforming society from earliest times to the present. Includes thought on society of preliterate peoples, ancient non-Western cultures, and every great movement in Europe, America, and modern Japan. Analyzes hundreds of great thinkers: Plato, Augustine, Bodin, Vico, Montesquieu, Herder, Comte, Marx, etc. Weighs the contributions of utopians, sophists, fascists and communists; economists, jurists, philosophers, ecclesiastics, and every 19th and 20th century school of scientific sociology, anthropology, and social psychology throughout the world. Combines topical, chronological, and regional approaches, treating the evolution of social thought as a process rather than as a series of mere topics. "Impressive accuracy, competence, and discrimination . . . easily the best single survey," *Nation.* Thoroughly revised, with new material up to 1960. 2 indexes. Over 2200 bibliographical notes. Three volume set. Total of 1586pp. 5⅜ x 8.
Vol. 1 Paperbound $2.75, Vol. 2 Paperbound $2.75, Vol. 3 Paperbound $2.50
The set $8.00

A HISTORY OF HISTORICAL WRITING, *Harry Elmer Barnes*
Virtually the only adequate survey of the whole course of historical writing in a single volume. Surveys developments from the beginnings of historiography in the ancient Near East and the Classical World, up through the Cold War. Covers major historians in detail, shows interrelationship with cultural background, makes clear individual contributions, evaluates and estimates importance; also enormously rich upon minor authors and thinkers who are usually passed over. Packed with scholarship and learning, clear, easily written. Indispensable to every student of history. Revised and enlarged up to 1961. Index and bibliography. xv + 442pp. 5⅜ x 8½. Paperbound $2.50

JOHANN SEBASTIAN BACH, *Philipp Spitta*
The complete and unabridged text of the definitive study of Bach. Written some 70 years ago, it is still unsurpassed for its coverage of nearly all aspects of Bach's life and work. There could hardly be a finer non-technical introduction to Bach's music than the detailed, lucid analyses which Spitta provides for hundreds of individual pieces. 26 solid pages are devoted to the B minor mass, for example, and 30 pages to the glorious St. Matthew Passion. This monumental set also includes a major analysis of the music of the 18th century: Buxtehude, Pachelbel, etc. "Unchallenged as the last word on one of the supreme geniuses of music," John Barkham, *Saturday Review Syndicate.* Total of 1819pp. Heavy cloth binding. 5⅜ x 8.
Two volume set, clothbound $13.50

BEETHOVEN AND HIS NINE SYMPHONIES, *George Grove*
In this modern middle-level classic of musicology Grove not only analyzes all nine of Beethoven's symphonies very thoroughly in terms of their musical structure, but also discusses the circumstances under which they were written, Beethoven's stylistic development, and much other background material. This is an extremely rich book, yet very easily followed; it is highly recommended to anyone seriously interested in music. Over 250 musical passages. Index. viii + 407pp. 5⅜ x 8. Paperbound $2.00

THREE SCIENCE FICTION NOVELS,
John Taine

Acknowledged by many as the best SF writer of the 1920's, Taine (under the name Eric Temple Bell) was also a Professor of Mathematics of considerable renown. Reprinted here are *The Time Stream*, generally considered Taine's best, *The Greatest Game*, a biological-fiction novel, and *The Purple Sapphire*, involving a supercivilization of the past. Taine's stories tie fantastic narratives to frameworks of original and logical scientific concepts. Speculation is often profound on such questions as the nature of time, concept of entropy, cyclical universes, etc. 4 contemporary illustrations. v + 532pp. 5⅜ x 8⅜.

T1180   Paperbound $2.00

SEVEN SCIENCE FICTION NOVELS,
H. G. Wells

Full unabridged texts of 7 science-fiction novels of the master. Ranging from biology, physics, chemistry, astronomy, to sociology and other studies, Mr. Wells extrapolates whole worlds of strange and intriguing character. "One will have to go far to match this for entertainment, excitement, and sheer pleasure . . ."*New York Times*. Contents: The Time Machine, The Island of Dr. Moreau, The First Men in the Moon, The Invisible Man, The War of the Worlds, The Food of the Gods, In The Days of the Comet. 1015pp. 5⅜ x 8.

T264   Clothbound $5.00

28 SCIENCE FICTION STORIES OF H. G. WELLS.

Two full, unabridged novels, *Men Like Gods* and *Star Begotten*, plus 26 short stories by the master science-fiction writer of all time! Stories of space, time, invention, exploration, futuristic adventure. Partial contents: *The Country of the Blind, In the Abyss, The Crystal Egg, The Man Who Could Work Miracles, A Story of Days to Come, The Empire of the Ants, The Magic Shop, The Valley of the Spiders, A Story of the Stone Age, Under the Knife, Sea Raiders* etc. An indispensable collection for the library of anyone interested in science fiction adventure. 928pp. 5⅜ x 8.   T265   Clothbound $5.00

THREE MARTIAN NOVELS,
Edgar Rice Burroughs

Complete, unabridged reprinting, in one volume, of Thuvia, Maid of Mars; Chessmen of Mars; The Master Mind of Mars. Hours of science-fiction adventure by a modern master storyteller. Reset in large clear type for easy reading. 16 illustrations by J. Allen St. John. vi + 490pp. 5⅜ x 8½.

T39   Paperbound $2.50

AN INTELLECTUAL AND CULTURAL HISTORY OF THE WESTERN WORLD,
Harry Elmer Barnes

Monumental 3-volume survey of intellectual development of Europe from primitive cultures to the present day. Every significant product of human intellect traced through history: art, literature, mathematics, physical sciences, medicine, music, technology, social sciences, religions, jurisprudence, education, etc. Presentation is lucid and specific, analyzing in detail specific discoveries, theories, literary works, and so on. Revised (1965) by recognized scholars in specialized fields under the direction of Prof. Barnes. Revised bibliography. Indexes. 24 illustrations. Total of xxix + 1318pp.

T1275, T1276, T1277   Three volume set, paperbound $7.50

HEAR ME TALKIN' TO YA, *edited by Nat Shapiro and Nat Hentoff*
In their own words, Louis Armstrong, King Oliver, Fletcher Henderson, Bunk Johnson, Bix Beiderbecke, Billy Holiday, Fats Waller, Jelly Roll Morton, Duke Ellington, and many others comment on the origins of jazz in New Orleans and its growth in Chicago's South Side, Kansas City's jam sessions, Depression Harlem, and the modernism of the West Coast schools. Taken from taped conversations, letters, magazine articles, other first-hand sources. Editors' introduction. xvi + 429pp. 5⅜ x 8½.   T1726   Paperbound $2.00

THE JOURNAL OF HENRY D. THOREAU
A 25-year record by the great American observer and critic, as complete a record of a great man's inner life as is anywhere available. Thoreau's Journals served him as raw material for his formal pieces, as a place where he could develop his ideas, as an outlet for his interests in wild life and plants, in writing as an art, in classics of literature, Walt Whitman and other contemporaries, in politics, slavery, individual's relation to the State, etc. The Journals present a portrait of a remarkable man, and are an observant social history. Unabridged republication of 1906 edition, Bradford Torrey and Francis H. Allen, editors. Illustrations. Total of 1888pp. 8⅜ x 12¼.
                    T312, T313   Two volume set, clothbound $25.00

A SHAKESPEARIAN GRAMMAR, *E. A. Abbott*
Basic reference to Shakespeare and his contemporaries, explaining through thousands of quotations from Shakespeare, Jonson, Beaumont and Fletcher, North's *Plutarch* and other sources the grammatical usage differing from the modern. First published in 1870 and written by a scholar who spent much of his life isolating principles of Elizabethan language, the book is unlikely ever to be superseded. Indexes. xxiv + 511pp. 5⅜ x 8½. T1582 Paperbound $2.75

FOLK-LORE OF SHAKESPEARE, *T. F. Thistelton Dyer*
Classic study, drawing from Shakespeare a large body of references to supernatural beliefs, terminology of falconry and hunting, games and sports, good luck charms, marriage customs, folk medicines, superstitions about plants, animals, birds, argot of the underworld, sexual slang of London, proverbs, drinking customs, weather lore, and much else. From full compilation comes a mirror of the 17th-century popular mind. Index. ix + 526pp. 5⅜ x 8½.
                    T1614   Paperbound $2.75

THE NEW VARIORUM SHAKESPEARE, *edited by H. H. Furness*
By far the richest editions of the plays ever produced in any country or language. Each volume contains complete text (usually First Folio) of the play, all variants in Quarto and other Folio texts, editorial changes by every major editor to Furness's own time (1900), footnotes to obscure references or language, extensive quotes from literature of Shakespearian criticism, essays on plot sources (often reprinting sources in full), and much more.

HAMLET, *edited by H. H. Furness*
Total of xxvi + 905pp. 5⅜ x 8½.
                    T1004, T1005   Two volume set, paperbound $5.25

TWELFTH NIGHT, *edited by H. H. Furness*
Index. xxii + 434pp. 5⅜ x 8½.   T1189   Paperbound $2.75

LA BOHEME BY GIACOMO PUCCINI,
translated and introduced by Ellen H. Bleiler
Complete handbook for the operagoer, with everything needed for full enjoyment except the musical score itself. Complete Italian libretto, with new, modern English line-by-line translation—the only libretto printing all repeats; biography of Puccini; the librettists; background to the opera, Murger's La Boheme, etc.; circumstances of composition and performances; plot summary; and pictorial section of 73 illustrations showing Puccini, famous singers and performances, etc. Large clear type for easy reading. 124pp. 5⅜ x 8½.
                                        T404   Paperbound $1.00

ANTONIO STRADIVARI: HIS LIFE AND WORK (1644-1737),
W. Henry Hill, Arthur F. Hill, and Alfred E. Hill
Still the only book that really delves into life and art of the incomparable Italian craftsman, maker of the finest musical instruments in the world today. The authors, expert violin-makers themselves, discuss Stradivari's ancestry, his construction and finishing techniques, distinguished characteristics of many of his instruments and their locations. Included, too, is story of introduction of his instruments into France, England, first revelation of their supreme merit, and information on his labels, number of instruments made, prices, mystery of ingredients of his varnish, tone of pre-1684 Stradivari violin and changes between 1684 and 1690. An extremely interesting, informative account for all music lovers, from craftsman to concert-goer. Republication of original (1902) edition. New introduction by Sydney Beck, Head of Rare Book and Manuscript Collections, Music Division, New York Public Library. Analytical index by Rembert Wurlitzer. Appendixes. 68 illustrations. 30 full-page plates. 4 in color. xxvi + 315pp. 5⅜ x 8½.   T425   Paperbound $2.25

MUSICAL AUTOGRAPHS FROM MONTEVERDI TO HINDEMITH,
Emanuel Winternitz
For beauty, for intrinsic interest, for perspective on the composer's personality, for subtleties of phrasing, shading, emphasis indicated in the autograph but suppressed in the printed score, the mss. of musical composition are fascinating documents which repay close study in many different ways. This 2-volume work reprints facsimiles of mss. by virtually every major composer, and many minor figures—196 examples in all. A full text points out what can be learned from mss., analyzes each sample. Index. Bibliography. 18 figures. 196 plates. Total of 170pp. of text. 7⅞ x 10¾.
                            T1312, T1313   Two volume set, paperbound $4.00

J. S. BACH,
Albert Schweitzer
One of the few great full-length studies of Bach's life and work, and the study upon which Schweitzer's renown as a musicologist rests. On first appearance (1911), revolutionized Bach performance. The only writer on Bach to be musicologist, performing musician, and student of history, theology and philosophy, Schweitzer contributes particularly full sections on history of German Protestant church music, theories on motivic pictorial representations in vocal music, and practical suggestions for performance. Translated by Ernest Newman. Indexes. 5 illustrations. 650 musical examples. Total of xix + 928pp. 5⅜ x 8½.   T1631, T1632   Two volume set, paperbound $4.50

THE METHODS OF ETHICS, *Henry Sidgwick*
Propounding no organized system of its own, study subjects every major methodological approach to ethics to rigorous, objective analysis. Study discusses and relates ethical thought of Plato, Aristotle, Bentham, Clarke, Butler, Hobbes, Hume, Mill, Spencer, Kant, and dozens of others. Sidgwick retains conclusions from each system which follow from ethical premises, rejecting the faulty. Considered by many in the field to be among the most important treatises on ethical philosophy. Appendix. Index. xlvii + 528pp. 5⅜ x 8½.
T1608   Paperbound $2.50

TEUTONIC MYTHOLOGY, *Jakob Grimm*
A milestone in Western culture; the work which established on a modern basis the study of history of religions and comparative religions. 4-volume work assembles and interprets everything available on religious and folkloristic beliefs of Germanic people (including Scandinavians, Anglo-Saxons, etc.). Assembling material from such sources as Tacitus, surviving Old Norse and Icelandic texts, archeological remains, folktales, surviving superstitions, comparative traditions, linguistic analysis, etc. Grimm explores pagan deities, heroes, folklore of nature, religious practices, and every other area of pagan German belief. To this day, the unrivaled, definitive, exhaustive study. Translated by J. S. Stallybrass from 4th (1883) German edition. Indexes. Total of lxxvii + 1887pp. 5⅜ x 8½.
T1602, T1603, T1604, T1605   Four volume set, paperbound $10.00

THE I CHING, *translated by James Legge*
Called "The Book of Changes" in English, this is one of the Five Classics edited by Confucius, basic and central to Chinese thought. Explains perhaps the most complex system of divination known, founded on the theory that all things happening at any one time have characteristic features which can be isolated and related. Significant in Oriental studies, in history of religions and philosophy, and also to Jungian psychoanalysis and other areas of modern European thought. Index. Appendixes. 6 plates. xxi + 448pp. 5⅜ x 8½.
T1062   Paperbound $2.75

HISTORY OF ANCIENT PHILOSOPHY, *W. Windelband*
One of the clearest, most accurate comprehensive surveys of Greek and Roman philosophy. Discusses ancient philosophy in general, intellectual life in Greece in the 7th and 6th centuries B.C., Thales, Anaximander, Anaximenes, Heraclitus, the Eleatics, Empedocles, Democritus, Anaxagoras, Leucippus, the Pythagoreans, the Sophists, Socrates, Democritus (20 pages), Plato (50 pages), Aristotle (70 pages), the Peripatetics, Stoics, Epicureans, Sceptics, Neo-platonists, Christian Apologists, etc. 2nd German edition translated by H. E. Cushman. xv + 393pp. 5⅜ x 8.
T357   Paperbound $2.25

THE PALACE OF PLEASURE, *William Painter*
Elizabethan versions of Italian and French novels from *The Decameron*, Cinthio, Straparola, Queen Margaret of Navarre, and other continental sources — the very work that provided Shakespeare and dozens of his contemporaries with many of their plots and sub-plots and, therefore, justly considered one of the most influential books in all English literature. It is also a book that any reader will still enjoy. Total of cviii + 1,224pp.
T1691, T1692, T1693   Three volume set, paperbound $6.75

SHAKESPEARE AS A DRAMATIC ARTIST, *Richard G. Moulton*
Analyses of *Merchant of Venice, Richard III, King Lear, The Tempest,* and
other plays show Shakespeare's skill at integrating story plots, blending light
and serious moods, use of such themes as judgment by appearances, antithesis
of outer and inner life, repeated use of such characters as court fool, and
other important elements. "Only notable book on Shakespeare's handling of
plot . . . one of the most valuable of all books on Shakespeare," Eric Bentley.
Introduction by Eric Bentley. Appendix. Indexes. xviii + 443pp. 5⅜ x 8.
T1546 Paperbound $2.50

THE ENGLISH AND SCOTTISH POPULAR BALLADS, *Francis James Child*
A great work of American scholarship, which established and exhausted a
whole field of literary inquiry. "Child" ballads are those 305 ballads and their
numerous variants preserved orally from medieval, Renaissance and earlier
times. Every known variant (sometimes several dozen) of these ballads known
at the time is given here. Child's commentary traces these ballads' origins,
investigates references in literature, relates them to parallel literary traditions
of other countries. This edition also includes "Professor Child and the Ballad,"
an essay by Prof. Walter Morris Hart. Biographical sketch by G. L. Kittredge.
Appendixes. Total of lxvii + 2694pp. 6½ x 9¼.
T1409–T1413 Five volume set, Paperbound $13.75

WORLD DRAMA, *edited by B. H. Clark*
The dramatic activity of a score of ages and eras—all in two handy, compact
volumes. More than one-third of this material is unavailable in any other current edition! In all, there are 46 plays from the ancient and the modern worlds:
Greece, Rome, Medieval Europe, France, Germany, Italy, England, Russia,
Scandinavia, India, China, Japan, etc.; classic authors such as Aeschylus, Soph-
ocles, Euripides, Aristophanes, Plautus, Marlowe, Jonson, Farquhar, Gold-
smith, Cervantes, Molière, Dumas, Goethe, Schiller, Ibsen. A creative collection
that avoids hackneyed material to include only completely first-rate plays which
are relatively little known or difficult to obtain. "The most comprehensive
collection of important plays from all literature available in English," *Saturday
Review.* Vol. I: Ancient Greece and Rome, China, Japan, Medieval Europe,
England. Vol. II: Modern Europe. Introduction. Reading lists. Total of
1,364pp. 5⅜ x 8.
T57, T59 Two volume set, paperbound $6.00

HISTORY OF PHILOSOPHY, *Julián Marías*
One-volume history of philosophy by a contemporary Spanish philosopher.
Major, perhaps the most important post-war philosophical history. Strong
coverage of recent and still-living philosophers (in many cases the only coverage of these figures available at this level) such as Bergson, Jaspers, Buber,
Marcel, Sartre, Whitehead, Russell and Boas; full coverage of Spanish philosophers (particularly the pre-W.W. II School of Madrid) such as Suárez,
Sanz del Río, Santayana, Unamuno and Ortega. Thoroughly organized, lucidly
written for self-study as well as for the classroom. Translated by S. Appelbaum
and C. C. Strowbridge. Bibliography. Index. xix + 505pp. 5⅜ x 8½.
T1739 Paperbound $2.75

THE WONDERFUL WIZARD OF OZ, *L. F. Baum*
All the original W. W. Denslow illustrations in full color—as much a part of
"The Wizard" as Tenniel's drawings are of "Alice in Wonderland." "The
Wizard" is still America's best-loved fairy tale, in which, as the author expresses
it, "The wonderment and joy are retained and the heartaches and nightmares
left out." Now today's young readers can enjoy every word and wonderful picture of the original book. New introduction by Martin Gardner. A Baum
bibliography. 23 full-page color plates. viii + 268pp. 5⅜ x 8.
T691 Paperbound $1.75

THE MARVELOUS LAND OF OZ, *L. F. Baum*
This is the equally enchanting sequel to the "Wizard," continuing the adventures of the Scarecrow and the Tin Woodman. The hero this time is a little
boy named Tip, and all the delightful Oz magic is still present. This is the
Oz book with the Animated Saw-Horse, the Woggle-Bug, and Jack Pumpkin-
head. All the original John R. Neill illustrations, 10 in full color. 287pp.
5⅜ x 8.
T692 Paperbound $1.50

ALICE'S ADVENTURES UNDER GROUND, *Lewis Carroll*
The original *Alice in Wonderland*, hand-lettered and illustrated by Carroll
himself, and originally presented as a Christmas gift to a child-friend. Adults
as well as children will enjoy this charming volume, reproduced faithfully
in this Dover edition. While the story is essentially the same, there are slight
changes, and Carroll's spritely drawings present an intriguing alternative to
the famous Tenniel illustrations. One of the most popular books in Dover's
catalogue. Introduction by Martin Gardner. 38 illustrations. 128pp. 5⅜ x 8½.
T1482 Paperbound $1.00

THE NURSERY "ALICE," *Lewis Carroll*
While most of us consider *Alice in Wonderland* a story for children of all
ages, Carroll himself felt it was beyond younger children. He therefore provided this simplified version, illustrated with the famous Tenniel drawings
enlarged and colored in delicate tints, for children aged "from Nought to
Five." Dover's edition of this now rare classic is a faithful copy of the 1889
printing, including 20 illustrations by Tenniel, and front and back covers
reproduced in full color. Introduction by Martin Gardner. xxiii + 67pp.
6⅛ x 9¼.
T1610 Paperbound $1.75

THE STORY OF KING ARTHUR AND HIS KNIGHTS, *Howard Pyle*
A fast-paced, exciting retelling of the best known Arthurian legends for young
readers by one of America's best story tellers and illustrators. The sword
Excalibur, wooing of Guinevere, Merlin and his downfall, adventures of Sir
Pellias and Gawaine, and others. The pen and ink illustrations are vividly
imagined and wonderfully drawn. 41 illustrations. xviii + 313pp. 6⅛ x 9¼.
T1445 Paperbound $1.75

Prices subject to change without notice.

Available at your book dealer or write for free catalogue to Dept. Adsci,
Dover Publications, Inc., 180 Varick St., N.Y., N.Y. 10014. Dover publishes more
than 150 books each year on science, elementary and advanced mathematics,
biology, music, art, literary history, social sciences and other areas.